スーパーCD **4**枚付き

ネイティブ英会話

フレーズ集 phrase index
3240

監修 佐々木 隆

西東社

はじめに

　インターネットやそれに付随するソーシャルネットワークの普及により、いま、誰もが世界中の人と簡単にコミュニケーションがとれるようになりました。また、ビジネスにおいても、英語でやり取りする機会が格段に増え、英会話は不可欠な時代といえるでしょう。

　そこで本書では、みなさんが普段の生活の中でほんとうに言いたかったことを表現できるように、生活、学校、仕事、旅行など、さまざまなテーマに基づいた3240のフレーズを集めました。どれも、ネイティブがよく使うフレーズなので、自然な英語で表現できます。

　学習をさらに深めるために、本書にはさまざまな工夫が施されています。
　例えば、フレーズの下の注釈では、同意表現や入れ替え語句などを紹介。併せて読むことで、各フレーズの理解力がより深まることでしょう。
　自分が言いたい表現を探すには、INDEX（12～24ページ）を活用してください。数あるフレーズの中から、目当てのフレーズが効率的に探し出せます。
　付属のスーパーＣＤには、掲載されているすべてのフレーズが日本語→英語の順で録音されています。DISC4には、標準速度のほか1.5倍と２倍速の音声も付いているので、レベルに合わせて使い分けができます。さらに、確認問題も収録されているので、パソコン画面やプリントを通して、学習効果をチェックすることができます。

　さあ、自分が言いたかったフレーズを見つけ、そこからスタートしてみましょう。
　本書を活用し、楽しみながら学習することで、あなたの英語力が格段にアップすることを願っています。

目次 CONTENTS

本書の見方……6
CDのしくみ……7
DISC4の操作の進め方……8
テストページのしくみ……10
言いたいフレーズがすぐ見つかる！ INDEX……12

Part1 | 基本の会話　25▶96

1 あいさつ……26
2 会話の間をつなぐ……38
3 感情を表す……50
4 気持ちを伝える……62
5 考えを表す……86

Part2 | 日常生活の会話　97▶192

1 家族との会話……98
2 学校での会話……122
3 ビジネス会話……140
4 オフィスでの会話……162
5 つき合う、恋愛……176

Part3 | オフタイムの会話　193▶272

1 レジャー、娯楽……194
2 ドライブ……208
3 美容院、ジム、エステ……216
4 ショッピング……228
5 外食……240
6 飲み会、カラオケ……252
7 招待、訪問、パーティ……260

Part4 | 話題別の会話　273▶352

1 趣味、娯楽……274
2 ファッション、グルメ……292
3 美容、健康……300
4 パソコン、携帯……304
5 エコ、環境……320
6 結婚、育児、教育……324
7 政治、経済、宗教……338
8 日本文化……344

Part5 | 場面別の会話　353▶415

1 旅行……354
2 公共の場所……382
3 冠婚葬祭、年中行事……408

本書の見方

本書は3240のフレーズと、必要なものには
注釈やアイコンなどを記載しています。
ここでは、それぞれの表示の意味を説明します。

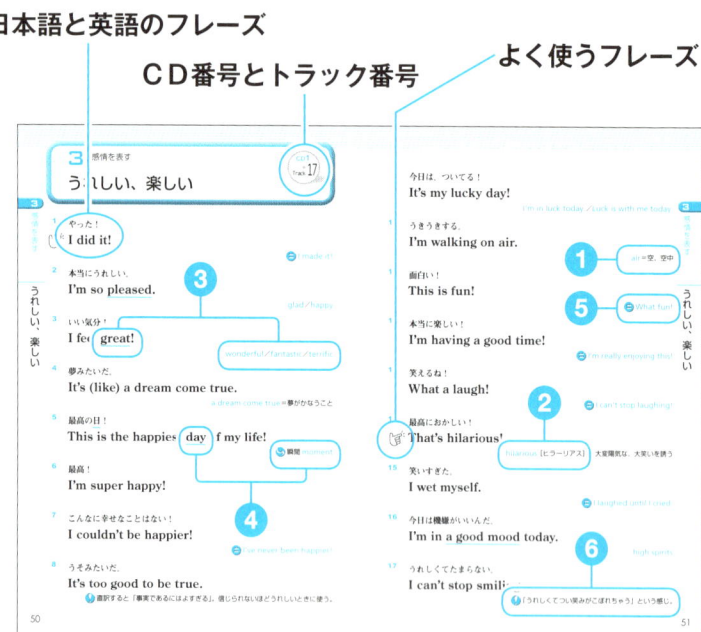

① 語句の意味
フレーズ内にある、とくに知っておきたい単語やイディオムの意味。

② 単語の読み方
フレーズ内にある、とくに読み方が難しい単語のカタカナ読み。＊ネイティブの発音は、付属の音声を参考にしてください。

③ 入れ替えられる類義語
下線部分と同じ意味の単語や句の例を紹介。

④ 意味の異なる句の入れ替え
下線部分を入れ替えることで別の意味を表す、単語や句の例を紹介。

⑤ 同意表現
同じような意味を表す別のフレーズを紹介。＊とくに使用頻度の高いフレーズを表示しています。

⑥ 補足説明
語句の説明や成り立ち、応答文など、役に立つ情報を紹介。

CDのしくみ

本書にはCDが4枚付いています。DISC1～3はオーディオCD、DISC4はオーディオCDとCD-ROM機能を併せ持つエンハンスドCDです。

●DISC1～4の内容

DISC1～3とDISC4のオーディオCD部分には、本書のフレーズを収録（日本語とネイティブ）。

DISC1…**P25～P161**のフレーズ
DISC2…**P162～P272**のフレーズ
DISC3…**P273～P381**のフレーズ
DISC4…**P382～P415**のフレーズ

パソコンで使うDISC4のCD-ROM部分には、次の①～③のコンテンツが収録されています。
①**パソコンの画面上で勉強できる確認テスト**
②**通常スピードと、1.5倍速、2倍速の高速リスニング音声(mp3形式)**。＊英語のみ
③**iPodやiPhoneで聴くことができるオーディオブックデータ(m4b形式)**。＊日本語・英語の両方
パソコンのCD/DVDドライブにセットして使います（Windows、Macintoshの両方に対応）。

DISC4のOS別の使い方

Windows8/7／Vistaの場合
1. CDをドライブにセットすると「自動再生ウィンドウ」が現れます。
2. 「オーディオCDのオプション」(オーディオCDの再生)をクリックすると、Windows Media Playerなどの再生ソフトが起動し、音声CD部が再生されます。「拡張コンテンツの実行」のAUTORUN.EXEの実行をクリックすると、CD-ROM部のトップメニューが表示されます。

「自動再生ウィンドウ」が表示されないとき
1. 「コンピュータ」▶「CD/DVDドライブ：ネイティブ英会話フレーズ集」アイコンを右クリック。
2. 「自動再生を開く」を選択し、クリックすると、上記1の「自動再生ウィンドウ」が表示されます。

Windows XPの場合
1. CDをドライブにセットすると、自動的にCD-ROM部のトップメニューが表示されます。
2. 音声CDを再生するには、①「マイコンピュータ」▶「CD/DVDドライブ：ネイティブ英会話フレーズ集」アイコンを右クリック。②「再生」を選択し、クリックすると、Windows Media Playerなどの再生ソフトが起動し、音声CDが再生されます。

Macintoshの場合
1. CDをドライブにセットすると、「オーディオCD」と「ネイティブ英会話フレーズ集」の2つのアイコンが表示されます。
2. iTunesなどの音声再生ソフトを起動すると、音声CD部が再生されます。
3. 「ネイティブ英会話フレーズ集」のアイコンをクリックし、その中にある「ネイティブ英会話フレーズ集.app」をダブルクリックすると、CD-ROM部のトップメニューが表示されます。

動作確認済みのOS／CD-ROM部、動作確認済みOSは、Windows:XP/Vista/7(32bit&64bit)/8(32bit&64bit)／Macintosh:OS10.4/10.5/10.6です。

DISC4の操作の進め方

ここでは、DISC4のCD-ROM部分に収録されている
コンテンツを使うときの、操作の進め方と内容を見ていきます。

 パソコンを使って
学習できるコンテンツ

[TOP画面]

音声を聴く場合は「音声を聴く」ボタンを、テストを受ける場合は「テストを受ける」ボタンをクリックします。

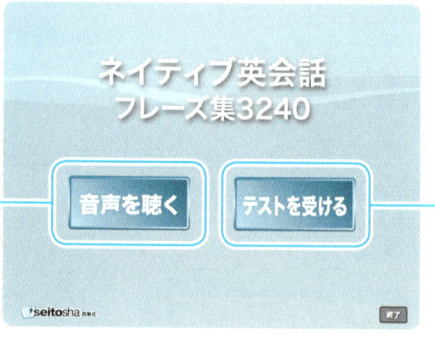

高速リスニングのあとに
通常スピードを聴くことで
リスニング力アップを実感！

音声を聴く場合は、「通常スピード」「1.5倍速」「2倍速」「オーディオブックデータ」から、目的のボタンを押します。＊「戻る」ボタンを押すと、「TOP画面」に戻ります。

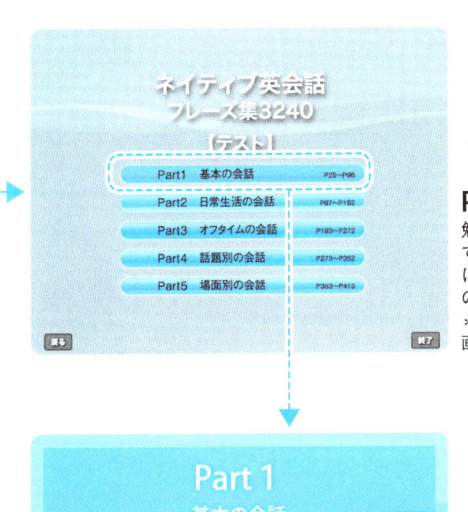

1
Partを選択する
勉強したいPartを選択します。それぞれのボタンの右端に記してあるページは、本書の該当ページです。
＊「戻る」ボタンを押すと、「TOP画面」に戻ります。

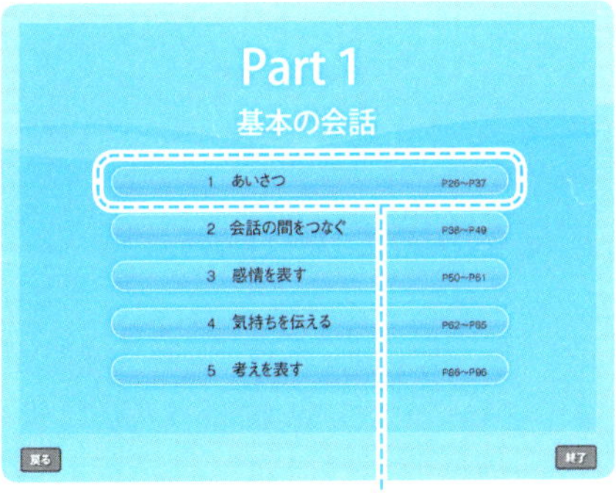

2
項目を選択する
勉強したい項目を選択します。それぞれのボタンの右端に記してあるページは、本書の該当ページです。
＊「戻る」ボタンを押すと、1の画面に戻ります。

[テストページの画面]

3
テストを受ける
選択した項目のテストページが開きます。下線に入る語句を考えて埋めましょう。
詳しい使い方▶P10〜P11

テストページのしくみ

下線の問題を解くことで学習効果を実感することができます。
フレーズ横の「音声ボタン」をクリックすれば、
ネイティブの発音を聴くことができます。

音声ボタン
フレーズの左の音声ボタンをクリックすると、ネイティブの発音でフレーズを聴くことができます。

便利なショートカットを活用して！
パソコンのTabキーを押すと、カーソルが次のフレーズの音声ボタンに移動。そのままスペースキーを押せば、そのフレーズの音声が聴けます。片手で簡単に操作できるので、テスト用紙に答えを埋めながらの学習にもぴったりです。
※パソコンの入力設定を英語入力にしてお使いください

[テストページの画面]

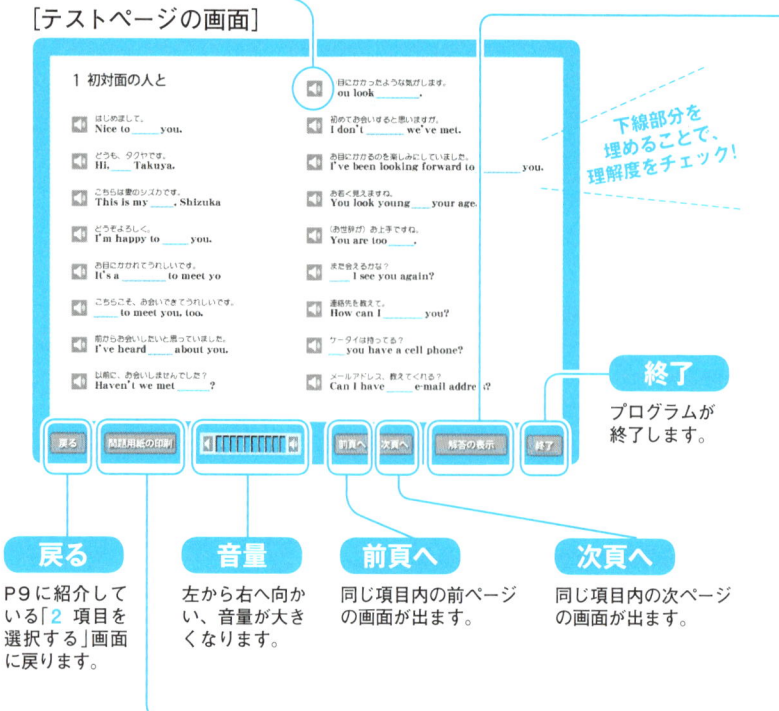

下線部分を埋めることで、理解度をチェック！

終了
プログラムが終了します。

戻る
P9に紹介している「2 項目を選択する」画面に戻ります。

音量
左から右へ向かい、音量が大きくなります。

前頁へ
同じ項目内の前ページの画面が出ます。

次頁へ
同じ項目内の次ページの画面が出ます。

解答の表示

ボタンをクリックすると、下線の部分に解答が表示されるので、答えをすぐに確認できます。
＊フレーズによっては、別の答えが考えられる場合もありますが、本書と同じ語句が表示されます。

答えを一発で確認できる！

---

1 初対面の人と

はじめまして。
Nice to <u>meet</u> you.

どうも、タクヤです。
Hi, <u>I'm</u> Takuya.

こちらは妻のシズカです。
This is my <u>wife</u>, Shizuka

どうぞよろしく。
I'm happy to <u>meet</u> you.

お目にかかれてうれしいです。
It's a <u>pleasure</u> to meet yo

こちらこそ、お会いできてうれしいです。
<u>Nice</u> to meet you, too.

前からお会いしたいと思っていました。
I've heard a <u>lot</u> about you.

以前に、お会いしませんでした？
Haven't we met <u>before</u>?

お目にかかったような気がします。
You look <u>familiar</u>.

初めてお会いすると思いますけど。
I don't <u>believe</u> we've met.

お目にかかるのを楽しみにしていました。
I've been looking forward to <u>meeting</u> you.

お若く見えますね。
You look young <u>for</u> your age.

(お世辞が)お上手ですね。
You are too <u>kind</u>.

また会えるかな？
<u>Can</u> I see you again?

連絡先を教えて。
How can I <u>contact</u> you?

ケータイは持ってる？
<u>Do</u> you have a cell phone?

メールアドレス、教えてくれる？
Can I have <u>your</u> e-mail address?

問題用紙の印刷

ボタンをクリックすると、パソコンに接続してあるプリンターから問題用紙をプリントできます。実際に答えを書き込むことで、記憶の定着やフレーズを覚える勉強にも役立ちます。

書くことでフレーズも覚えられる！

---

1 初対面の人と

はじめまして。
Nice to ____ you.

どうも、タクヤです。
HI, ____ Takuya.

こちらは妻のシズカです。
This is my ____, Shizuka

どうぞよろしく。
I'm happy to ____ you.

お目にかかれてうれしいです。
It's a ____ to meet yo

こちらこそ、お会いできてうれしいです。
____ to meet you, too.

前からお会いしたいと思っていました。
I've heard ____ about you.

以前に、お会いしませんでした？
Haven't we met ____ ?

お目にかかったような気がします。
You look ____ .

初めてお会いすると思いますけど。
I don't ____ we've met.

お目にかかるのを楽しみにしていました。
I've been looking forward to ____ you.

お若く見えますね。
You look young ____ your age.

(お世辞が)お上手ですね。
You are too ____ .

また会えるかな？
____ I see you again?

連絡先を教えて。
How can I ____ you?

ケータイは持ってる？
____ you have a cell phone?

メールアドレス、教えてくれる？
Can I have ____ e-mail address?

INDEX
言いたいフレーズがすぐ見つかる!

言いたいフレーズが簡単に見つかるように、キーワードとなる言葉を五十音順に並べました。
目的のフレーズが掲載されているページがすぐにわかります。

あいさつ… 26、27、103、106、108、110、114、151、155、160
あいづちを打つ ……………………… 41、42、43
相手に任せる ………………………………… 93
相手のことを尋ねる…122、128、131、139、148、155、182、256、267、268、274、276
会う ……………………………………… 28、29、30
赤ちゃん ………………………………… 331、332
アカデミー賞 …………………………………… 196
赤点 ……………………………………………… 128
あきらめる ……………………………………… 61
飽きる …………………………………………… 286
アクセサリー・小物を買う …………………… 234
味 ………………………………………… 109、249
焦る ……………………………………………… 74
暖かい …………………………………………… 32
暑い ……………………………………………… 33
圧縮 ……………………………………………… 305
アニメ …………………………………… 346、347
アプリケーション ……………………………… 318
アポイントを取る ……………………………… 153
雨 ………………………………………………… 322
あやしい ………………………………………… 94
謝る……30、64、65、140、148、149、153、154、187、212、261
あり得ない ……………………………………… 57
アルバイトをする ……………………… 132、133
アレルギー ……………………………… 247、390、394
慌ただしい ……………………………………… 106
安産 ……………………………………………… 330
暗証番号 ………………………………………… 370
安心する ………………………………… 53、398
安全 ……………………………………………… 321
案内する ………………………………………… 242

い

言い訳 ……………………………………… 80、185
家の中を案内する ……………………… 264、265
意外 ……………………………………………… 197

息苦しい ………………………………………… 392
行き先を伝える ………………………………… 373
行きたい ………………………………………… 354
育児休暇・産休 ………………………… 330、332
育児ノイローゼ ………………………………… 332
いくらか尋ねる ………………………… 366、406
意見を言う ………………………………… 68、90
意見を聞く ………………………………… 75、86、89
居心地 …………………………………………… 264
居酒屋で ………………………………… 252、253
いじめ …………………………………… 335、342
医者を呼ぶ ……………………………………… 371
異常気象 ………………………………………… 323
意思を伝える ……………………………… 82、83
忙しい …………………………… 27、138、161、182
急ぐ ……………………………………………… 247
痛い ……………………………………………… 400
痛み止め ………………………………………… 401
一生懸命 ………………………………………… 128
異動 ……………………………………………… 166
委任状 …………………………………………… 404
いびきをかく …………………………………… 98
違法な …………………………………………… 339
違法薬物 ………………………………………… 342
嫌な予感 ………………………………………… 94
依頼する…66、111、114、119、123、126、142、143、144、145、146、148、149、153、157、159、209、211、224、225、226、233、235、248、257、269
イライラする …………………………… 55、331
依頼を受ける …………………………………… 67
依頼を断る ……………………………………… 67
印鑑 ……………………………………………… 402
印鑑証明 ………………………………………… 404
インターネット…198、238、276、280、290、308、309、346、368、370、403

う

ウォーキング …………………………………… 283
うきうきする …………………………………… 51
受け取る ………………………………………… 311
後ろ ……………………………………………… 78

疑う……………………………………94
打ち合わせ…………………………140、160
美しい…………………………………374
うまくいく……………………………328
海……………………………………205
敬う…………………………………343、411
うらやましい……………………………177、326
うるさい………………………135、166、338、371
うれしい…………………27、28、50、51、72、262、270
上書きする……………………………306
浮気…………………………………192、328
うわさ話……………………………134、135、163、170
うんざり…………………………49、175、188、201、399
運転講習………………………………405
運転する…………208、209、210、211、212、401
運転免許………………………………130、405
運動会………………………………415
運動する……………………………282、303
運動不足………………………………217

え

映画………40、112、115、194、195、196、197、286、287、363
影響…………………………………323、341
営業時間……………………………368、378
ATM…………………………………403
駅……………………………141、217、382、384、387
駅で…………………………………386、387
エステ……………222、223、224、226、227、300、369
X線…………………………………393
FX……………………………………341
選ぶ…………………………………362
演奏する………………………………277
円高…………………………………341

お

おいしい………………………………249
わいとをする……………………………271
大げさ…………………………………286
オートロック……………………………368
おかげ…………………………………62
お金を引き出す………………………402、403
おかわりする……………………………109
お悔やみ……………………………412、413
怒る………………………………54、182、186、187
お酒………87、103、106、113、174、175、248、250、252、253、254、269、343、362、369
教える…………………………………344

お辞儀をする…………………………352
おしゃべり………………………………40
おしゃれ………………………………293
汚職事件………………………………339
押しまちがい……………………………306
お世辞………………………………29、72、270
お互いさま………………………………63
オタク………………………………296、303、346
落ち込む………………………………60、77
落ち着く………………………………74
夫…………………………………173、266、327
お通夜…………………………………412
お釣りを断る……………………………373
お年寄り………………………………314
落とす…………………………………314
驚く…………………………27、42、43、413
音を立てて食べる………………………352
おなかいっぱい…………………………110
おなかがすく……………………………130
お似合い………………………………409
お風呂に入る……………………………113
お盆……………………………………411
お見舞い……………………………398、399
お土産…………………………263、360、376、377
オムツ…………………………………331
思い出す……………………………48、85
思い出…………………………………177
面白い………………………………51、112、310
泳ぐ…………………………………205、219、283
お礼への返答……………………………63
お礼を言う………62、72、149、151、155、183、190、255、271、360、379、398、409
終わる………………………………160、161、339
音楽………………………………200、276、277、319
温泉…………………………………182、350

か

ガーデニング……………………………281
絵画…………………………………270
外貨…………………………………041
海外旅行………………………………291
改革…………………………………342
会議・プレゼンテーション……………150、151、152
解決しない……………………………307
介護………………………………172、173、337
外国人登録……………………………404
介護保険制度…………………………342
解除する………………………………322

13

改善する	96
快速電車	387
快適	366
解凍する	305
買い物	115、228、229、230、231、232、233、234、235、376、377
解約する	216
外来	388、397
帰る	161、183
替える	371
顔色	116、399
顔のシミ	301
顔のシワ	300、301
顔を洗う	100
価格	158、159
各駅停車	387
学園祭	138
覚悟する	78
格差	342
学食で	130
確認する	45、94、142、157、355、358
学費	132
かさばる	377
家事	104、327
カジノ	369
風邪	116、117、261
稼ぐ	172、173
画像を取り込む	305
家族サービス	115
家族のこと	172、173
家族を紹介する	266、267、268
ガソリンスタンド	213
肩こり	227
片付ける	111
形見	411
がっかりする	197、256
楽器	349
かっこいい	71、73
学校での会話	122、123、124、125
カップル	324、350
合併症	395
家電製品	235、319
華道	348
悲しい	59
加入する	355
株	341
株価	341
歌舞伎	348
花粉症	32
我慢する	197
髪の傷み	301
髪を切る	220、221
髪を染める	221
辛い	109、249
カラオケ	130、257、347
カロリー	219、302
かわいい	182、255、295
為替	341
考え直す	66
考える	79、139、292
環境にいいこと・エコ	320
環境問題	321
関係ない	47、81
観劇に行く	198、199、200
観光案内所	374
観光地	350、351
観光名所	374、375
頑固な	167
感謝する	53、62
慣習	415
鑑賞する	407
感心する	52、71
感染する	306
乾燥した	362
感想を聞く	196、197
感動する	52、196
乾杯	253、409
がんばる	69、70

き

企画書	142
危機・恐怖に直面する	57、58
聞き返す	44
企業献金	339
効く	303
機嫌が悪い	185
帰国子女	336
儀式	410
機種変更	312
起床	98、99
傷口	395
帰社する	160、161
帰省	130、268、411、415
期待外れ	197
帰宅する	106
気づかう	74

きっかけ	324
切符を買う	386
機内で	361、362、363
気にならない	93
気になる	414
記入する	389、396
機能	313、319
希望を聞く	181、192、194、204、205、206、252、269、399
気持ちいい	227
気持ち悪い	58
客を迎える	262、263
キャンセルする	245
キャンセル待ち	359
休暇を取る	354
急行電車	387
休日	115、121
給湯室での会話	169、170、171
給料	133、136、162、163、165
教育	333
行儀が悪い	334
凶作	323
教室での会話	122、123、130
行政改革	339
興味がない	88、338
許可されている	316
許可を求める	113、160、181、184、208、209、229、263
距離	382
嫌い	88
記録する	219
気をつける	78、79
禁煙	243、355
緊急	381、397
近況を尋ねる	26
銀行	402、403
禁酒	259
緊張する	56
金融危機	341

く

空港	355、356、357、358、359、360、361、362、363、364、365、366、384
空港でのチェックイン	356、357、358、359、360
苦情を言う	96、98、239、245、246、247、251
くすぐったい	227
薬	390、401
薬を飲む	401

口ごたえをする	335
口を開ける	400
グチを言う	175
靴	234、295、297、352
クリーニング	369
クリスマス	272
車	162、181、208、209、210、211、212、213、214、215
グルメ	298、299
クレジットカード	236、372

け

景気	340
景気対策	340
敬語	352
経済	340、341
警察	342、381、405
携帯電話	29、194、312、313、314、315、316
携帯のマナー	316
経費で落とす	143
警報	322
契約	157
経理	305
ゲーム	290
ケガをする	117
景色がいい	264
化粧する	101、169
血液検査	393
欠航	360
結婚	191、192、324、325
結婚記念日	325
結婚式で	408、409
結婚生活	326、327
決心する	82、83、139、327
下痢	363
原因	328、342
けんか	185、186、327
圏外	315
元気	26、69、116、334
現金	236
健康	303、330
健康保険	389
原作	347
減税	340
倦怠期	326
現地時間	363

15

こ

恋をする	178、179、180
後遺症	395
後悔する	61、68
合格祈願	352
交換	312
公共料金	402
合コン・飲み会	255、256
交差点	384
口座を解約する	402
口座を開く	402
交渉	158、159、168
洪水	322
高速道路	212
交通渋滞	143、214、215、385、415
交通トラブル	214、215
購読する	318
興奮する	53
誤解	95
互換性	307
国技	349
国内旅行	291
告白・プロポーズ	176、179、180
国宝	351
国連	378、379
ご祝儀	408
故障する	362、371
故人の遺志	412
コスプレ	346
子育て	331、332
子どもの世話	120
断る	180
好み	86、87、88、171、195、230、233、249、255、286、294、298
コピー	144
困る	96
ゴミを出す	103
怖い	58、204
婚姻届	404
コンタクトレンズ	101
コンビニエンスストア	158、228、382
コンピューター	88
コンピューターウイルス	306、307
婚約	324
混乱する	93

さ

サークル・部活動	131
最悪	27、60
再会する	29、30
再現する	319
最高	26、50、168、184、196、242、271、287、294、350
再婚	326
最新の	304
サイズ	239
再配達	406
探す	260、309、346、407
下がる	386
差し入れ	130
座席	359、361、363
誘う	123、130、174、179、194、201、202、208、222、228、252、256、257、260、271
撮影禁止	407
茶道	348
寂しい	59、413
サビ抜き	345
作法	344
さぼりがち	219
寒い	34
三回忌	411
残業	160、162
酸性雨	321
賛成する	89

し

幸せ	50、182、191、270、324、326
幸せを祈る	409
シートベルト	361
死因	413
資格	136、275、336
時間	99、102、114、152、183、208、355、377
時間がかかる	371、385、394
時間を尋ねる	195、199、360、363
時期	92、336
敷金・礼金	352
時候のあいさつ	32、33、34
自己紹介	28、148、256
仕事	268、304、327、332、336
事故に遭う	380
自殺	342
時差ぼけ	363
指示する	146、147

支持率	339	手術	289、394、395
地震	322	出血	400
自然災害	322、323	出社する	140、141、160、161
〜したい	115、121、165、175、183、184、204、284	趣味・習い事	274、275
時代遅れ	319	腫瘍	394
〜したくない	188	順番	407
七五三	415	順路	407
試着する	231	省エネ	158、320
実感がわかない	410	紹介する	28、155、266、267、268
失業率	340	条件	157、159
しつけ	334、335	上司	142、143、153、166、167、168
しつこい	81	症状	391、392
質問する	106、107、109、110、112、116、117、118、119、121、124、151、152	昇進	163、170
		招待状	408
失礼	79	招待する	260、324
失恋、別れ話	188、189、190	商談	158、159
自動販売機	373	使用中	363
辞任する	339	情緒	350
始発	386	消灯	396
支払い	236、237、238、251、253、296、368、372	初期化	307
		ジョギング	283
しばらく会えないとき	37	職業	364
地味	294	食事	99、108、109、110、111、179、241、246、247、248、249、250、269、270、302、344、345、397、399
自民党	339		
事務処理をする	144、145	助言する	68、82、83、218、303、336
指名	333	初診	388
社会福祉制度	342	初対面のあいさつ	28、29
社会問題	342	処方箋	401
謝罪への返答	65	署名する	157
写真	279、311、313	所要時間	366、372、373、379、382
車内放送	387	書類	358
じゃまする	38	知らせる	329
写メール	313	調べる	194
宗教	343	尻に敷く	326
就職活動	136、137、336	視力検査	405
就職難	342、336	城	351
就寝前に	114	進学	336
集中豪雨	323	新幹線	386
充電	315	信号	383、385
宗派	343	申告する	358、364、365、404
週末	115、283	新婚	326
重要文化財	351	新婚旅行	192、325
重量	357	診察	388、389、391、392、393、397
授業参観	121、333	診察券	389
塾通い	333	神社	351、352、415
宿題	125	信じる	94
祝福する	73、121、324、330、409、410	新鮮	167
受験	128、336	身長	330

新調する	408
陣痛	329
心電図	393
震度	322
心配する	132、169、332、361
進路	139、336
新郎新婦	408、409

す

酢	320
水泳	205、219、283
推測する	122、150
好き	86、87、171、178、180、195、200、233、249、274、278、280、286、298
スキー・スノーボード	206
過ごしやすい	33
寿司	241、242、344、345
頭上	78
すすぐ	400
すすめる	217、224、245、277、303、377
ストーカー	405
スピーチ	408
スポーツ	284、349
スポーツ観戦をする	202、203
スマートフォン	317、318
住まい	172
〜するつもり	165
〜するべき	188、189

せ

性格	166、167、168、177、274
税関	364
税金	237、341、377、404
政権	339
成功する	170
正座	352
政治・選挙	338、339、343
政治不信	338
成人式	410
成績・単位	129
成長する	335
政党	338
セーフティボックス	368、370
精密検査	393
生理	169、335
世界遺産	351
赤外線通信	312
咳が止まらない	391
責任	410
世代	347
接続する・つなぐ	308、318、370
接待する	161
せつない	178
節分	414
説明する	151、394
責める	185、186
世話になる	412
選挙	338、339
専業主婦	327
選挙権	410
センス	292、293
先生	134
先祖	411
洗濯物	105
前夫	326

そ

葬式	412、413
掃除する	104
早退する	160
相談する	75、143、403
相場	408
速達	406
卒業	139
尊敬する	52
損をする	341

た

ダイエット	170、250、302
対応を求める	321
大学	336
大気汚染	321
大恐慌	341
退屈	197、255
体型	217、219、282、302
体験する	350
滞在場所	364
滞在予定	364
大事	333
大使館	381、405
退社する	160、161
体重	302、330
大丈夫	69、76、119
大切にする	321
体調が悪い	27、116、117、140、169、371、380、391、392

態度……………………………………79
台風…………………………33、323、360、415
大変……………………………………106
代理人…………………………………404
体力……………………………………217
ダウンロードする……………………314
高い……………………………………234
妥協する………………………………91
タクシー………………………………385
他社を訪問する………………154、155、156
助けを呼ぶ……………………………381
七夕……………………………………414
楽しい………36、50、51、124、183、200、249、255、
　　　　　　　　　　　　　271、275、279
楽しみにする(待ち遠しい)……29、53、162、219、
　　　　　　　　　　　　　360、369
タバコ……………………………213、243
旅先でのトラブル…………………380、381
たぶん…………………………………92
食べすぎ………………………………392
食べ物……………………………291、298
試しに…………………………………82
試す……………………………224、300、317
足りない………………………………111
だるい…………………………………390
誕生日……………………73、121、182、272
暖冬……………………………………323

ち

地下鉄…………………………………387
地球温暖化…………………………321、323
チケット………………………198、199、373、379
遅刻する………………………140、143、181
地図………………………………211、373
チップ…………………………………352
着メロ……………………………314、316
注意する………65、78、79、98、99、100、101、103、
　　　　104、106、108、109、112、113、114、120、124、209、
　　　　　　　　　　　　　212、403
注意を促す………………………208、210
駐車する………………………………215
昼食……………………………………130
超過料金………………………………357
(機械の)調子が悪い……………144、145
朝食……………………………………99

つ

ツイッター……………………………310

通勤電車………………………………141
通帳……………………………………402
通販…………………………………238、309
使い方………………………………304、344
使いこなす……………………………313
疲れる…………………………………211
つき合う………………………………182
突き刺す………………………………344
続ける…………………………………327
津波が発生する………………………322
妻…………………………………172、173、174
つまらない……………………………43
梅雨…………………………………32、33、323
釣り…………………………………205、285
つわり…………………………………329

て

提案する…68、83、151、156、176、183、184、187、
　　　　　　　206、252、270、272
TPOに合わせる…………………294、295
DVD………………………………287、319
定期的…………………………………397
定期預金………………………………402
テイクアウトする……………………240、249
定形外郵便……………………………406
定刻通り……………………358、359、360、363
停電……………………………………323
定年……………………………………165
データが消える………………………306
デート………171、176、179、181、182、183、184
出かける……………………………102、103、115
手がしびれる…………………………391
デザート…………………………110、111、250
デザイン…………………………232、264
手数料……………………………366、403
テスト・試験…………………126、127、128
手伝う……………………………66、68、332
徹夜する……………………………125、290
手荷物検査……………………………357
手配……………………………………375
寺…………………………………351、375、412
テレビ……………112、114、134、287、313、319、347
電化製品………………………………346
天気……………31、32、33、34、105、174、206、208
天気予報………………………………323
転勤になる……………………………164
電源を切る……………………………305
伝言……………………………………368

電子書籍	318
電車	316、386、387
電車の遅延	387
天寿	413
転職	165
転送する	311
点滴	399
伝統芸能・文化	348
転入	404
電波	315
伝票	369
添付する	311
電話	118、119、148、149、185、187、198、314
電話が切れる	315

と

トイレ	104、214、263、289、361、363、370
トイレが詰まる	370
同意書	394
同意する	89
動悸	391
陶芸	275
登校拒否	335
倒産	340
投資	341
搭乗券	365
同情する	43、76
搭乗手続き	358、359、360
到着する	212、367
到着予定	363
投票	338
同僚	168
登録	351
とがめる	80、81
時	74、76
ドキドキする	53、56
特産品	377
独身	327
特別な日に	121
登山	206、284
図書館	407
途中まで	387
突然の	413
届く	408
友達・仲間	131
ドライブ	208、209
トラブルに巻き込まれる	380
トラベラーズチェック	367、372

とりあえず	252
取り込む	305
取り締まる	342
トレーニング	282

な

内定	137
直す	215、371
仲直りをする	187
泣き虫	334
泣く	196
なぐさめる	76、77
亡くなる	411、412、413
なごむ	167
名前	289
～ならいいのに	166
並ぶ	204、359
何回目	354

に

似合う	71、169、231、293、294、295、296、324
苦手	124、255、269、270、278、286
二次会	409
日時を尋ねる	125
似ている	267
日本文化	270、275、344、345、346、347、348、349、352
荷物を預ける	356、357、372
入院	396、397
入院生活	399
入院手続き	396
入国審査	364、365
入場料	375
尿検査	393
人気がある	158、230、281、297、299、346、347、349、350
妊娠・出産	191、327、329、330
認知症	337

ね

ネイルサロン	225
願いが叶う	414
値下げする	318
寝すごす	98
寝たきり	337
値段	199、201、213、216、231、236、237、242、265、299、354
熱が出る	117、331、371、391

ネット検索	308、309
寝不足	331
眠気	401
年中行事	414、415
年末年始	272、415

の

納品	157
のどが渇く	362
飲み物をもらう	362
乗り換え	387
乗り継ぐ	359
乗り物から降りる	384、385
乗り物酔い	366
のんびりする	115

は

バー	254
バーゲンセール	169、228、229、231
パーティ	260、272
バーベキュー	269、272
パーマ	221
排気ガス	321
歯医者	400
配送	235、237
バイト探し	132
ばかばかしい	43
墓参り	411
歯茎	400
迫力がある	200
はぐれる	380
励ます	69、74、76、77、206
初めて	354、394
初めての街で	382、383
場所を尋ねる	125、194、198、199、236、251、364、365、366、368、372、373、374、379、382、404
走る	141
恥じる	176、181
箸を使う	344
破水	330
バスに乗る	364
パスポート	358、381、404
パスワード	308、317
パソコン	146、147、235、276、304、305、306、307、319、361
パソコンのトラブル	306、307
肌のトラブル	222、223、301
バツイチ	327

バックアップ	307
抜糸する	397
発生する	322
バッテリー切れ	315
発明	345
話をうながす	40
話を終わらせる	49
話を切り出す	39
鼻づまり	392
歯の矯正	400
歯みがき	100
払い戻し	377
バレンタイン	414
ハロウィーン	272
反抗期	334
反対・否定	90
パンフレット	374

ひ

PTA	333
PDF	305
冷え性	227
惹かれる	283
ひきつけ	331
引き取る	405
ビザ	405
久しぶりに会ったとき	30
美術館	201、407
ひったくり	381
必要	333
否定する	95
ひどい	42
人見知り	334
ひとり	59、189
ひな祭り	414
秘密	84、142
日焼け	205
美容	222、223、224、300、301
病院で	388、389、390、391、392、393、394、395、396、397、398、399
美容院	220、221
評判	170、195、241、369
貧血	169

ふ

ファクスをする	144、145
ファストフードで	240
ファッション	292、293、294、295、296、297

フィットネスクラブ	216、217、218、219
フェイスブック	310
吹き出物	301
副作用	401
服装	71、169、182、231、232、233、294、295
不景気	340
不幸	323
不公平	342
不在通知	406
部署名	154、155
不審者	405
不足	332
負担	337
ふだんのあいさつ	26、27
不通	381
ふつう	326
二日酔い	259
復帰する	332
仏教	343
仏像	351
不動産	352
太る	302
不満	55
ブランド	297
フリーズ	306
振り込め詐欺	403
プリントアウト	146、147、305
プレゼント	237
ブログ	279、309、310、313
ブログが炎上する	310
プロポーズ	191、192
紛失する	365、381
分担する	327、337
分別する	320

へ

ペット	266、288、289
勉強する	126、128
変更する	153、157、245
返答に困ったとき	46、47
便秘	117
返品する	239
便利	317、384

ほ

宝庫	351
報告書	305
報告する	143
放任	333
忘年会	174
奉納する	348
訪問する	154、155、156、261
ボーナス	162、172
ホームページの開設	309
保険証	388
誇りに思う	71
欲しい	129、224、376
ほっとする	53
募集する	132
保証人	396
ポップカルチャー	346、347
ホテルで	367、368、369、370、371、372
ホテルでのトラブル	370、371
ホテルのチェックアウト	372
ホテルのチェックイン	367
ホテルの予約	354、355
歩道橋	383
母乳で育てる	331
ほめられたとき	72
ほめる	52、70、71、73、161、166、182、200、207、264、265、270、292、294
保留する	92、93
盆踊り	415
本気	82

ま

まあまあ	26、72、196、326
マイホーム	172
任せる	208
麻酔	395
まだ早い	316
待ち受け画面	314
間違いを指摘する	95
街を楽しむ	373
待つ	243
マッサージ	223、224、226、227
マナーモード	316
学ぶ	347
まもなく	362、363
守る	192、325
マンガ喫茶	346
漫才	349
満席	242、359
満腹	110

み

見送る	156、360
身支度	100、101
道案内する	382、383、384
道なり	383
道に迷う	210、211、382
道を尋ねる	372、382、384
見積もり	159
見所	374
ミュージカル	199、200

む

向かい側	383
むかつく	54
むくみ	301
蒸し暑い	33
虫歯	400
無宗教	343
難しい	201、304
ムダ	61、190
夢中	281、284
むなしい	60
無料	318

め

名刺をいただく	154
命令する	80
メール	29、147、311、312、313、314
目印	383
めまいがする	392
面会	398
面会謝絶	398
免許の更新	405
面接	137
めんどくさい	55
面倒見がいい	166

も

もうすぐ	123、138、139、263
目的	364
目標	219
文字化け	311
持ち込む	356、357
もてなす	262
喪に服す	411
物忘れ	337
もはや〜でない	291

盛り上がる	255、272
文句を言う	54、55
問題外	90

や

役所で	404、405
約束する	84
役割を果たす	339
夜景	243
やけどをする	391
安い	232、238、384
休み時間に	130
休む	140、143、209、354
安らかな	413
やせる	219
家賃	342
やつあたり	81
薬局	228、401
やってみる	82

ゆ

憂鬱	60
遊園地で	204
融資	403
優柔不断	83
夕食	107、108、109
夕食後	110、111
夕食の用意	107
郵便局で	406
輸血	390
夢	139、164、291
許さない	65
許して	64
許す	65

よ

要求する	66
様子を尋ねる	74、106、125、143、361
様子をみる	92
腰痛	104
洋服を買う	231、232、233
容量	307、319
よかった	52
汚れる	104
予算	354、377
酔っぱらう・二日酔い	258、259
予定を伝える	102、118、121、123、133、140、143、150、154、160、272、344

予定を尋ねる…………………………260
予定を立てる……………………………115
夜泣き………………………………331
呼びかける………………………………38
予防接種…………………………390
予約する………………161、198、241、242
よろしく……………………28、35、156

ら

ライブ……………………………200
落語………………………………349
ラッキー……………………………51
ラッピング………………………237
ラベル………………………………105

り

離婚…………………………………328
離婚届………………………………328
リサイクル…………………………320
リスクが高い………………………341
利息…………………………………402
立派…………………………………413
リフォームする……………………265
留学する……………………………139
流行……………230、283、292、296、297、350
留年・落第……………………129、139
理由を尋ねる………………………55、59
両替する……………………………365
料理する……………………………107
料理を注文する……244、245、246、247、362
旅行……………………115、291、354〜381
旅行の準備………………………354、355
リラックス………………………69、74
履歴書……………………………136、137

る

ルームサービス……………………369

れ

礼儀正しい…………………………168
レストラン………241、242、243、244、245、246、247、248、249、325、368
恋愛…87、88、171、176、177、178、179、180、181、182、183、184
レンタカー………………………366、369
レントゲン…………………………389
連絡先を聞く………………29、149、256
連絡する……………………30、92、143

ろ

老後…………………………………337
浪費する…………………………380、326
労をねぎらう………………………70
ローン……………………………172、403
録画…………………………………319
ロックする…………………………370

わ

わからない………44、47、93、127、162、186、380
わかる………………………………45
別れのあいさつ………………35、36、37、271
別れ話……………………………188、189、190
わくわくする………………………53
忘れっぽい…………………………85
忘れ物………………………………103
忘れる………………85、177、215、290、381、389
話題を変える………………………48
笑う……………………………51、185、349
割り勘………………………………251
割引き…………………………237、309

Part 1 基本の会話

1 あいさつ ……………… 26
2 会話の間をつなぐ …… 38
3 感情を表す ……………… 50
4 気持ちを伝える ……… 62
5 考えを表す ……………… 86

1 あいさつ

ふだんのあいさつ

1 元気？
How's it going?
🟰 How are you? / How's life?　＊「あなたは？」と聞き返すときは How about you?

2 調子はどう？
How's <u>everything</u>?
things

3 最近、どう？
What's <u>up</u>?
new

4 最近どうしてた？
What have you been up to lately?
🟰 How have you been?

5 元気だよ。
Pretty good.
💡「すごく元気」なら Excellent! と言おう。

6 調子いいよ。
It's going pretty well.
🟰 Everything's fine.

7 最高！
Couldn't be <u>better</u>!
happier

8 まあまあだね。
Not too bad.
🟰 All right. / Can't complain.

9 相変わらずだよ。
 Same as usual.

always

10 変わりないよ。
Nothing much.

special

11 具合が悪くて。
I'm not (feeling) very well.

≡ Not too well.

12 とても忙しくて。
Things are really hectic.

héctic [ヘクティック]

13 最悪！
I feel awful!

terrible／lousy　＊こう言ったら What happened?「どうしたの？」と聞かれる。

14 会えてうれしいなあ。
I'm so happy to see you.

≡ Great to see you.

15 会えるとは思わなかった。
I wasn't expecting to see you.

expect＝予期する

16 ここで会えるなんてびっくり。
I'm surprised to bump into you here.

bump into ～＝～にばったり出会う　＊run into ～も同じ意味。

17 これは驚いた！
 **What a pleasant surprise!**

a pleasant surprise は「うれしい驚き」。思いがけずいいことがあったときに使おう。

1 あいさつ

初対面の人と

1 はじめまして。
Nice to meet you.
= How do you do? ＊やや堅苦しい感じ。

2 どうも、タクヤです。
Hi, I'm Takuya.
「タクヤと呼んでください」なら Call me Takuya.

3 こちらは妻のシズカです。
This is my wife, Shizuka.
Have you met my wife, Shizuka ? と紹介するのも自然。

4 どうぞよろしく。
I'm happy to meet you.
pleased／glad 「お会いできてうれしいです」という定番表現。

5 お目にかかれてうれしいです。
It's a pleasure to meet you.
相手が2人（3人）いて、それを強調したいときは pleasure to meet you two (three) と言う。

6 こちらこそ、お会いできてうれしいです。
Nice to meet you, too.
= The pleasure's mine.

7 前からお会いしたいと思っていました。
I've heard a lot about you.
「お噂はかねがね聞いている」の意味から「会ってみたかった」という感じで使われる。

8 以前に、お会いしませんでした？
Haven't we met before?
= Have we met before? ＊こちらのほうが、会ったことへの確信が弱い感じ。

9 お目にかかったような気がします。
You look familiar.
= Haven't I seen you somewhere before?

10 初めてお会いすると思いますが。
I don't believe we've met.
think

11 お目にかかるのを楽しみにしていました。
I've been looking forward to meeting you.

12 お若く見えますね。
You look young for your age.
= You don't look it.

13 (お世辞が) お上手ですね。
You are too kind.
so／very

14 また会えるかな？
Can I see you again?
💡 婉曲に断るときは See you around.「またどこかでね」と返そう。

15 連絡先を教えて。
☞ How can I contact you?
= How can I get in touch with you?

16 ケータイは持ってる？
Do you have a cell phone?

17 メールアドレス、教えてくれる？
Can I have your e-mail address?

1 あいさつ

初対面の人と

1 あいさつ
久しぶりに会ったとき

1 久しぶり。
Long time no see.
　Hey there, stranger.　＊よりカジュアルな表現。

2 ごぶさたでしたね。
It's been a long time.
　「そうですね」と返すときは It sure has.

3 久しぶり、どうしてた？
Where have you been hiding?
　Where have you been keeping yourself?

4 最後にお会いしたのはいつでしたかね？
When was the last time we met?

5 全然変わらないね。
You haven't changed at all.
　「雰囲気が変わったね」は You look different today.

6 元気そうですね。
You look great.

7 連絡しなくてごめんね。
I'm sorry for losing touch.
　Sorry for being such a bad friend.

8 これからは連絡を取り合おうよ。
Let's stay in touch in the future.
　「いいね」と返すときは Sure. / Will do.

1 あいさつ
天気の話をする

1 気持ちのいい日だね。
Beautiful day, isn't it?

嫌な Disgusting／Nasty

2 雲ひとつない空だ。
There isn't a single cloud in the sky.

3 曇ってきたよ。
It's getting cloudy.

overcast／gloomy

4 雨、降るのかな？
Is it going to rain today?

「たぶんね」と返すなら Looks like it.　「降らないんじゃない」は I doubt it.

5 雨がぽつぽつきた。
It's sprinkling.

6 やっと雨があがったね。
The rain has finally lifted.

7 明日の天気は？
What's the weather like tomorrow?

What's the forecast for tomorrow?／What's tomorrow's forecast?

8 また天気予報ははずれだ。
The weather forecast was wrong again.

forecast＝天気予報

1 あいさつ
時候のあいさつ

1 春らしくなりましたね。
It feels like spring is already here.
= It feels like spring has already started.

2 春一番が吹きました。
The spring's first south wind blew.

3 花粉症の季節がやってきましたね。
This is the time of year we suffer from hay fever.
hay fever＝花粉症　suffer from ～＝～を患う、～に苦しむ

4 暖かくなってきましたね。
It's getting warmer and warmer, isn't it?

5 お花見にはうってつけの陽気ですね。
This is the perfect weather for cherry blossom viewing.

6 もう桜を見ましたか？
Have you seen the cherry blossoms yet?

7 梅雨入りしたらしいよ。
It looks like the rainy season has kicked in.
kick in＝始まる

8 じめじめして、気が滅入るよ。
It's damp and depressing.
damp＝湿気のある、じめじめした　depressing＝まったく嫌な、うんざりする

9 洗濯物が全然乾かなくて。

My laundry never gets dry.

láundry [ローンドリー]

10 まあでも、カタツムリは喜んでるんじゃないの。

Well, at least snails are happy.

↪ カエル frogs／植木 plants／木 trees／子どもたち children

11 梅雨が明けました。

The rainy season has ended.

is over

12 この暑さ、耐えられない。

The heat is killing me.

= I can't bear the heat.／I'm so hot I could die.

13 今日の最高気温は40℃だって。

The maximum will be 40 degrees today.

14 暑くてムシムシする。

It's so hot and stuffy.

stuffy＝息が詰まる ＊humid より、湿気によって「自分が不快である」感じが出せる。

15 今日は過ごしやすい。

It's a pleasant day, isn't it?

= The weather is nice today, isn't it?

16 冷房病になりそう。

I'm getting sick from the air conditioning.

air conditioner

17 台風が近づいてるらしいよ。

A typhoon is on the way, I heard.

= It looks like a typhoon's coming.

あいさつ 1

時候のあいさつ

18 日が短くなってきましたね。

The days are getting shorter.

↻ 長く longer

19 秋らしくなってきましたね。

I can smell autumn.

💡「秋の匂いがする」という意味。それぞれの季節に使える。

20 小春日和だね！

It's like an Indian summer!

an Indian summer＝秋晴れ　＊秋なのに初夏のように快晴で暖かい日を指す。

21 紅葉が色づいてきましたね。

The autumn leaves are changing color.

↻ 黄色くなって turning yellow

22 今年は暖冬だって。

It's going to be a warm winter this year.

↻ 厳冬 severe winter

23 今朝は冷えますね。

It's chilly this morning.

24 息が白いよ。

I can see my breath.

25 寒くて凍えそう。

It's freezing, isn't it?

＝ I'm chilled to the bone.

26 雪になるかも。

There may be snow.

💡「雪が降りそうなくらい寒いね」という感じで使おう。

1 あいさつ
別れ際のあいさつ

CD1 Track 6

1 さようなら（バイバイ）。
Bye.
＝ Goodbye.

2 またね。
See you soon.
later ＊「また明日」は See you tomorrow.

3 それじゃあ、また。
See you later, alligator.
alligator＝ワニ　later と alligator が韻を踏んでいるのを面白おかしく言う。

4 じゃあ、また。
In a while, crocodile.
crocodile＝大型ワニ　See you later, alligator. と言われて、こう答えられたら楽しい。

5 元気でね。
☞ **Take care (of yourself).**
＝ Take it easy.　＊どちらも軽い別れ際のあいさつとしてよく使われる。

6 彼女によろしく。
☞ **Please say hello to your girlfriend.**
家族 family／同居人 flat mate／お母さん mom

7 行かなくちゃ。
I've got to go.
＝ I have to get going.

8 じゃあ、行くね。
I'm off now.
家を出るときには「行ってきます」として使える。

あいさつ

別れ際のあいさつ

9 またすぐ会えるといいね。
See you again soon, I hope.
= Let's meet again soon.

10 よい1日を。
Have a nice day.
💡 dayは、夜なら eveningに変えて。

11 あなたもね。
You, too.
= Same to you. ＊どちらも Have a nice day. と言われたときの応答。

12 おしゃべりができてよかった。
Nice talking to you.
🔄 会えて meeting you／知り合えて knowing you

13 楽しかった。
I (really) enjoyed meeting you.

14 また近いうちにやりましょう。
☞ Let's do it again soon.
sometime／very soon

15 次回はまたすぐやりましょう。
Let's not leave it so long next time.
💡「今度はあまり長いこと放っておかないようにしよう」という意味。

16 がんばって！
Good luck!
💡 I wish you good luck.「幸運を祈る」の意味。

17 よい旅を！
Bon voyage!
💡 フランス語で旅立つ人に言う言葉。Have a good trip. よりも、こなれた感じ。

1 あいさつ

しばらく会えないとき

1. 寂しくなるな。
I'll miss you.
= I'm going to miss you.

2. きっと帰ってきて。
You must come back.
= Please come back.

3. たまには電話して。
Give me a call sometime.
= Call me from time to time.

4. 手紙ちょうだいね。
Please write to me.
= Please write me a letter.

5. 連絡して。
Drop me a line.
a line＝1行　＊「手紙やメールでのひと言」を指す。

6. 忘れずに電話ちょうだい。
Don't forget to call.
「わかった」は I won't.

7. またいつか会おうね。
Let's get together again sometime.

8. 無理しないでね。
Don't work too hard.

2 会話の間をつなぐ
呼びかける

CD1 Track 8

1 ねえ！
Hey!

2 こんにちは！
Hello, there!

💡「すみません」と呼びかけるときなどに使う。

3 すみません。
Excuse me.

= Pardon me.

4 ちょっといいですか？
Have you got a minute?

= Got a minute? ＊よりくだけた表現。

5 少しお話しできますか？
Could I talk to you (for a minute)?

May

6 今、暇？
Are you free now?

↔ 忙しい busy

7 じゃまして悪いんだけど。
☞ **Sorry to interrupt you.**

💡 話しかけるときの決まり文句。

8 おじゃまかな？
Am I bothering you?

bóthering you [バーザリンユウ]

2 会話の間をつなぐ

話を切り出す

CD1 Track 9

1 ねえ、知ってる？
☞ **Guess what?**

= You know what ?

2 ねえ、聞いた？
Have you heard about that?

3 聞いて！
Listen (to me)!

4 すごいこと、聞いちゃった。
You'll never guess what I heard.

💡「私が何を聞いたか、あなたには想像もできない」の意味。奇想天外なニュースを伝えるときに。

5 びっくりしないでね。
Are you ready for this?

be ready for 〜 =〜の覚悟ができている

6 ねえ、聞いて。
I tell you what.

💡 正式には I'll tell you what. だが、会話では will を省略することが多い。

7 話したいことがあるんだけど。
There's something I want to tell you.

need>have ＊悪い知らせの場合は need や have を使うことが多い。

8 言いにくいんだけど。
I don't know how to put this.

= I'm not sure how to put this. ＊いずれも歓迎されないことを言わなければならないときに。

2 会話の間をつなぐ
話をうながす

1 何か言ってよ。
Tell me something.
≡ Say something.

2 もっと詳しく教えて。
Tell me more about it.
≡ I want to know more about it.／I'd love to know more details.

3 その話、聞きたいなあ。
I'd like to hear the story.
≡ I'd love to hear about it.

4 映画はどうだった？
How was the movie?
↻ 旅行 your trip／試験 the exam／お出かけ your day out

5 楽しかった？
Did you like it?
≡ Did you enjoy yourself?

6 おしゃべりしようよ。
Let's have a chat.
a chat＝雑談

7 何、ニコニコしちゃって。
What are you smiling about?
💡「何を考えてニコニコしてるの？」の意味。「言いたいことがあるんでしょ」と、からかい口調で聞き出そう。

8 話を続けてよ。
☞ I'm all ears.
≡ I'm listening. ＊直訳は「私は今、全身が耳です」。

2 会話の間をつなぐ

あいづちを打つ

CD1 Track 11

1 うんうん。
Uh-huh.

uh-húh [アハー]

2 なるほどね。
I see.

⊜ Oh, yeah?

3 へえ、そうなんだ。
Is that right?

so／true

4 そうだといいね。
I hope so.

💡 反対は I hope not. 「そうじゃなきゃいいけど」。

5 そのとおり。
That's right.

⊜ Exactly!

6 そうなの？
You are?

were／do／did／haveなど　＊相手の動詞に合わせて使い分ける。

7 わかるわ。
I know.

understand／bet

8 いいねえ。
Sounds good.

alright＜good＜great＜excellent　＊右に行くほど「いい」と思っている度合いが強まる。

41

9 いいんじゃない？
Why not?

10 びっくりね！
What a surprise!

= How surprising!

11 ええっ！
Oh my!

12 びっくり！
That's amazing!

= Wow!／How about that!

13 ショック！
I'm astonished!

shocked／surprised

14 ショックだよ。
It gave me a jolt.

jolt＝激しい上下運動、精神的ショック

15 冗談でしょ？
☞ **Are you kidding?**

joking

16 本当に？
Are you serious?

sure

17 ひどい！
What a shame!

= How terrible!

18 信じられない！
(That's) unbelievable!

≡ I can't believe it!

19 まさか！
☞ No way!

💧「うそでしょう」「あり得ない」というニュアンスで使う。

20 それはお気の毒に。
That's too bad.

💧 人からよくない話を聞いたときに、同情を込めて言う。

21 ばかばかしい。
That's <u>stupid</u>.

ridiculous／crazy

22 ばかなこと言わないで。
Don't be <u>silly</u>.

stupid／ridiculous

23 くだらないこと言わないで。
Stop talking nonsense.

≡ What nonsense!

24 つまんないの！
How boring!

25 いつになったら話は面白くなるの？
When does the fun start?

💧 ちょっと皮肉っぽい意地悪な言い方。友達にからかい口調で言おう。

26 それがどうしたの？
So what?

≡ And?　＊強い言い方をすると、反抗的な表現になる。

会話の間をつなぐ 2

あいづちを打つ

2 会話の間をつなぐ

聞き返す

1 えっ、何ですか？

Sorry?
= What?／Pardon?　＊相手の話が聞き取れなかったときに、語尾を上げて聞き返す。

2 もう1回言って。

Say that again.
= Can you say that again?　＊こちらのほうが、よりていねいな言い方。

3 よくわからなかったよ。

☞ I didn't quite catch that.

get／understand

4 話についていけなくなっちゃった。

I'm not quite following you.
= I can't keep up (with you).　＊話についていけていないときは早めに相手に伝えよう。

5 もう少し ゆっくりしゃべってくれませんか？

Can you speak more slowly, please?

大きな声で loudly／小さい声で quietly

6 全然わかんないんだけど。

I'm totally lost.
= I didn't get the point.　＊「何て言ったの？」は What did you say?

7 どういう意味？

What does it mean?
= What do you mean?／What are you trying to say?

8 もうちょっと具体的に言ってくれない？

Can you be more specific?

specific＝明確な、具体的な

2 会話の間をつなぐ

確認する

1 意味がわかる？

Does this make sense?

make sense=意味をなす　＊全然わかってなさそうな相手には any sense と強調してもいい。

2 わかった？

(Do you) understand?

≒ Understood?　＊少し強い言い方。

3 私の言ってることがわかりますか？

Do you know what I mean?

see／understand

4 私の話についてきていますか？

Are you with me?

≒ Are you following me?

5 よくわかった？

Is that clear?

≒ All clear?

6 ねえ、わかるでしょ。

You know what I'm talking about.

≒ You know what I mean.

7 前に言いましたよね。

I said that, didn't I?

8 だいたいわかった？

(Do you) get the picture?

the picture=状況、事態

2 会話の間をつなぐ

返答に困ったとき

1 そうだなぁ…。
Let me see.
= Well, ... / Let's see.　＊このように言って、言葉につまったときに時間を稼ごう。

2 そんなところかな。
Sort of.
= Kind of.

3 まあそんなところです。
It's something like that.
= It's something of that sort.

4 そうだと思う。
I guess so.
「そうでないと思う」は I guess not.

5 そうかもしれないね。
It could be.
= Maybe.

6 何とも言えないなあ。
☞ It depends.
It all depends on circumstances. を省略した表現。「時と場合によるよ」という感じ。

7 さあ、どうかな。
Yes and no.
「どちらとも言いがたい」という意味。

8 何と言ったらいいか。
How should I put this?
= What should I say?

9 うーん、わかんないけど。
Well, I don't know.

10 見当がつかないよ。
Beats me.
= I'm not sure. ＊聞かれたことの答えが思い浮かばないようなときに使う。

11 関係ないよ。
Who cares?
「誰もそんなこと気にかけちゃいないよ」という感じ。

12 誰にもわかんないよ。
Nobody knows.

God

13 全く見当もつかないよ。
I don't have a clue.
clue＝手がかり、糸口

14 ちんぷんかんぷんだ。
☞ It's all Greek to me.
「まるでギリシャ語のように見当もつかない」という言い方。

15 つじつまが合わないよ。
That makes no sense.
= That doesn't make sense.

16 理解できない。
I can't figure it out.
figure out＝計算する、解く

17 さっぱりわからない。
I can't make heads or tails of it.
heads と tails は硬貨の「表」と「裏」。

2 会話の間をつなぐ

話題を変える

1 話題を変えよう。
Let's change the subject.
topic

2 さて、ほかの話をしようか。
Well, let's talk about something else.
different

3 もっと楽しい話をしようよ。
Let's talk about something more fun.
面白い interesting／まじめな serious

4 その話はしたくないな。
I don't want to talk about it.
I'd prefer not to talk about it.　＊こちらのほうが、少しやわらかい言い方。

5 話は変わるけどさ…。
To change the subject, ...
By the way, ...

6 ああ、そうそう。
That reminds me.
「それで思い出したんだけど」という感じ。人の話にのって、話題を変えるときに使える。

7 そういえばさ…。
Now that you mention it, ...
「その話のついでなんだけど」という感じ。

8 それはさておき…。
Putting it aside, ...
That aside, ...／Moving on, ...

2 会話の間をつなぐ

話を終わらせる

CD1 Track 16

1 この話はこれまで。
Let's drop the subject.
drop＝落とす　＊かなり強い言い方。Drop it! で「やめて！」。

2 これで終わり。
That's about it.
= That's it.

3 話すのをやめませんか。
Why don't we stop talking?
Why don't we stop ~ ing ?＝～するのをやめにしないか？　＊比較的、やわらかい表現。

4 もう、これ以上は話したくない。
I don't want to talk any more.
状況によってはかなりきつい言い方になるので要注意。話したくない理由を添えるとよい。

5 もう、それ以上言わないで。
I've heard enough about it.
うわさ話や悪口などに飽き飽きしたときに使おう。

6 もうたくさん。
Enough already.
= That's enough.／Enough is enough.

7 もう聞いたよ。
You've already told me.
Somebody's already told me.「誰かから聞いた」と言った方が婉曲的で使いやすい。

8 もうその話はうんざりよ。
I'm sick of hearing it.
tired

3 感情を表す

うれしい、楽しい

CD1 Track 17

1 やった！
☞ **I did it!**

= I made it!

2 本当にうれしい。
I'm so pleased.

glad／happy

3 いい気分！
I feel great!

wonderful／fantastic／terrific

4 夢みたいだ。
It's (like) a dream come true.

a dream come true＝夢がかなうこと

5 最高の日！
This is the happiest day of my life!

瞬間 moment

6 最高！
I'm super happy!

7 こんなに幸せなことはない！
I couldn't be happier!

= I've never been happier!

8 うそみたいだ。
It's too good to be true.

直訳すると「事実であるにはよすぎる」。信じられないほどうれしいときに使う。

9 今日は、ついてる！
It's my lucky day!
I'm in luck today.／Luck is with me today.

10 うきうきする。
I'm walking on air.
air＝空、空中

11 面白い！
This is fun!
≡ What fun!

12 本当に楽しい！
I'm having a good time!
≡ I'm really enjoying this!

13 笑えるね！
What a laugh!
≡ I can't stop laughing!

14 最高におかしい！
☞ That's hilarious!
hilárious［ヒラーリアス］＝大変陽気な、大笑いを誘う

15 笑いすぎた。
I wet myself.
≡ I laughed until I cried.

16 今日は機嫌がいいんだ。
I'm in a good mood today.
high spirits

17 うれしくてたまらない。
I can't stop smiling.
「うれしくてつい笑みがこぼれちゃう」という感じ。

3 感情を表す

感動する

CD1 Track 18

1 感動しちゃった。
I was (deeply) moved.

= How moving!

2 とてもよかった。
It was great.

wonderful／fantastic／super／fabulous

3 胸を打たれたよ。
☞ **It touched me.**

= I cried buckets.

4 感心したよ。
I was impressed.

= How impressive!

5 君って天才！
You are a genius!

génius [ジーニアス]

6 一生忘れない。
It will stay in my heart.

= I will never forget it.

7 あなたを尊敬します。
I respect you.

admire／look up to

8 目を見張ったよ。
It was a real eye-opener for me.

eye-opener＝目を見張らせる(驚くべき)こと、びっくりするような発見

3 感情を表す

興奮する、ほっとする

1 待ち遠しいなあ。
I'm really looking forward to it.

= I can't wait.

2 すごいことになるよ。
It's going to be great.

3 ドキドキする。
My heart is pounding.

4 ありがたい！
Thank heavens!

heaven「天国」にいる神に感謝する気持ちから。

5 やれやれ！
Whew!

Whew! [ヒュー]

6 ああ、ほっとした！
What a relief!

That's

7 よかった。
I feel a lot better now.

8 それを聞いて安心したよ。
I'm relieved to hear that.

= I feel much better now that you've told me.

3 感情を表す

イライラする、不満が募る

CD1 Track 20

1 腹が立つ。
It's driving me crazy.
💧 人に対して「腹が立つ」ときは You're (She's) driving me crazy. のように言う。

2 あなたには**本当に頭にくる**。
You're driving me round the bend.
round the bend＝気の狂った（口語）

3 むかつくなあ。
That's disgusting.
🟰 That disgusts me.

4 もう**限界**だ。
I blew my top.
🟰 I lost my temper.　＊頭の先から蒸気が出るように、ひどく怒ること。

5 よくもまあ！
How dare you!
💧 How dare you say that!「よくもそんなことが言えるな」の略。

6 あっちへ行け！
Get lost!
🟰 Go away!／Get out of my sight!

7 ほっといてよ。
Leave me alone.
🟰 Stop bothering me.　＊どちらもかなり強い言い方。相手を怒らせたくないときは言わない。

8 やめてよ。
👉 Give me a break.
a break＝小休止、好意ある扱い　＊「勘弁してよ」の意味にも使える便利なフレーズ。

9 イライラする。
I'm in a bad mood.
= I'm irritated with (人). ／I'm irritated at (物).

10 イライラしてきた。
It's getting on my nerves.
nerves＝神経過敏（な状態）

11 イラつかないで。
Don't fret.
= Don't let it get to you.

12 何が気に入らないの？
What's eating you?
eat＝困らせる、イライラさせる

13 イライラさせないで！
Stop pestering me!
bugging／nagging

14 その音、イライラする。
The noise irritates me.
annoys／frets

15 めんどくさいなあ。
☞ What a hassle.
hassle＝骨の折れること

16 不満だね。
I'm not satisfied.
= This isn't good enough.

17 それじゃ納得できないね。
That doesn't explain it.
= It's not acceptable.

3 感情を表す

イライラする、不満が募る

3 感情を表す
緊張する、恥じる

1 胸がドキドキする。
My heart is beating so fast.

2 緊張してきた。
I'm getting nervous.
> しだいに緊張が高まる様子は I'm getting more and more nervous. と言う。

3 落ち着かないよ。
I can't relax.
= I have butterflies. ／ I'm on pins and needles.

4 あせっちゃう。
I feel flustered.
> 「逃げ出したい気分だ」なら I feel like running away.

5 どうすればいいんだろう？
☞ What am I supposed to do?
= I don't know what to do. ／ What should I do?

6 人見知りで。
I'm shy.
> 性格的なこと。もじもじして人見知りするような恥ずかしさ。

7 すごく恥ずかしい。
I'm so embarrassed.
> 行いによること。ファスナーが空いたまま出掛けてしまったときのような恥ずかしさ。

8 恥を知れよ！
Shame on you!
= What a shame!

3 感情を表す

危機・恐怖に直面する

CD1 Track 22

1 まずい。
I'm in a big mess.

mess＝めちゃくちゃに散らかっていること

2 ただごとではないよ！
This is serious!

≒ disaster

3 あり得ない！
It can't be!

＝ It can't be true! ／ Impossible!

4 困ってるんだ。
I'm in a pickle.

pickle＝困った立場、苦境

5 もうダメだ。
The game is up.

6 お手上げだ。
It's over my head.

💡「もう何も考えられない」といった状態。

7 もう、あとがない。
I'm at the end of my rope.

💡「万策尽きた」「万事休す」といった感じ。

8 もうおしまいだ。
I'm doomed.

doomed＝運が尽きた、破滅する運命にある

危機・恐怖に直面する

9 やっちゃったね。
You've done it now.

10 不意打ちを食らっちゃって。
It took me by surprise.
= I got caught with my pants down.

11 怖いよ。
I'm scared.
terrified／horrified／frightened

12 気味が悪いな。
That's creepy.
💡 動詞 creep は「這う」「忍び寄る」の意味。creepy は「ぞっとするような、不気味な」。

13 鳥肌が立っちゃった。
I've got goose bumps.
= It gave me goose bumps.

14 ぞっとする。
I'm petrified.
= I'm scared stiff.／I've got cold feet.

15 おどかさないでよ。
You gave me a fright.
= You startled me.／You made me jump.

16 気持ち悪い！
That's gross!
gróss［グロウス］＝不快な、ぞっとする、気味の悪い

17 吐きそう。
I'm going to puke.
púke［ピューク］ ＊「オエーッと吐く」という感じ。

3 感情を表す

悲しい、寂しい

1 悲しい。
I'm so sad.

very

2 とても悲しいんだ。
I'm down in the dumps.

dump＝ごみ捨て場　＊I'm sad. よりも深い悲しみが表せる。

3 それ聞いたら悲しくなってきた。
Your story is making me sad.

4 いったいどうしちゃったんだよ。
What's the matter with you?

5 立ち直れない。
☞ **I can't get over it.**

＝ I can't seem to cheer up.／I feel like I'll never be happy again.

6 寂しい。
I'm lonely.

＝ I feel alone.

7 ひとりぼっちだ。
I feel cut off.

isolated

8 あなたがいなくて寂しい。
I feel lost without you.

＝ I wish you were here.／I miss you.

3 感情を表す

落ち込む、後悔する

1 憂鬱(ゆううつ)だ。
I feel blue.
= I'm blue.／I have the blues.

2 最悪だよ。
It's a no-win situation.
何をやってもうまくいかないときに使う。

3 へこむよ。
I'm disappointed.
disappointed＝失望した、がっかりした

4 落ち込んじゃって。
I'm depressed.
= I feel depressed.／I'm feeling down.

5 ボロボロだよ。
I feel miserable.
heartbroken

6 むなしいな。
I feel empty.
「空っぽで無意味」な感じ。I feel incomplete. と言うと、さらにむなしい感じが出る。

7 何でそうご機嫌ななめなの？
What makes you so grumpy?
= Why the long face?

8 何でそう暗いわけ？
Why so moody?
glum／gloomy

9 もうあきらめた。

I've (completely) given up on it.

≡ I give up. ／ Not a chance.

10 やってもムダだ。

There's no use in trying.

≡ We don't have a chance in hell.

11 もうどうでもいいや。

It doesn't matter any more.

≡ I don't care any more.

12 後悔してる。

I regret it.

≡ I regret what I've done. ／ I'm sorry for what I did.

13 大きな間違いだったんだ。

It was a big mistake.

≡ What a mistake!

14 あんなこと言わなきゃよかった。

☞ **I shouldn't have said that.**

≡ I regret what I've said. ／ I feel bad about what I've said.

15 何であんなことしちゃったんだろう。

Why did I do that?

≡ How on earth could I have done that?

16 やり直せたらいいのに。

I wish I could do it over again.

💡 仮定法 could で、現実にはやり直せないことが強調される。

17 そのことが頭から離れないんだ。

I can't get it off my mind.

≡ I can't get it out of my head.

4 気持ちを伝える
お礼を言う

1 どうもありがとう。
Thanks a lot.
million = Thank you very much.

2 先日はどうも。
Thanks for the other day.

3 感謝するよ。
Much obliged.
obliged [オブライジド]

4 いろいろありがとうございます。
☞ **Thank you for everything.**

5 助かったよ。
It was a great help.
= You helped me a lot.

6 あなたのおかげです。
I couldn't have done it without you.
= I wouldn't have been here without you.

7 あなたの援助に助けられました。
Your help was invaluable.
評価 feedback／意見 opinion／助言 advice

8 そんなふうに言ってくれてありがとう。
That made my day.
お世辞やうれしいことを言われて、「あなたのお陰で素敵な1日になったよ」という気持ち。

4 気持ちを伝える

お礼を言われたとき

1 どういたしまして。
You're welcome.
> Thank you. に対して言う、最も一般的なフレーズ。

2 お安い御用だ。
My pleasure.
> Don't mention it.

3 どうってことないよ。
It was nothing.
> No problem. ／ Not at all.

4 いいって。
That's alright.
> That's okay. ／ Don't worry about it.

5 役に立ててよかった。
I'm glad I could help.
> I was happy to help.

6 いつでもどうぞ。
Anytime.
> Whenever.

7 お互いさまだよ。
The feeling's mutual.
> mutual＝相互の、双方の

8 つけとくよ。
You owe me one.
> 直訳すると「君は僕に1つ借りを作ったね」。友達に冗談っぽく言う。

4 気持ちを伝える

謝る

1 本当にごめんなさい。
I'm so sorry.
awfully／very／terribly

2 私のせいよ。
All my fault.
= My mistake.／I take all the blame.／I was (very) wrong.

3 ご迷惑をおかけして申し訳ありません。
I'm sorry for all the trouble.

4 謝らせて。
Let me apologize.
apólogize [アポロジャイズ] = I owe you an apology.

5 申し訳なくてたまらない。
I feel terrible about it.
awful／horrible

6 そんなつもりじゃなかったんだけど。
I didn't mean to do this.
= I didn't mean it.

7 許してくれる？
Can you forgive me?
= Please forgive me.

8 どうしたら許してくれる？
What can I do to make it up to you?
= Is there anything I can do to make you feel better?

4 気持ちを伝える
謝られたとき

1. 気にしないで。
(It's) no big deal.
Don't worry about it. / Never mind. / Forget it.

2. 謝る必要ないよ。
No need to apologize.

3. あなたのせいじゃない。
It wasn't your fault.
You didn't do anything wrong.

4. 仕方なかったんだよ。
Anyone could have done the same.
「誰でも同じようにしたよ」の意味。

5. もういいよ。
☞ **Apologies accepted.**
I accept your apology. / I forgive you.

6. 謝るのはこっちだよ。
I should be the one to apologize.
be blamed

7. ごめんじゃ済まないよ。
Sorry isn't (good) enough.
It's unforgivable.

8. 次からは気をつけてくださいね。
Please don't let it happen again.
Please be more careful next time.

4 気持ちを伝える
依頼・要求をする

1 お願いがあるんだけど。
Do me a favor.
> Will you ～?／Can you ～?／Could you ～? で始めれば、ていねいな印象になる。

2 お願いがあります。
I have a favor to ask.
= May I ask you a favor?

3 手伝ってくれる？
Can you give me a hand?
= Will you help me?

4 助けが必要なの。
I need some help.
a hand

5 あなたがいなければできない。
I can't do it without you.

6 無理なお願いかな？
Is that asking too much?
= Is that too much to ask?

7 考え直してくれない？
Won't you reconsider?

8 そんなことしないでください。
Please don't do that.

4 気持ちを伝える
依頼・要求に応える

1 いいよ。
Okay.
= Sure./Sure thing./Of course./Certainly./No problem./Anytime./With pleasure.

2 喜んで。
I'd be glad to.
happy／pleased

3 あなたのためなら何なりと。
☞ Anything for you.
↪ 親友 a good friend／妻 my loving wife／愛する我が子 my little princess

4 やってあげたいけど、できない。
I'd love to, but I can't.
= I wish I could.

5 ごめん、手が離せない。
Sorry, I'm tied up now.
be tied up＝忙しい

6 絶対に無理。
☞ Not in a million years.
💡「100万年たってもない」という意味から、「絶対にできない」感じを表現。

7 それについては力になれないよ。
I can't do anything about it.
= There is nothing I can do about it.

8 またの機会にね。
Maybe some other time.

↪ 次の next

4 気持ちを伝える
提案・助言をする

CD1 Track 31

1 ひとつ提案してもいい？
Can I make a suggestion?
＝ I want to make a suggestion.

2 手伝おうか？
Do you need some help?
＝ Do you want a hand?

3 私に何かできることはある？
Anything I can do (for you)?
Is there anything … ? の略。

4 もう一度やってみたらどう？
Why don't you try again?

5 個人的な意見だけど。
That's just my two cents.
two cents＝価値のないもの　＊自分の考えを言うときの控えめな表現。

6 そうしたほうが君のためだ。
You'd better do it or else.
or else＝さもないと（ひどいことになる）

7 自分の気持ちに正直になったほうがいいよ。
I think you should follow your heart.

8 あとで後悔することになるよ。
You're going to regret it later.

4 気持ちを伝える

励ます

1 がんばれ！
Way to go!
Hang in there! ＊何かをしている人に「いいぞ」「がんばり通して」と声援を送るときに使う。

2 あなたなら大丈夫、がんばって！
You can do it!
Go for it! ＊これから何かを始めようとする人を励まして言う。

3 リラックスしてがんばって！
☞ Take it easy!
「気楽にね」という意味。これから試験を受ける人などを励ます表現。

4 元気を出して！
Cheer up!
Come on!

5 あきらめちゃダメ。
Don't give up.
Never say never. ／ Never give up.

6 もうちょっとだったのにね。
It was really close.
clóse [クロウス] You're nearly there.

7 明日があるさ。
Things will look better tomorrow.
Tomorrow is another day. ／ There's always tomorrow.

8 いいこともあるよ。
Look on the bright side.
「物事の明るい面も見てごらんよ」「悪いことばかりじゃないよ」といった意味。

4 気持ちを伝える

ほめる

1 すばらしい！
Great!
= Excellent! / Fantastic! / Brilliant!

2 たいしたもんだね。
That's really something.
You're / He's / They'reなど

3 やるね！
Nice going!
= Good going! / Nice job!

4 よくやってくれたよ。
I think highly of you.
think highly of ～=～を尊敬する

5 努力の甲斐があったね。
It was worth the effort.
= Your effort finally paid off.

6 あなたのがんばりのおかげです。
All the credit goes to you.
credit=手柄、功績

7 君の手柄だ。
You deserve all the credit.
deserve ～=～を受ける価値がある

8 君の貢献は大きい。
You were a big help.

9 うまくいったね。

It came out great.

どうなるかわからなかったものが、「結果的にうまくいった」という感じ。文末に in the end をつけても。

10 でかした！

Well done!

11 君を誇りに思うよ。

I'm proud of you.

娘 my daughter／父親 my father／自分 myself／そのミュージシャン the musician

12 感心するよ。

I admire you.

13 あなたって本当にかっこいい！

You're really cool!

魅力的 attractive／頭がいい smart／器用 clever／人気者 popular

14 すごくうまくなったね。

You're making a lot of progress.

＝ You've improved a lot.

15 その髪型いいね！

I like your hairstyle.

シャツ shirt／ドレス dress／靴 shoes／イヤリング earrings

16 その服、とても似合ってるよ。

That dress looks really good on you.

nice／great

17 料理上手だね。

You're an excellent cook.

聞き listener／教え teacher／運転 driver／泳ぎ swimmer

4 気持ちを伝える

ほめられたとき

CD1 Track 34

1 おほめの言葉、ありがとう。
I appreciate the compliment.

compliment＝ほめ言葉

2 (お世辞が) お上手ですね。
☞ You flatter me.

flatter＝お世辞を言う　≡ That's very flattering.

3 お世辞でもうれしいな。
I'm happy, even if it's just flattery.

flattery＝お世辞、おべっか

4 そんなふうに言ってくれるなんてうれしい。
That's really nice of you to say.

≡ I'm happy that you'd say that.

5 もっと言って、もっと言って。
Oh, go on.

go on＝続ける、進む

6 まあまあのできだったかも。
It didn't turn out too badly.

≡ It wasn't too bad.

7 まだまだこれからよ。
I'm not quite there yet.

💡「自分が目指すゴールへはまだ到達していない」という意味。

8 ありがとう。でも運がよかっただけ。
Thank you. It was pure luck.

≡ I was just lucky.

4 気持ちを伝える

祝福する

1. おめでとう！

   Congratulations!

   ❗ 何かを達成したときなどに使う。お正月や誕生日には使わない。

2. <u>結婚</u>おめでとう。

   Congratulations on your <u>marriage</u>.

   🔄 婚約 engagement／昇進 promotion／新しい仕事 new job／全快 recovery

3. よかったね！

   Good for you!

   ＝ I'm (really) happy for you.

4. やったね！

   Good job!

   ＝ Well done!／Excellent!／Fantastic!

5. 君なら、やると思っていたよ。

   I knew you could do it.

   ＝ I knew it.

6. かっこよかった！

   You're my hero!

   ＝ Bravo!

7. お誕生日おめでとう！

   Happy birthday!

   🔄 新年 New Year／ハロウィーン Halloween／クリスマス Christmas（当日25日の言い方）

8. よい1年になりますように。

   All the best for the new year.

   ❗ All the best! は、別れ際や手紙の最後などにも使う。「幸せを(祈る)」の意味。

4 気持ちを伝える
気づかう

1 大丈夫？
Are you okay?

alright

2 落ち着いて。
Calm down.

= Keep your calm.

3 ちょっと落ち着いてよ。
Hold on a second.

= Slow down for a minute.

4 あせらなくていいよ。
Take your time.

= No rush.／No hurry.

5 リラックスして！
Just relax!

= Take it easy!

6 なるようになるさ。
☞ **Take things as they come.**

「起きるできごとをそのまま受け入れよう」の意味。

7 時がたてばわかるよ。
Time will tell.

= You'll see.

8 あわてない、あわてない。
No need to panic.

panic＝うろたえる　＊Don't panic! で「あわてるな！」。

4 気持ちを伝える

相談する

CD1 Track 37

1 相談したいことがあって。
I've got something I want to talk about.
I'd like ＊ややていねいな感じ。

2 聞いてもらいたいことがあるの。
I have something I want you to know.
💧「あなたに知ってもらいたいことがある」の意味。うちあけ話を始める前に言う。

3 あなたならどうする？
👉 What would you do if you were me?
💧「もしあなたが私だったとしたら」という仮定法を使った表現。

4 私の立場だったら、どうしてた？
What would you have done in my situation?
situation＝立場、境遇

5 どう思う？
Tell me what you think.
💧「あなたの思っていることを言って」の意味。

6 正直に言って。
I want your honest opinion.
🔵 率直 frank

7 言わなくちゃいけないことがあるの。
I have a confession.
confession＝白状、告白 ＊言いにくい事実を伝えるときに。

8 本当のことを言うよ。
I'll tell you the truth.
truth＝真実、真相

4 気持ちを伝える
なぐさめる

1 お気の毒に。
I'm sorry about that.
= I'm sorry to hear that. ／ My heart goes out to you. ／ My soul is with you.

2 かわいそうに。
You poor thing!
= There! There! ＊泣いている人を「よし、よし」と慰めるときなどに。

3 力になりたいな。
☞ If you ever need a shoulder to cry on …
💡 直訳すると「泣くための肩が必要なら」。「話を聞くよ」といった感じ。

4 大丈夫だよ。
Don't worry.
= Don't sweat it.

5 つらいでしょうね。
It must be tough for you.
tough [タフ]　hard／difficult

6 気持ちはわかるわ。
☞ I know how you feel.
= I know this must be a difficult time for you.

7 何て言ったらいいのか。
I don't know what to say.

8 時が解決してくれるよ。
Time heals all wounds.
heal＝治す、いやす　= Time heals most troubles. ／ Time is a great healer.

9 すぐによくなるって。

Everything will soon be okay.

= It'll be over soon.／You'll feel better soon.

10 気にしすぎだよ。

I think you're overreacting.

overreact＝大げさに反応する

11 たいしたことじゃないよ。

I don't think it's that serious.

❗ that にストレスを置いて、「そんなに」深刻ではないと強調する。

12 そういうこともあるって。

It happens.

happen＝予測できないことが起こる

13 ましなほうですよ。

☞ I've seen worse.

❗「もっとひどい状態を見たことがある」という意味。慰めの気持ちを込めて。

14 泣くほどのことじゃない。

It's not worth crying over.

cry over 〜＝〜のことを嘆く

15 なるべくしてなったんだよ。

It was meant to happen.

= It was fate.

16 そのことで落ち込まないで。

Don't let it get you down.

= Don't let it get to you.

17 君のせいじゃないよ。

Don't blame yourself.

= It's not your fault.

気持ちを伝える

なぐさめる

4 気持ちを伝える
注意する

1 気をつけて！
Watch out!
= Be careful!

2 頭上に気をつけて。
Mind your head.
↻ 足元 step／後ろ back

3 後ろを見て！
Behind you!
💡 後ろに、人や自転車・車などが迫ってきているのに気づかない人などに注意を喚起する。

4 右を見て！
To your right!
↻ 左 left

5 しっかりつかまってね。
Hold on tight.
= Don't let go.

6 覚悟しておいてね。
Be prepared.
💡 散らかっている部屋に招待するときなどに「びっくりしないでね」という感じ。

7 彼には気をつけて。
Watch out for him.
= Keep your eye on him.

8 罠があるわ。
There's a (little) catch.
= There's something to it.

9 よくよく考えてね。

Think twice.

> Think twice before you do it. の略。「行動する前に二度考えろ」の意味。

10 早まらないで！

Don't jump to conclusions!

> conclusion＝結論　＊「結論を急がないで」といった意味。

11 バカなまねはよして。

Don't make a fool of yourself.

> ＝ Don't play the fool.／Stop acting like a fool.

12 口のきき方に気をつけなさい。

Watch your tongue.

> language／mouth　＊汚い言葉づかいを注意する。

13 態度が悪いよ。

You have a bad attitude.

> ＝ You have an attitude problem.

14 年を考えて。

Act your age.

> act＝行動する、ふるまう

15 失礼だよ。

That's (very) rude.

> rude＝無作法な、失礼な　＊Don't be rude! で「失礼な振るまいはやめて」。

16 割り込まないで。

Don't jump the queue.

> queue [キュー]＝(人や車の) 待っている列　＝ Don't cut into the line.

17 行儀よくして。

Behave yourself.

> ＝ Behave!／Don't be naughty.／Where are your manners?

4 気持ちを伝える

命令する、とがめる

1 やめろ！
Hold it!
= Cut it out!

2 やめて！
Stop it!
= Don't do that!

3 動くな！
Freeze!
freeze＝凍る　＊Halt!「停止しろ！」も同意。警察官や強盗にこう言われたら動かないこと。

4 手を上げろ！
Hands up!
= Hands in the air!／Reach for the sky!

5 放してよ！
Let go (of me)!
= Let me go!

6 何とかしてよ！
Do something (about it)!

7 言い訳は、もうたくさん。
No more excuses.
excuse＝弁解、理由

8 そんなの言い訳にならないよ。
That's not a good excuse.
= You have no excuse.

9 そんな目で見ないでよ。

Don't look at me like that.

≒ Don't give me a dirty look.

10 しつこいなあ！

Stop nagging!

nag＝がみがみしつこく小言を言う　＊Stop complaining! は「文句言うな」。

11 やつあたりしないでよ。

Don't take it out on me.

take it out on ~＝~に当たり散らす

12 私の身にもなってよ。

☞ Put yourself in my shoes.

≒ Can you see it from my point of view?

13 君には関係ないよ。

☞ None of your business.

≒ Mind your own business.／Keep your nose out of this.

14 あなたには聞いてない。

Who asked you?

💡「口をはさむな」という感じ。

15 ムリムリ！

Not a chance!

≒ No way!

16 もう済んだことだ。

It's all over.

≒ It's history.／It's in the past.／That's it.

17 そういうものだよ。

That's the way it goes.

≒ That's always the way.／That's how it works.／I can't help it.

4 気持ちを伝える
決心する、意思を伝える

1 決めたよ。
I've made up my mind.
make up one's mind＝決心する

2 決心したよ。
I've decided.
= I've made my decision.

3 本気よ。
I mean it.
= I'm serious.／I'm positive.

4 もう気は変わらない。
It's the final decision.
= My decision is final.

5 試しにやってみるよ。
I'll give it a go.
= I'll give it a try.／I'll have a go at it.／I'll go for it.

6 やるだけやってみたら？
Why not take a chance?
Why not ～?＝～してみてはどうだろう？

7 やっても損はないんじゃない。
It's worth a try.
worth ～＝～に値する

8 君ならできるって。
I know you can do it.
= I'm sure you can do it.／I have confidence in you.

9 やるなら今だよ。

(It's) now or never.

「今やらなければ永久にできない」の意味。

10 やるなら早い方がいい。

The sooner, the better.

決断を迷う相手(または自分自身)に、はっぱをかけるように言う。

11 あとには引けないよ。

There's no turning back.

turn back＝引き返す

12 今、思い直せばまだ間に合うよ。

It's not too late to change your mind.

change one's mind＝気が変わる

13 決められないよ。

I can't make up my mind.

It's so difficult to decide.

14 優柔不断なんだ。

I'm too indecisive.

indecisive [インディサイシヴ]

15 あなたが決めてよ。

You decide.

I'll follow you.／It's all up to you.／It's your call.

16 くじを引いて決めよう。

Let's draw lots.

I think we should draw lots.

17 よし、決まった。

It's a deal.

deal＝取引　＊「商談成立」の意味。ふざけた感じで使う。握手を求めても楽しい。

気持ちを伝える

決心する、意思を伝える

4 気持ちを伝える

約束する

1 約束する。
I promise.
> I can't promise. で「約束はできない」。

2 約束を守ってね。
Hope you keep your promise.
> Hope you don't break your promise. で「約束を破らないで」。

3 誰にも言わないでよ。
Don't tell anyone.
= Don't breathe a word.

4 ふたりだけの秘密だよ。
☞ This is just between you and I.

5 内緒だよ。
Keep this quiet, OK?
= Mum's the word, eh?　＊シェイクスピアの戯曲に出てくるセリフから。

6 誰にも言わないよ。
I won't say a word.
> 「ひとことも言わない」の意味。「絶対しゃべらない」と約束するときの表現。

7 それは秘密だよ。
It's a secret.

8 つい口がすべっちゃって。
It was a slip of the tongue.
> 「口が軽いのね」は You have a big mouth.

4 気持ちを伝える
忘れる、思い出す

CD1 Track 43

1 最近忘れっぽくて。
I've been forgetful lately.

these days

2 ど忘れしちゃった。
It slipped my mind.

💡「私の意識から滑り落ちてしまった」の意味。

3 物忘れが激しい。
I have a terrible memory.

💡「ひどい記憶力を持っている」の意味。

4 覚えた端から忘れちゃって。
I have a memory like a sieve.

sieve=ふるい、こし器

5 ここまで出かかってるんだけど。
It's on the tip of my tongue.

💡「舌の先まできている」という意味。

6 どうしても思い出せない。
I can't remember for the life of me.

for the life of me=どうしても

7 それで思い出した！
That rings a bell!

= That reminds me!／Now I remember!

8 思い出させないで！
Don't remind me!

remind me (of ~)=私に(~を)思い出させる

5 考えを表す

好き、嫌い

1 大好き。
I love it.
🔊 I like it. より好きな度合いが強い。I love cats. は「猫が好きでたまらない」という感じ。

2 新しいCDが気に入ってるんだ。
I'm <u>happy</u> with my new CD.
pleased／satisfied／content

3 そのバンド、好きなんだ。
I'm fond of the band.
be fond of ～＝～が好きだ　🔊「そのバンドのファンなの」は I'm a big fan of the band.

4 どっちが好き？
Which one do you like better?
≒ Which do you prefer?

5 （これよりも）あっちのほうが好き！
I prefer that one (to this one).
≒ I'd rather have that one (than this).

6 これ、どう思う？
☞ How do you like this?
≒ What do you think of this?

7 いいねえ。
It's <u>great</u>.
fantastic／wonderful

8 カンペキ！
This is perfect.
≒ I couldn't ask for more.

9 タイ料理に目がなくて。

I'm crazy about Thai food.

be crazy about ~ = ~に夢中になっている、~がとても気に入っている

10 甘いものに弱いんだ。

I have a weakness for sweets.

weakness = 欠点、弱点　＊have a weakness for ~で「~に目がない、~が大好物だ」。

11 ファストフードが大好きなんだ。

I'm partial to fast food.

be partial to ~は、2つ以上あるもののうち、特にこれが好きというニュアンス。

12 ビールなしじゃ生きていけない。

I can't live without beer.

13 納豆が好きになった。

I came to like natto.

はじめは受けつけなかったものを、だんだん好きになった場合に使うフレーズ。

14 彼女にまいってるんだ。

I have a crush on her.

crushは「押しつぶすこと」の意。ハートが押しつぶされる感じの「ベタぼれ状態」を言う。

15 あの娘、そそられる。

She turns me on.

turn on = 興奮させる、性的に刺激する

16 好みにうるさいんだ。

I'm choosy.

picky／fussy

17 好きじゃない。

I don't like it.

≡ I dislike it.

考えを表す

好き、嫌い

好き、嫌い

18 好みじゃない。
I don't care for it.
care for ~ = ~を好む、欲する　*疑問文・否定文・条件文で使う。

19 大嫌い。
I hate it.
I don't like it. よりも嫌いな度合いが強い。

20 勉強なんか大嫌い。
I'm allergic to studying.
allérgic [アレージック]　*「勉強アレルギーだ」というニュアンス。

21 スポーツは苦手です。
I'm not good at sports.
歌を歌うこと singing songs

22 彼女はタイプじゃない。
She's not my cup of tea.
cup of tea = 好きなもの、好物　　She's not my type.

23 興味ないよ。
I'm not into it.
I'm not interested (in it).

24 コンピューターには興味ない。
I'm not a computer person.
本 book／音楽 music／勉強 academic／マンガ comic

25 どこがいいのかわからない。
I can't see the appeal.
It has little appeal to me.

26 趣味が悪い！
You have bad taste.
taste = 趣味、好み

5 考えを表す

賛成する、同意する

CD1 Track 45

1 同感です。
I agree.
= I think so, too.

2 賛成だ。
I'm with you.
💡 with は「一致」「調和」を表す。Are you with me? で「私に賛成なの？」。

3 異議なし！
No objection!
💡 議会などで使う固い表現だが、友人同士の会話で面白おかしく使われることもある。

4 僕は文句ないよ。
No problem here.
with me／on my side

5 いいんじゃない。
Sounds alright to me.
= Sounds good.／Good idea.

6 まさにそのとおり。
You can say that again.
= Well said.

7 そのとおり！
Absolutely!
💡 強い肯定の表現。強い否定は Absolutely not.

8 賛成、それとも反対？
Are you for it or against it?
= For or against?

5 考えを表す
反対する、否定する

1 賛成できません。
I don't agree.
> I can't agree. と言った方が、少しやわらかい表現になる。

2 反対だ。
I'm against it.
> I'm against you. は、個人に反対することになるので、避けたほうが無難。

3 納得できないな。
I can't buy that.
> buy＝信じる、受け入れる

4 僕たち、意見が違うね。
We don't see eye to eye.
> 主語を I にしたら I don't see eye to eye with you.

5 いい考えとは思えない。
That's not a good idea.
> ＝ That's no good.／No good.

6 問題外だね。
That's out of the question.
> ＝ That's nonsense.／That's bullshit.

7 うまくいきっこない。
It won't work.
> work＝機能する、具合よくいく

8 僕ならやらない。
I wouldn't do it if I were you.
> 「もし私があなただったら、そうはしない」の意味。

5 考えを表す

妥協する

1 妥協しよう。
Let's compromise.
≡ Let's meet halfway.

2 妥協点はあるはず。
There must be a happy medium.
médium [ミーディアム]

3 第三の方法があるかも。
There may be a third solution.
solution=(問題などの)解決、解明

4 妥協するよ。
I'm willing to be flexible.
flexible=しなやかな、柔軟な、融通の利く

5 話し合いしだいではね。
That's negotiable.
negótiable [ネゴウシャブル]

6 やっと妥協点を見出した。
We've reached a compromise.
≡ We've found some middle ground.

7 かなり譲ったよ。
☞ **I made some concessions.**
concession=譲歩

8 君って融通が利かないな。
You are very uncompromising.
≡ You are so stubborn.

5 考えを表す

保留する

1 たぶんね。
Maybe.
💧 possibly＜perhaps＜maybe＜probably　右に行くほど確信の度合いが強い。

2 おそらく。
Could well be.
💧「十分にあり得る」という感じ。Could be. より可能性が高い。

3 ちょっと様子をみよう。
Let's wait and see.
💧 wait and see what happens の略。

4 あせらないようにしよう。
Let's not be hasty.
hásty［ヘイスティ］

5 もう少し時間が必要だ。
I need more time.
💧「返事はちょっと待って」は Can it wait?

6 よく考えてから連絡する。
☞ I'll think it over and get back to you.
sleep／mull

7 時期尚早だ。
It's too soon.
💧「それをするには早すぎる」の意味。

8 何か気がのらないなあ。
I'm hesitant to do it.
hesitant＝躊躇した、ためらいがちな

9 さあ、どうかなあ。
I'm not sure.

10 どちらでも。
☞ **Either way is fine with me.**

> whatever. というと投げやりなニュアンスに。

11 全然気にならない。
I couldn't care less.

> 「これよりもっと気にしないことはできない」から「全く気にならない」の意に。

12 どれでも構わない。
It doesn't matter.

= It makes no difference (to me).

13 君しだい！
Anything you say!

= I'm easy.

14 君に従うよ。
You're the boss.

= You're in charge.

15 混乱してる。
I'm confused.

16 何が何だかさっぱりわからない。
I don't know what's what.

17 僕だってわからない。
Your guess is as good as mine.

> 「あなたの推測は私のと同じくらい」から「(あなたと同様)私だってわからない」の意味。

5 考えを表す
信じる、疑う

1 君の言うことを信じるよ。
I believe you.
= I believe what you said. ＊一時的に「人」「人の言うこと」を信じるときに使う。

2 君を信用している。
I believe in you.
一時的ではなく、「存在」「能力」「人柄」を信じるときに使う。

3 信頼しているよ。
I trust you.
= I'm counting on you. ／I have faith in you.

4 信じてよ。
☞ Take my word (for it).
= Believe me.／Trust me.

5 確かなの？
Are you sure (about that)?
= Is it true?

6 あやしいな。
I'm suspicious.
skeptical

7 うさんくさいなあ。
☞ That sounds fishy.
fishy＝あやしい、いかがわしい、まゆつばものの

8 嫌な予感がする。
I have a bad feeling about it.
= It's too good to be true. ＊「できすぎ(でおかしい)」といった意味。

5 考えを表す

間違いを指摘する

CD1 Track 50

1 悪いけど、違うよ。
I'm afraid you're wrong.
＊間違いを指摘するときは失礼にならないように I'm afraid や I'm sorry をつける。

2 ごめん、でも君は間違っているよ。
I'm sorry, but you're wrong.
= I think you're wrong.

3 誤解してるみたいだね。
I think you misunderstand.

4 何か誤解があったみたいだね。
I think there's been a misunderstanding.
misunderstanding＝誤解

5 そのことじゃないよ。
That's not the point.
issue／matter／ploblem

6 そうじゃなくて。
That's not how I see it.
「私はそういうふうには見ていない、考えていない」の意味。

7 そんなこと言ってないよ。
That's not what I'm talking about.
= That's not what I mean.

8 君のせいだろう？
Who's to blame?
= Whose fault is it?　＊いずれも「誰のせいだと思ってるんだよ？」という感じ。

5 考えを表す
苦情を言う

1 ちょっと困ってるんだけど。
I have a problem.
相手に気に障ることを伝えるときは、このフレーズで始めよう。

2 一つ言わせてもらうよ。
I have a complaint.
complaint=不平、苦情、ぐち　＊強い言い回しなので、相手は身構えることに。

3 もう我慢ならない。
I can't take it any more.
longer

4 欲しかったものと違うんだ。
It's not what I wanted.
聞いてた heard／思ってた thought／予想してた expected

5 これ、どこか変なんだ。
There's something wrong with this.
Is it supposed to be like this?

6 改善の余地があります。
There's room for improvement.
It can be improved.　＊婉曲に不満だったことを伝える表現。

7 うるさくて考えごともできやしない。
I can't even hear myself think.

8 困らせないでよ。
Don't be a pain in the neck.
pain in the neck=不快感、イライラ

Part 2 日常生活の会話

1 家族との会話……98
2 学校での会話……122
3 ビジネス会話……140
4 オフィスでの会話……162
5 つき合う、恋愛……176

1 家族との会話

起床、朝食をとる

1 起きて。
It's time to get up.
　= Rise and shine. ＊こちらは、特に子どもに対して使う。

2 まだ寝ぼけているの？
Are you still dreaming?

3 あと5分だけ寝かせて！
Just five more minutes!

4 もうこんな時間？
☞ **Is that the time?**
　= Look at the time!

5 寝過ごした！
I overslept!

6 もっと早く起こしてよ。
Why didn't you wake me up earlier?

7 遅くまでテレビを見ているからよ。
You sat up late watching TV.
　sit up late＝夜ふかしをする

8 昨夜、いびきをかいていたよ。
You were snoring last night.
　snore＝いびきをかく

9 朝食ができたわよ。
Breakfast is ready!

10 朝ご飯を食べる時間がないな。
I don't have time for breakfast.

11 オレンジジュースだけでいいわ。
Just orange juice is fine.

↪ トースト toast／コーヒー coffee

12 コーヒーはいかが？
Care for a cup of coffee?

13 トーストにジャムをぬって！
Put jam on the toast!

↪ バター butter

14 卵はどうする？
How would you like your eggs?

15 半熟にして。
I want my egg soft-boiled.

↪ 固ゆで hard-boiled／スクランブルエッグ scrambled／目玉焼き sunny-side up

16 食べちゃいなさい、遅刻するわよ。
Eat up, or you'll be late.

17 食べながら新聞を読まないで。
Don't read the paper at the table.

1 家族との会話

起床、朝食をとる

家族との会話

起床、朝食をとる

18 新聞を取ってきてくれる？
Can you go and get the newspaper?

19 顔を洗ってきなさい。
Go wash your face.

20 歯みがきしなきゃ。
I'll brush my teeth.

❗ teeth は tooth「歯」の複数形。

21 口がにおうよ。マウスウォッシュして！
You have bad breath. Gargle with mouthwash!

22 歯みがき粉、なくなっちゃったの？
Are you out of toothpaste?

be out of ～ = ～がない、～を切らしている

23 髪がボサボサ！
☞ **My hair's messy!**

messy = めちゃめちゃな、ぼさぼさの

24 今日は髪型が決まらないなあ。
My hair doesn't want to cooperate today.

25 さっとシャワーを浴びるよ。
I'm going to take a fast shower.

26 水、出しっぱなしだよ。
Somebody left the tap running.

27 せかさないで！ コンタクトつけてるんだから。
Don't rush me! I'm putting in my lenses.

28 早く着替えなさい。
Now get dressed.

= Hurry up and get dressed.

29 何を着ようかな。
What should I wear?

30 寒いから、コートが必要ね。
It's overcoat weather, isn't it?

31 このワイシャツ、しわくちゃだ。
This dress shirt is wrinkled.

wrinkled＝しわくちゃ

32 靴下が片方ない。
One sock is missing.

❗「靴下」は2枚で1組なので、ふつう socks。片方（1枚）は単数形 sock になる。

33 おっと、鼻毛が出てる。
Oh, I've got a lot of nose hair.

34 化粧のりが悪いわ。
My makeup doesn't feel right.

makeup＝化粧

35 ちょっとお化粧が濃過ぎるかも。
I'm wearing too much makeup.

1 家族との会話
出がけに

1 もう出る時間だ。
It's time to go.

2 急がなきゃ。
I'd better hurry.
had better 〜=〜したほうがよい、〜しないと困ったことになる　*I'd better=I had better

3 あれ、かばんはどこに置いたっけ？
Oh, where did I put my bag?

カギ key(s)／財布 purse

4 途中で何か食べるよ。
I'll get something to eat on the way.
on the way=途中で

5 帰りにパンを買ってきてくれる？
Can you get some bread on your way home?
one one's way home=家に帰る途中で

6 今日はちょっと遅くなるかも。
I may be a little late today.

7 夕飯食べないなら、電話して。
If you don't need dinner, will you call me?

8 夕飯までには戻るよ。
I'll be back by dinner time.

9 今日は会社の飲み会だ。

I'm going for a drink with my coworkers.

go for a drink＝飲みに行く　coworker＝同僚

10 飲みすぎないようにね。

Don't drink too much.

11 ゴミを出して。

Take out the garbage.

↪ 不燃ゴミ non-burnable garbage／可燃ゴミ combustible trash／資源ゴミ recyclable waste

12 傘、持っていったほうがいいね。

You should take your umbrella with you.

13 忘れ物はない？

Do you have everything?

= Are you sure you haven't forgotten anything?

14 お弁当を忘れてるわよ！

You forgot your lunch!

↪ 傘 umbrella

15 まっすぐ帰ってらっしゃい。

Come right home.

straight

16 行ってきます。

I'm leaving now. Bye!

❗「行ってらっしゃい」は Have a good day. や、See you (later). などでもよい。

17 車に気をつけてね。

Watch out for cars.

= Take care with the car.

1 | 家族との会話
掃除、洗濯をする

1 なに、この散らかりようは？
What is this mess?
mess＝散らかった状態

2 あなたの部屋はまるでブタ小屋みたいね！
Your room is a pigsty!
❗ 子どもの部屋が汚いときに親が言う。

3 あれ？掃除機が動かない。
Huh? The vacuum cleaner doesn't work.
vacuum cleaner＝掃除機　＊動詞「掃除機をかける」も vacuum。

4 コンセントにささっていないよ。
You've forgotten to plug it in.
plug＝(プラグを)差し込む、接続する

5 部屋を片づけなさい。
Clean your room.
Straighten up／Tidy up

6 トイレが汚れてるわ。
The toilet bowl is dirty.
toilet bowl＝便器

7 お風呂にカビが生えちゃった。
Mildew is growing in the bathroom.
mildew［ミルデュー］＝白カビ

8 家事は腰にくるわ。
☞ Housework is hard on my back.
be hard on ～＝～に負担がかかる、～に厳しい

9 今日は洗濯日和だわ。

Today is a good day to do the wash.

laundry

10 今日は部屋干しね。

I have to hang the clothes inside the house today.

11 洗濯物が山積み。

The laundry has really piled up.

12 あのシャツは手洗いしないといけなかったのに。

I should've hand-washed that shirt.

hand-wash＝手で洗う、手洗いする

13 ラベルには「柔軟剤を使わないでください」と書いてあるわ。

The label says, "Do not use fabric softener."

fabric softener＝柔軟剤

14 洗濯物は乾いたかな？

Is the wash already dry?

↩ まだぬれている still wet

15 湿気が多いから、なかなか乾かないわ。

It takes longer to dry because of the humidity.

16 洗濯物を取り込まなくちゃ。

☞ **I have to bring the wash in.**

❗「洗濯物を干す」は hang the wash out (to dry).

17 洗濯物をたたんでくれる？

Can you fold these clothes, please?

fold＝たたむ

1 家族との会話

帰宅する

1 ただいま！
I'm home!
　⊜ I'm back! ＊旅行などから帰ってきた場合は It's good to be back. とも言う。

2 おかえりなさい！
Welcome home!
　　　　　　　　　　　　　　　　　　　　　　　　⊜ Welcome back!

3 早かったね。
You're back early.
　　　　　　　　　　　　　　　　　　　　　　　↪ 遅かった late

4 学校はどうだった？
How was school?
　　　　　　　　　　　　　　　　　　　　　　　↪ 仕事 work

5 あわただしい一日だったよ。
☞ **Today was really hectic.**
　　　　hectic＝大変忙しい、大騒ぎの　＊I'm hectic. とは言わないので注意。

6 今日は大変だったよ。
I had a tough day.
　　　　　　　　　　　　　　　　　　　　　　　　　　　hard

7 また飲んできたの？
Are you drunk again?

8 門限を過ぎてるよ。
It's past your curfew.

cúrfew ［カーフュー］＝門限

1 家族との会話

夕食の用意をする

1 今日の夕飯は何？
What's for dinner tonight?
　= What are we having for dinner?

2 お米をといでくれる？
Can you wash the rice?

3 ジャガイモの皮をむいてちょうだい。
Peel the potatoes.
peel＝皮をむく

4 そろそろ鶏肉が焼けたみたい。
The chicken is almost done.

5 これを1分、電子レンジでチンしてちょうだい。
Microwave this for one minute.
microwave＝レンジでチンする

6 ちょっとお鍋を見ててくれる？
Can you keep an eye on this pan?
keep an eye on 〜＝〜から目を離さない

7 何か焦げてるにおいがする。
It smells like something's burning.
burn＝焦げる

8 食事の準備を手伝ってくれる？
Would you help me set the table?
set the table は、テーブルに箸や皿などを並べて食事の準備をすること。

1 家族との会話

夕食をとる

1 ご飯よ！
Come and get it!
　　It's time for dinner. ／ Dinner is ready!

2 いま行くよ。
I'm coming.
　　I'll be right there. ／ I'm on my way.

3 今日はカレーよ。
Today, we're having curry.

4 いただきます。
👉 Let's eat.
　　Shall we begin?

5 めし上がれ。
Help yourself.
　　Please go ahead. ／ Let's dig in.

6 また残り物？
Leftovers again?
　　「今日はごちそうだ」は We're going to have a feast tonight.

7 ちゃんと箸を持って。
Hold your chopsticks <u>right</u>.
　　　　　　　　　　　　　　correctly

8 食べながらテレビ見ちゃダメでしょ。
No TV during dinner.
　　Don't watch TV while you're eating.

9 ゆっくり食べなさい。
Take your time eating.

10 こぼさないの！
Don't spill it!

= Don't tip it over.

11 魚を食べるときは、骨に気をつけて。
When you eat your fish, watch out for bones.

12 これ、おかわりある？
Is there any more of this?

Do you have

13 これ、辛すぎるよ！
This is way too hot!

spicy　＊way too は「あまりに、すごく」という意味。

14 田中裕太！　食べながらおしゃべりしない！
Yuta Tanaka!　Don't talk with your mouth full!

❗ 親が子どもを叱るとき、このように、自分の子どもをフルネームで呼ぶこともある。

15 これいらない。まずいんだもん。
I don't want this.　It tastes awful.

terrible／bad／yucky

16 残さないで食べなさい。
☞ **Finish up your plate.**

= Clean your plate.／Don't leave any on your plate.

17 世界には、食べたくても食べられない子どもがたくさんいるのよ。
There are a lot of starving children in the world.

starving=飢えた、飢えて死にそうな

1 家族との会話

夕食をとる

1 家族との会話
夕食のあとで

CD1 Track 58

1 食べすぎた。
I ate too much.
❗「食べすぎでおなかが苦しい」は I ate too much and my stomach hurts.

2 おなかいっぱい。
☞ My tummy is full.
🟰 I'm full.／I'm stuffed.　＊「おなかがパンパン」は My stomach is about to explode.

3 ごちそうさま。
It was delicious, thank you.
❗「ごちそうさま」の決まった表現はないので、料理へのお礼や感想を言う。

4 おいしかった？
Was it good?

5 足りた？
Have you had enough?

6 デザート、食べる？
How about some dessert?
dessért［ディザート］　＊［デ］にアクセントを置くと、désert「砂漠」の意味になる。

7 ケーキを切りましょうか？
Shall I cut you a slice of cake?

8 シュークリームを作ったのよ。
I baked some cream puffs.
❗「シュークリーム」は和製英語。

9 デザートは別腹。

There's room for dessert.

I have

10 お茶でも入れましょうか？

Can I make you some tea or something?

Would you like

11 コーヒーを1杯もらえるかな。

Could you pour me a cup of coffee?

🔄 緑茶 green tea

12 テーブルの上を片づけてくれる？

Would you clear the table?

＝ Would you put the dishes away?

13 食器を水につけておいてくれる？

Can you soak the dishes in the sink?

soak＝浸す　sink＝流し、シンク

14 テレビを見る前に、台所にお皿を下げてね。

Take your dishes to the kitchen before you go watch TV.

15 お皿を洗うよ。

I'll do the dishes.

do the dishes＝皿洗いをする　🔄 拭く dry

16 このお茶わん、欠けてるよ。

This rice bowl is chipped.

chipped＝(陶器の縁などが)欠けた

17 洗剤が足りないよ。

There isn't enough detergent.

detergent＝(合成)洗剤

家族との会話 1

夕食のあとで

1 家族との会話

テレビを見る

1 テレビは宿題が終わってからよ。
No TV until you finish your homework.

2 何か面白い番組やってる？
Are there any good programs on TV?

3 どれどれ。あ、映画やるよ。
Let's see. Oh, there's a movie.

4 これ、再放送だ。
☞ **It's a rerun.**

5 それ何チャン？
What channel is it on?

chánnel [チャネル]　＊「チャンネル」と言わないように。

6 リモコン取って。
Hand me the remote (control).

Give／Pass

7 チャンネルをコロコロ変えるの、やめてよ！
Stop changing channels!

flipping

8 ちょっと音を小さくして。
Turn it down a little bit.

↻ 大きく up

1 家族との会話

お風呂に入る

1 お風呂に入っていい？
Can I take a bath?

「お風呂わいてる？」は Is the bath ready?

2 今、お母さんが入ってる。
Mom's in the bath right now.

「今、お風呂あいてるよ」は The bathroom is free now.

3 今夜は私が赤ちゃんをお風呂に入れようかな。
I think I'll give the baby a bath tonight.

4 ぬるいから、熱いお湯を足してね。
It's not hot enough.　Could you add more hot water?

5 ねぇ！　お風呂の水があふれてるよ！
Hey! The bath is overflowing!

overflow＝(液体が)あふれる、あふれ出る

6 お風呂から出たよ。
I'm through.

be through＝終わる

7 のぼせちゃった。
I feel dizzy.

dizzy＝目が回る、目まいがする、フラフラする

8 風呂上がりのビールは最高だね。
There's <u>nothing like</u> beer after taking a bath.

nothing better than／nothing as good as

113

1 家族との会話 — 就寝前に

1 明日も早いし、そろそろ寝るか。
I have to get up early. I guess I should get to bed now.

2 テレビを消して、もう寝なさい。
Turn off the TV and go to bed, right now.

3 寝る時間、過ぎてるわよ。何してるの？
It's past your bedtime. What are you doing?

4 テレビつけっぱなしだよ。
You left the TV on.
= You forgot to turn the TV off.

5 寝る前には歯みがきでしょ。何度言ったらわかるの！
How many times do I have to tell you to brush your teeth before you go to bed?

6 ちゃんと目覚ましかけて寝るのよ。
Make sure to set the alarm before going to sleep.
Don't forget

7 明日は6時に起こしてね。
☞ **Wake me up at 6:00 tomorrow.**

8 おやすみなさい。いい夢を！
Good night. Sweet dreams!
Have a pleasant dream!

1 家族との会話

休日のプランを練る

1 週末どうしようか？
What shall we do this weekend?

2 家でのんびりしたい気分。
I feel like staying at home and taking it easy.
feel like 〜 ing＝〜したい気分である　take it easy＝のんびりする、休む

3 ぶらっと買い物にでも行こうか。
Let's just go shopping.
just＝ちょっと、ともかく、ほんの〜だけ

4 週末、どこかへ出かけようよ。
Let's get away for the weekend.
get away＝(気晴らし・デートなどで)どこかへ行く

5 映画でも見に行く？
You want to see a movie or something?

6 早く、週末にならないかな。
☞ **The weekend seems so far away.**
❗「週末が遠く感じる」といった意味。

7 次の日曜日は家族サービスしないと。
I have paternal duties next Sunday.

8 今度の三連休は旅行に行きたいな。
I'd like to go on a trip during the next three-day weekend.　three-day weekend＝三連休　＊three days off in a row とも言う。

1 家族との会話

体調の話をする

1 元気ないね。
You don't look so good.
very well

2 顔色悪いな。
You look pale.
pale＝青白い、顔色が悪い

3 目が充血してるよ。
You have red eyes.
🔄 目が腫れて swollen eyes

4 ちょっとだるい。
I feel a little tired.

5 おなかが痛い。
I have a stomachache.
🔄 頭 headache／胃 bellyache／歯 toothache

6 吐きそう。
I'm going to throw up.
be sick／puke／vomit　❗「胸がむかむかする」は I'm sick at my stomach.

7 熱があるの？
Do you have a fever?
fever＝熱　❗「咳が止まらない」は I've had a bad cough.

8 風邪をひきかけてるみたい。
I think I'm coming down with a cold.

9 熱っぽいんだ。
I feel feverish.
= I have a bit of a fever. 「熱があるの？」は Do you have a fever?

10 寒気がする。
I feel chilly.

11 鼻が<u>詰まっちゃって</u>。
I have a <u>stuffy nose</u>.

↻ 鼻水が出る runny nose

12 薬を飲んだほうがよさそうだ。
I'd better take some medicine.

take medicine＝薬を飲む

13 ベッドで横になりなさい。
Go snuggle up in bed.

= Lie down on the bed.

14 その指どうしたの？
What happened to your finger?

15 ケガしちゃった。
I got hurt.

= I'm hurt.／I'm injured.

16 便秘気味なの。
I haven't had a bowel movement.

bowl＝腸　= I suffer from constipation.

17 下痢しちゃった。
I have <u>loose bowels</u>.

loose bowels＝下痢　＊bowel は通列〜s

家族との会話

体調の話をする

1 | 家族との会話
電話で話す

1 もしもし、お父さん？　お母さんに代わって。
Hello, Dad? Can I speak to Mom?

2 今、買い物に行っているよ。
She's out shopping now.
> 「出かけています」は She's out.　主語が男性なら He's out.

3 あと1時間くらいで戻ってくると思うけど。
I think she'll be back in about an hour.

4 帰りは7時頃って言ってたわ。
She said she'd be home around 7:00.

5 よく聞こえないんだけど。
I can't hear you very well.

6 電話が遠いみたい。
☞ **We have a bad connection.**
> Could you speak a little louder?「もっと大きな声で話してもらえる？」も、ほぼ同じ意味。

7 もしもし、**渡辺さんのお宅**ですか？
Hello. Is this the Watanabe's?

8 どちら様でしょうか？
Who's calling, please?

9 雅子さんはいますか？

Is Masako there?

> May I speak to Masako, please? は、少しかしこまった言い方。

10 私よ。

It's me.

= Speaking.

11 お待ちください。呼びますから。

Hold on.　I'll get her.

12 美咲、電話だよ。

Misaki, it's for you.

13 今、話して大丈夫？

Can I talk to you now?

14 電話があったことを伝えていただけますか？

Will you tell her that I called?

15 お帰りになったら、お電話をいただきたいのですが。

I'd like her to call me when she gets back.

would like（人）to ～ =（人）に～してもらいたい

16 私の外出中に電話くれた？

Did you call me while I was out?

17 ちょっと待って。キャッチが入った。

Just a second.　I'm getting another call.

1 家族との会話

電話で話す

1 家族との会話
子どもの世話をする

1 あら、オムツ換えてほしいの？ どれどれ。
Oh, you want me to change your diaper? Let me take a look.
diaper [ダイパー]＝オムツ

2 3歳までには、オムツが取れるといいけど。
I hope she'll be out of diapers by the time she's three.
❗ 男の子の場合は he を使う。

3 いないいないバア！
Peek-a-boo!
Péek-a-bòo! [ピーカブー]

4 おしっこしたいの？
Do you need to pee?

5 仲よくするのよ。
Be nice to each other.

6 ケンカしないの。
No fighting.
fight＝ケンカする

7 危ないからやっちゃダメ。
It's dangerous, so don't do that.
❗「お行儀よくしなさい」は Behave yourself.

8 宿題をしなさい。
Do your homework.

1 家族との会話
特別な日に

1 休日くらい、ゆっくり寝かせてよ。
Please let me sleep on my day off.

2 今日はずっと寝ていたいよ。
☞ **All I want to do today is sleep.**
> 本来なら All (that) I want to do today is (to) sleep. となるが、口語では省略。

3 来週の日曜日は友人の結婚式だ。
I'll be attending a friend's wedding next Sunday.
attend＝出席する、参列する

4 明日は授業参観よ。
Tomorrow is parents' day.

5 今日は何の日か覚えてる？
Don't you remember what today is?

6 遅れちゃったけど、お誕生日おめでとう！
A belated Happy Birthday!
belated＝遅ればせながら、少し遅れた

7 40歳になった気分はどう？
How does it feel to have finally reached the big four-O?
reach the big four-O＝40の大台に乗る

8 誕生日プレゼントは何がいい？
What would you like for your birthday?

2 学校での会話

教室で

1 何年生？
What grade are you in?

2 2年生。
I'm a sophomore.

↪ 1年 freshman／3年 junior／4年 senior　＊いずれも主に大学の場合。

3 現役で合格したの？
Did you go on to college directly?

4 専攻は何？
☞ **What's your major?**

❗ I major in economics.／I'm an economic major.「経済学だよ」のように答える。

5 何の科目が得意？
What subject are you good at?

↪ 苦手 poor

6 ビジネス英語は選択科目だよ。
The business English class is an elective.

↪ 必修科目 a required course／a required subject

7 卒論のテーマは決めた？
Have you decided on the subject of your thesis?

subject＝論題、主題　thesis＝論文　thésis［シーサス］

8 僕のカンでは、次の講義は休講だね。
My instinct says that the next class will be canceled.

9 この席あいてる？

👉 **Is this seat taken?**

❗ 席があいているときは No. あいていないときは Yes.

10 今日の最初の講義は英文学だよ。

English literature is the first class of the day.

class＝講義　of the day＝今日の

11 前回休んだから遅れをとっているんだ。

I got left behind when I was absent last class.

get left behind＝置き去りにされる、あとに残される

12 もうすぐチャイムが鳴るよ。

The bell is going to ring soon.

13 授業サボらない？

👉 **Do you want to cut class?**

skip

14 悪いけど、代返しておいてよ。

Can you answer for me at roll call?

roll call＝出欠、点呼

15 出席を取ります。

Let me call the roll.

call the roll＝出席を取る

16 授業で眠らないようにしないと。

I should keep awake during class.

keep awake＝起きたままでいる

17 １０時３０分から１０時４０分まで、休み時間です。

We have a break from 10:30 to 10:40.

break＝休憩時間

2 学校での会話　教室で

18 質問3の答え、何になった？
What did you get for question three?

19 文学部にはかわいい子が多いなあ。
There are a lot of cute girls in the faculty of letters. ➥ 法学 law／経済学 economics／政治学 politics／神学 theology

20 そこ！ 私語は慎むように。
Hey! No talking over there.

21 この英語の講義についていけないよ。
☞ **This English course is beyond me.**

beyond＝理解できない、力が及ばない

22 誰かにノートを写させてもらおうっと。
I'll ask someone to share their notebook.

＝ I'd like to copy someone's notebook.

23 今日の授業はこれまで。
That's all for today.

＝ So much for today.

24 誰かわかる人？
Does anyone know the answer?

25 質問があります。
I have a question.

26 今日の講義は本当に楽しかった。
I really enjoyed today's lecture.

❗「今日の授業は退屈だった」は I didn't enjoy today's lesson.

学校での会話

教室で

27 次の授業、どの教室だっけ？

Where should we go for next period?

> 「次の授業何だっけ？」は What's the next class?

28 レポートの提出、いつか知ってる？

☞ **Do you know when the report is due?**

the deadline for the report is

29 宿題、終わった？

Finish your homework?

30 レポートはだいたい半分できた。

My report is almost halfway done.

halfway＝途中で、中間で

31 宿題がたまっているんだ。

I've got a lot of homework to do.

32 何についての作文を書いているの？

What theme are you writing on?

33 このレポート、コピー&ペーストばっかり。

This report is nothing but copy and paste.

34 レポートを仕上げるのに徹夜したよ。

I was up all night writing my report.

be up all night＝徹夜する

35 私のレポートはどうでしたか？

How was my report?

2 学校での会話
試験を受ける

1. 試験勉強しないと。
I have to prepare for the test.
prepare for 〜＝〜の準備をする

2. テストも近いし、図書館で勉強するかな。
Exams are coming up. I think I'll go to the library and study.

3. この**必修科目**の単位は落とせないんだ。
I can't afford to fail this required course.
can't afford to 〜＝〜する余裕がない、〜できる状態にない

4. いつも一夜漬けなんだ。
I always cram overnight for exams.
cram＝詰め込む

5. ヤマが当たった！
☞ **I guessed right about what would be on the exam!**
↩ ハズレた wrong

6. テスト、教科書の持ち込み可だよ。
It's going to be an open book test.

7. 名前と学生番号を忘れずに書いてください。
Be sure to write your name and student number on the paper.
be sure to 〜＝必ず〜する

8. 答案用紙は後ろから集めてください。
Collect the exam papers starting from the back of the room.

9 やっと試験が終わった。

My exams are finally over.

be over＝終わる

10 あんな問題が出るなんて思わなかったよ。

I had no idea there would be questions like that on the exam.

11 試験に合格したと思う？

Do you think you'll pass the exam?

❗「ダメだと思う」は I don't think so.

12 2つ目の問題がわからなかった。

I couldn't answer the second question.

13 英語のテスト、70点か。

Seventy points on the English test.

marks

14 僕の答案はほとんど白紙だ。

My paper is almost blank.

blank＝空白の

15 君、この授業を落としたら卒業できないよ。

You can't graduate if you flunk this class.

flunk＝失敗する、落第する

16 いくつか追試を受けなくてはならないんだ。

I'm retaking my finals a few times.

retake＝再度（試験などを）受ける　final＝最終試験、期末試験

17 今日、抜き打ちテストがあったんだ。

We had a pop quiz today.

🟰 They gave us a surprise quiz.

試験を受ける

18 赤点にちがいない。
I must have failed the exam.

19 第一志望はどこ？
Which school is your first choice?

20 文系か理系か決めた？
Have you decided whether to go into arts or sciences?

21 いくつの学校に申し込むつもり？
How many schools are you applying to?

22 昨日、願書を送ったんだ。
I sent off my application yesterday.

23 合格できそう？
What are your chances of getting into the school, you think?

24 そう、やっぱり就職することにしたのか。
So you decided to get a job after all?

25 入試に受かった！
I passed the entrance exam!

❗「落ちた」は The school rejected me. / I wasn't accepted.

26 もっと一生懸命に勉強すればよかった。
☞ **I should've studied harder.**

❗後悔は仮定法〈should have＋過去分詞〉を使う。

2 学校での会話

成績、単位

1 彼女はいつもオールAだ。
She always gets all A's.

2 法学が落第点だった。
I got a failing grade in law.

failing grade＝(試験の)落第点、赤点

3 成績がどんどん落ちているんだ。
My grades are dropping.

4 単位を落としちゃうかも。
I might flunk the course.

5 Cでもいいから、単位が欲しい！
I don't care if I get a C, I just want the credits.

6 進級できていなかったら、どうしよう。
What should I do if I can't move up to the next grade?

move up to the next grade＝進級する

7 落第しちゃう。
I'll be a repeater.

repeater＝再履修者

8 留年だ。
I can't graduate on time.

＝ I have to stay at college one more year.

2 学校での会話

休み時間に

1 おなかペコペコだね。
We're starving, aren't we?
be starving＝腹ペコである、ひどくおなかが空いている

2 学食の日替わりランチは何かな？
I wonder what the lunch special in the student cafeteria is today?

3 これ、ケンからの差し入れ。
This is compliments of Ken.
compliment＝心づけ、チップ、あいさつ

4 学部の掲示板は見た？
Have you seen the department bulletin board?
❗「休講と補講が貼られていたわよ」は It listed canceled and extra classes.

5 放課後、カラオケに行かない？
How about going to karaoke after school?
go to karaoke＝カラオケに行く

6 渋谷のことならまかせてよ。
I know Shibuya like the back of my hand.
know（物）like the back of one's hand＝（物）を熟知している

7 夏休みに帰省する？
Are you going home during summer vacation?

8 車の免許、簡単に取れたよ。
Getting my driver's license was a piece of cake.
a piece of cake＝簡単なこと、楽にできること

2 学校での会話

サークル・部活動

1 何かサークルやってる？
Are you in any clubs?

2 テニス部に入っているよ。
I'm on the tennis team.
= I'm a member of the tennis club. ／I belong to the tennis club.

3 部員は何人いるの？
How many members are on your team?
club

4 友達を作るためにサークルに入ったんだ。
I joined the club to make friends.

5 ほかのサークルとの掛け持ちもできるよ。
You can join other clubs, too.

6 くだらないサークルはいやだな。
I don't want to have anything to do with silly clubs.

7 後輩に慕われているんだね。
You're very popular with the juniors.
junior＝後輩

8 彼らはサークル仲間なんだ。
Those are my club chums.
chum＝親しい友人、仲間

2 学校での会話

アルバイトをする

1 学費がいくらかかるか心配だよ。

I'm worried about how much college is going to cost.

2 学費は親が払っているよ。

My parents pay my (school) tuition.

school tuition＝学費

3 学業とアルバイトは両立できると思うよ。

I think I can study and work part-time.

4 バイトを探しているんだ。

I'm looking for a part-time job.

part-time job＝アルバイト

5 あの店、いつもバイトの学生を募集しているよ。

That store is always looking for students to work.

6 バイトの経験は面接のときに有利らしいよ。

I heard part-time jobs look good in job interviews.

7 バイト探しはどうなった？

☞ **How's the job hunting going?**

8 いくつか受けたけど、全部だめだった。

I've had some job interviews, but I keep getting beat out.

beat out＝打ち負かす

9 これからバイトなんだ。

I'm going to work after this.

10 ハンバーガーショップでバイトを始めたんだ。

I started working part-time at a burger shop.

work part-time at ～＝～でアルバイトをする

11 時給いくら？

☞ **How much is your hourly pay?**

hourly pay＝時給

12 時給９００円。

I get 900 yen an hour.

13 週に1回は夜勤しなければならないんだ。

I have to work the night shift once a week.

night shift＝夜勤

14 その日はシフトが入っているよ。

I have to work that day.

15 ほら、土曜日はアルバイトって言ったじゃない。

I have a part-time job on Saturday, remember?

❗ 一度言ったことを相手に思い出させたいときは、文末に remember? をつける。

16 高校生の家庭教師をしているんだ。

I tutor a high school student.

17 週に3日働くのは結構きつい。

Working three days a week is very draining.

draining＝疲れさせる、くたくたにさせる

2 | 学校での会話

先生や友達のうわさ話

1 先生、テレビに出るらしいよ。
I hear he's going to be a TV star.
> 先生が女性なら she's を使おう。

2 あの先生、わかってくれるんだよな。
That teacher identifies with us.
identify with（人）=（人）に共感する、（人）を支持する

3 あの教授、ほとんど四六時中、大学にいるみたいだよ。
The professor seems to spend nearly all his time at the college.

4 彼、女の子にもてるな。
He's popular with girls.

5 彼女は高嶺の花だよ。
I can't hold a candle to her.
can't hold a candle to ～=～の足元にも及ばない、～とは比べものにならない

6 彼女ってキャリア志向が強いみたい。
She seems career-oriented.
career-oriented=キャリア志向の

7 彼女は国際感覚が身についているね。
She's an international-minded person.
international-minded=国際感覚のある

8 彼、大学対抗弁論大会に出場したんだ。
He <u>participated in</u> an intercollegiate speech contest.
entered

9 あいつ、最近学校で見かけないな。何してるのかなあ？

I haven't seen him in school recently. I wonder what he's doing.

10 あいつ、ちょっとうるさいよ。

He's a bit annoying.

11 彼女、頭がいいのを鼻にかけているね。

She's <u>boastful</u> of her cleverness.

She boasts

12 みんな彼のこと、空気を読めないと思ってるよ。

Everyone thinks he is a dork.

13 彼、筋肉バカだから。

He seems like a jock.

jock＝運動選手、スポーツ狂　＊「運動はできるが頭が弱い人」という意味も含む、嫌味っぽい表現。

14 人の陰口言うの、やめなよ。

☞ **Don't talk behind his back.**

⚠ 女性なら her back となる。

15 君が好きそうなゴシップがあるよ。

I have some juicy gossip for you.

juicy gossip＝興味深いうわさ話

16 君にしか、このことは言っていないから。

You're the only one that knows.

17 僕から聞いたって言うなよ。

☞ **You didn't hear this from me.**

2 学校での会話

先生や友達のうわさ話

2 学校での会話
就職活動に取り組む

1 そろそろ就職活動を始めないと。
It's time to start hunting for a job.
hunt for a job＝職探しをする　＊「就職活動」は job hunting。

2 まずはその茶髪、黒く染めたら？
First, why don't you dye your brown hair black?

3 マスコミ業界を中心に就職活動するつもりなんだ。
I'm mainly going to hunt for a job in the mass media field.
金融業界 financial sector

4 給料がいいから、外資系を狙うつもり。
I'm interested in applying to foreign companies because they pay well.
foreign-affiliated

5 資格がないから、この仕事はできないな。
I don't think I can do this as I'm not qualified.

6 英語の教員免許を持っているよ。
I have the qualifications to be an English teacher.
an English teacher's license

7 自己PR、書いた？
Have you written the self-promotion report?

8 自分自身についてや、自分の能力について書くんだよ。
You should write what you're made of and what you can do.

9 履歴書に、もっと詳しく自己PRを書いたほうがいいよ。

You should write more detail about yourself in your resume.

detail＝詳細　resume＝履歴書

10 面接はどういう形式なのかな？

What form does the interview take?

form＝形式、スタイル

11 人前で話すのは苦手だな。

☞ **I'm not a good public speaker.**

public speaker＝人前で話をする人、演説家

12 面接官の質問は厳しかったな。

The interviewer asked some tough questions.

13 書類で落とされちゃったよ。

They turned me down after just seeing my resume.

turn down＝断る

14 面談の日にち、間違えちゃった。

I just got the date of the interview mixed up.

get（物）mixed up＝（物）をごちゃごちゃにする、間違った順序にする

15 最終面接までいったけど、だめだった。

I got to the final interview but was passed over.

be passed over＝（仕事などの対象から）外される

16 内定取れたって、誰かに言った？

Told anyone you got a job offer?

job offer＝求人、採用通知

17 内定が取り消された。

My informal job offer was canceled.

informal job offer＝内定　＊「formal（正式）ではない採用通知」という感じ

2 学校での会話

就職活動に取り組む

2 学校での会話
学園祭

1 もうすぐ学園祭だね。
It's almost time for the school festival.
= The school festival is just around the corner.

2 学園祭で芝居をやるつもりなんだ。
We're planning to perform a play at the school festival.
put on／stage

3 最後の学園祭だから、好きなことやろうよ！
Since this is our last festival, let's do something everyone wants to do!

4 学園祭の準備で忙しいよ。
I'm really busy preparing for the cultural festival.
be busy ～ing=～するのに忙しい

5 もう気分は学園祭だね！
I'm getting in a festival mood already!
be (get) in a ～ mood=～の気分になる

6 ライブのチケット、買わない？
Do you want to buy a ticket for the live concert?

7 うちのサークル、学園祭でクレープ売るんだ。
Our club is selling crepes at the school festival.

8 売上金で打ち上げしようよ。
Let's have a party with the profits from the sales.

2 学校での会話

卒業したら…

1 もうすぐ卒業だよ。

It suddenly seems like the rest of the school year is coming up so fast. the rest of the school year=残りの学生生活

2 卒業したらどうする？

What do you think you'd like to do after college?

3 自分の夢について、じっくり考えなきゃね。

We should dig deep and think about our aspirations for the future. dig deep=深く掘り下げる　aspiration=熱望していること、抱負

4 自分の将来は自分で決めたいよ。

☞ **I want to decide my own future.**

5 卒業後はニューヨークに留学するんだ。

I'm going to study in New York after graduation.

6 できれば大学院に進みたいな。

I'd like to go to graduate school, if possible.

7 留年しようかな。

I'm thinking about staying here one more year.　❗「実家に戻るかも」は I guess I'm back my parents' house.

8 卒業旅行はパリに行こうよ！

Let's all go to Paris for our graduation trip!

3 ビジネス会話

出社する

1 少し遅れます。
I'm going to be a little late.
🔴 「遅れてすみません」は I'm sorry, I'm late.

2 10分遅れるので、ホワイトボードに書いておいてもらえる？
Would you write on the whiteboard that I'll be ten minutes late?

3 病院に立ち寄るので、午前中、休ませてください。
I'll have to stop in at the hospital, so could I take the morning off?

4 得意先に直行します。
I'll go straight to one of our customers.

5 打ち合わせに10分ほど遅れます。
I'll be about ten minutes late for our meeting.

6 体の具合が悪いので、今日は休みます。
I'm not feeling well. I think I'll take the day off today.

7 遅刻してしまい、申し訳ありません。
I apologize for the delay.
🟰 I'm sorry to be late.

8 また、ギリギリかい？
In the nick of time again?

in the nick of time＝ギリギリ間に合って、間一髪で

9 彼はまだ出社していません。

He hasn't got to the office yet.

10 タイムカードは押しましたか？

Did you punch in?

> 退社時は Did you punch out?

11 自動改札でひっかかっちゃった。

I got stopped by an automatic ticket gate.

12 今日は、いつもと違う路線で来たよ。

Today, I took a different route for a change.

> Unusually for me, I took a different route today.

13 駅から会社まで走ったら、息が切れたよ。

I ran to the office from the station and I'm out of breath now.

14 電車で寝すごして、隣りの駅まで行っちゃった。

I went to the next station because I fell asleep on the train.

15 かばんをドアにはさんじゃった。

I got my bag caught in the train doors.

16 電車の中、冷房が効きすぎだね。

The train's air conditioning is working full blast, and it's freezing.

17 今日は電車が空いていたよ。

The train was not crowded today.

3 ビジネス会話

報告・連絡・相談

1 高橋社長がお呼びです。
President Takahashi wants to talk to you.

2 さっき、柴田部長が探してたよ。
Mr. Shibata was here to see you.

3 予定表を見ておいてください。
Take a look at the schedule board, please.

4 来週のスケジュールを確認してください。
Can you check the schedule for next week?

5 できるだけ早く、これを仕上げてください。
☞ **Please have this completed ASAP.**

❗ ASAP=as soon as possible「できるだけ早く」。[エイ エス エイ ピー]または[エイサップ]と発音。

6 2週間で企画書を作成してください。
Please draw up a plan in two weeks.

7 企画書には目を通していただけましたでしょうか？
Have you taken the time to look over my proposal?

8 この企画書は社外秘です。
This project proposal should not be shown to anyone outside of the company.

9 ２、３分で戻ります。

I'll be back in a couple of minutes.

a couple of ～＝２、３の～

10 交通渋滞に巻き込まれて、到着が３時になります。

I'm delayed by the heavy traffic and I won't get there until 3:00.

not ～ until ...＝…になってやっと～

11 先方に連絡を取ろうとしましたが、つかまりませんでした。

I tried to get hold of him, but I couldn't.

get hold of（人）＝（人）と接触する、連絡を取る

12 佐藤課長、今、よろしいですか？

☞ **Mr. Sato, are you available now?**

available＝（人が）手が空いている、時間がある

13 プロジェクトは順調？

How's the project going?

＝ Is the project going along well?

14 これは経費で落とせますか？

Can we put this down as an expense?

put ～ down as an expense＝～を経費で落とす

15 上司に相談させて。

Let me talk to my boss.

let me ～＝（私に）～させて

16 何か問題があったら知らせてください。

If there are any problems, please let me know.

❗「はい。必ず知らせます」は Sure, I will.

17 今週の金曜日、お休みをいただきたいのですが。

I'd like to take the day off this Friday.

Friday off

ビジネス会話

報告・連絡・相談

3 ビジネス会話

事務処理をする

CD1 Track 79

1 10部コピーしてくれる？
☞ **Can you make ten copies?**

2 コスト削減のため白黒コピーにしよう。
We should print materials in black and white since it costs less. material＝資料　in black and white＝白黒で

3 コピー機を<u>拡大</u>のままにしたの、誰？
Who left the copier on <u>enlarge</u>?
　　　　　　　　　　　　　　　　　　↩ 縮小 reduce

4 またコピーが紙詰まりだ。
The copy machine paper got jammed again.
get jammed＝(紙などが)詰まる

5 コピー機の紙がなくなりそう。
The copy machine is running out of paper.

6 ファクス、まだ来ない？
☞ **Hasn't the fax come in yet?**

7 この地図をシドニー支店にファクスしてください。
Can you fax this map to the Sydney office?
fax＝ファクスする(動詞)

8 9時までにファクスを送らなければなりません。
I have to send a fax by 9:00.
send a fax＝ファクスを送る

9 ファクスの調子が悪い。

The fax machine isn't working well.

10 これファイルしておいて。

Can you file these?

file=書類をファイルする、整理する

11 請求書はホチキスでとめてくれませんか？

Would you please staple these invoices together?

staple=ホチキスでとめる、とじる

12 ホチキスの針が入っていないよ。

The stapler is empty.

⊖ The stapler is out of staples.

13 セロテープで封をしてください。

Please seal the envelope with Scotch tape.

Scotch tape=セロハンテープ

14 ボールペン何本かとメモ用紙が必要です。

We need some ballpoint pens and memo pads.

❗「ボールペン」は和製英語。

15 この画びょうで図表を貼ってください。

Please put up this chart with these thumbtacks.

thumbtack=画びょう、押しピン

16 封筒から中身を取り出してください。

Please remove the letters and enclosures from the envelope.

enclosure=同封(物)、封入されたもの

17 クリップで手紙をまとめておいて。

☞ **Please fasten the letters together with a paperclip.**

fasten=(ピンやひもなどでしっかり)とめる、結び付ける

3 ビジネス会話

事務処理をする

3 ビジネス会話

パソコンやメールを使う

1 ファイルを開いてデータを処理してください。

Can you open the file and process the data?

2 これをデータ化してくれませんか？

Could you convert this to digital format for me?

convert A to B＝AをBに変換する

3 スプレッドシートを拡大してください。

Please enlarge the spreadsheet.

spreadsheet＝計算表

4 そのデータをエクセルのグラフにしてください。

☞ **Would you please transfer the data to a graph on Excel?**

5 そのグラフをワード文書に貼り付けてください。

Would you please paste the graph onto the Word document?

paste A onto (into) B＝AをBに貼り付ける

6 そのビデオ、DVDに焼けますか？

Can I burn the video onto a DVD?

burn＝CDやDVDに焼き付ける、記録する

7 パワーポイントで資料を作って、僕のUSBに入れておいて。

Can you prepare our documents with Power Point and save the data onto my USB drive?

8 プリントアウトしてくれる？

☞ **Can you print it out, please?**

9 プリンターがつながっていないみたいだけど。

It looks like the printer isn't connected.

10 この書類はカラーでプリントしないと。

This document has to be printed in color.

= We want this document printed in color.

11 あなたのノートパソコンに文書を保存しておいてください。

Save the document onto your laptop, please.

save A onto B＝AをBに保存する

12 文書がウイルスに感染していないことを確認してください。

Please make sure the document doesn't have a virus.

the document is not infected with a virus

13 メールが送信できません。

I can't send e-mail.

⇔ 受信 receive

14 そのEメールの添付を開いてください。

Open the attachment on the e-mail, please.

attachment＝添付書類、(Eメールなどの)添付ファイル

15 添付書類をダウンロードしてください。

Can you download the attachment?

16 上司にメールを転送しておきます。

I'll forward the e-mail to my boss.

forward A to B＝AをBに転送する

17 コンピュータの電源を切っておいてね。

Please shut off the computer.

turn off／power off

3 ビジネス会話

電話を取る

1 はい、フェニックス社です。
Hello. This is Phoenix Inc.

2 どちら様でしょうか？
☞ **May I ask who's calling, please?**
May I ask 〜?＝〜を聞いてもよろしいでしょうか？、失礼ですが〜ですか？

3 こちらは、ABCオンラインの渡辺です。
This is Watanabe from ABC Online.

4 コリンズさんをお願いいたします。
Could I speak to Mr. Collins?

5 かしこまりました。すぐにおつなぎします。
Sure. I'll put you through now.
put through＝電話をつなぐ

6 申し訳ありませんが、いま電話に出られません。
Sorry, but he's not available now.

7 申し訳ありません、コリンズはただ今、他の電話に出ております。
Sorry, but Mr. Collins is on another line now.
be on another line＝電話中である、話し中である

8 お急ぎですか？
Is it urgent?

9 そのままお待ちください。

Hold the line, please.

= Hold on, please.

10 電話を切らないでください。

Please don't hang up the phone.

hang up the phone＝電話を切る

11 折り返しお電話するように伝えましょうか？

Shall I ask him to call you back?

= Shall I ask him to return your call?

12 お電話番号を頂戴できますか？

May I have your phone number, please?

13 伝言を承りますが。

Would you like to leave a message?

leave a message＝伝言を残す　❶「伝言をお願いできますか？」は Can I leave a message?

14 お電話があったことを伝えておきます。

I'll tell him you called.

15 すみません、何度もお電話いただいて。

I'm sorry to have made you call so many times.

16 お電話ありがとうございます。

Thank you for calling.

❶ 電話を切るときは Good bye.／Have a nice day.

17 宅配サービスに、集荷の電話をしてください。

Would you please call the express delivery service for a pickup?

express delivery service＝宅急便

3 ビジネス会話
会議・プレゼンテーション

1 会議はどこで行われますか？
Where's the meeting going to be held?
be held=（行事、会議などが）実施される、行われる

2 議題は何ですか？
What's going to be discussed?
❗「会議の議題は～についてです」は The meeting agenda will cover ～.

3 会議は、来週火曜日の午後1時から3時です。
The meeting will be held from 1 p.m. to 3 p.m. on Tuesday next week.

4 会議はどのくらいで終わりますか？
How long is the meeting going to last?
= When will the meeting be over?

5 午後の<u>役員会議</u>は取りやめになった。
The executive meeting in the afternoon has been canceled.
🔄 営業会議 sales meeting

6 今日の会議は長引くかもしれない。
Today's meeting could run long.

7 事前に、会議の打ち合わせをしておこう。
We have to talk about the meeting in advance.

8 誰が議事録をまとめるのですか？
Who's going to type up the minutes?
type up ～=～をまとめる、清書する　minutes [ミニッツ]＝議事録

9 これについては、もう少し検討したほうがよいと思います。

I think this matter needs to be discussed further.

10 この企画はぜひ通したいですね。

☞ **I really want this plan to go through.**

11 プレゼンには、レーザーポインターが必要です。

I need a laser pointer to give the presentation.

12 本題に入ります。

Now we're going to get to the main point topic.

13 本日はご出席いただき、ありがとうございます。

I'd like to thank you all for coming here today.

14 お手元に資料は回りましたでしょうか？

Did everyone receive the handouts?

＝ Does everybody have the handouts?

15 質問はプレゼンの最後にお願いします。

☞ **Please save your questions for the end of the presentation.**

save A for B＝AをBのためにとっておく

16 そろそろ始めましょうか？

Shall we start now?

17 プロジェクトの基本方針についてご説明いたします。

I'd like to explain the basic principles underlying this project.

18 明確にしておきたい点が1つあります。

Please allow me to clarify one thing.

19 プロジェクターにあります、こちらの棒グラフをご覧ください。

Please look at this bar graph on the projector.

↪ 線グラフ line graph／円グラフ pie chart

20 この線グラフで、9月に最高の売り上げを記録したことがわかります。

This line graph shows that the best sales were recorded in September.

21 これには、理由が3つあります。

There are three reasons for this.

22 いくつか例を挙げてみましょう。

☞ **Let me give you some examples.**

23 簡単に言えばこういうことです。

I can summarize it like this.

24 賛成の方は挙手をしてください。

Raise your hand if you approve.

25 どなたか、ご質問がありますか？

Does anyone have any questions?

26 残念ですが、時間がなくなってしまいました。

I'm afraid we're out of time.

3 ビジネス会話

アポイントを取る

1 ごあいさつに伺いたいのですが、お時間をいただけないでしょうか？

I'd like to do a proper greeting. Could you give me some time?

greeting=あいさつ

2 貴社にお伺いしてよろしいでしょうか？

I'm wondering if I could visit your office.

❗ I was wondering 〜にすると、ていねい度が増す。

3 支店長と一緒に伺います。

I'm planning to go with the head of our branch office.

4 明日はご都合がよろしいですか？

Would some time tomorrow be convenient?

convenient=都合のよい、うってつけの

5 明日の午後は予定通りですよね？

Are we still on for tomorrow afternoon?

on=予定通りで、約束されて（形容詞）

6 明日の約束を、来週に変更していただきたいのですが。

I'd like to change my appointment tomorrow to next week.

change A to B=AをBに変える

7 申し訳ないのですが、その日は別の約束があります。

I'm afraid I have another appointment that day.

8 約束を午前11時から午後3時に変更できますか？

Could I reschedule the appointment from 11 a.m. to 3 p.m.?

reschedule the appointment=予定を再調整する

3 ビジネス会話
他社を訪問する

1 お約束ですか？

Do you have an appointment?

2 11時にケネディさんと約束をしています。

I have an appointment with Ms. Kennedy at 11:00.

have an appointment with (人) at (時刻)＝(人)と(時)に約束がある

3 名刺をいただけますか？

Could I have your business card, please?

Could I have ～?＝～をいただけますか？

4 受付にフェニックス社のスミスさんがいらっしゃっています。

Mr. Smith from Phoenix Inc. is here at the receptionist counter.

5 申し訳ありませんが、ケネディは席を外しております。

I'm sorry, but Ms. Kennedy is not at her desk now.

6 ケネディは数分で戻ってまいります。

Ms. Kennedy will be back in a few minutes.

7 こちらでお待ちいただけますか。

Could you wait here?

8 経理部は16階になります。

The accounting department is on the 16th floor.

be on the 16th floor＝16階にある

9 左手のエレベーターをご利用ください。

Please take the elevator on the left.

take the elevator＝エレベータに乗る

10 本日はお時間を頂戴し、ありがとうございます。

Thank you very much for your time today.

11 こちらが広報部長のスミスさんです。

This is Mr. Smith, the public relations manager.

12 ベンソンさんは販売課の責任者です。

☞ **Ms. Benson is in charge of the sales section.**

be in charge of ～＝～を担当している、任されている

13 ABCオンラインのジェームズ・ブラウンです。

I'm James Brown from ABC Online.

14 遠いところ、わざわざありがとうございます。

Thank you for coming all the way.

15 ABCオンラインにはどのくらいお勤めですか？

How long have you been with ABC Online?

16 ABCオンラインでは何をなさっているのですか？

What do you do at ABC Online?

＝ What is your position at ABC Online? ＊どちらも職種などを尋ねる表現。

17 市場調査の担当です。

☞ **I take care of market research.**

I'm in charge of／I take charge of

3 ビジネス会話

他社を訪問する

3 ビジネス会話

他社を訪問する

18 日本でビジネスを始めようと思っています。

We're setting up business in Japan.

set up business＝企業を設立する、事業を始める

19 私は田中の仕事を引き継ぎました。

I've taken over Tanaka's job.

take over ～＝～を引き継ぐ

20 加藤さんによろしくお伝えください。

Please give my regards to Mr. Kato.

give one's regards to ～＝～によろしく伝える

21 あなたの事業について、もっとお話しする必要がありますね。

We need to talk more about your business.

22 来週、打ち合わせのあとにランチでもいかがですか？

Could we meet for lunch after the meeting next week?

❗ Could we ～?は、ていねいな提案としても使える。

23 来週の火曜日はどうでしょう？

Would Tuesday next week be all right?

convenient

24 何時がよろしいですか？

☞ **What time would suit you?**

suit＝～に合う、都合がよい

25 昼の12時でしたら大丈夫です。

Twelve noon would be OK.

26 玄関までお送りしますよ。

I'll see you off at the entrance.

see ～ off＝～を見送る

3 ビジネス会話
契約を結ぶ

1 契約内容をチェックさせてください。
Let me go over the contract.
go over ～＝～を(綿密に)調べる　contract＝契約

2 そちらの条件はどうなっていますか？
What are your terms?

3 その契約書は細部に変更が必要です。
We need to change the details of the contract.

4 契約書に書き入れましょうか？
Would you like me to fill out the contract?
fill out＝記入する、書き込む

5 納品はいつですか？
When can you deliver our order?

6 納品日を少し早めていただきたいのですが。
Could you make the delivery date a little earlier?
delivery date＝納品日、納期

7 注文事項を確認していただけますか？
Could you confirm the details of the order?
confirm the details＝詳細を確認する

8 ここにご署名をお願いします。
Would you please sign here?
＝ Would you put your signature here, please?

3 ビジネス会話
商談・交渉

1 わが社の提案については、いかがお考えですか？

What are your thoughts about our proposal?

thoughts about ～＝～についての考え

2 火曜日の話について、ちょうど考えていたところです。

I was just thinking about our conversation on Tuesday.

3 わが社の製品は、NY社のものよりも省エネ効果があります。

Our model has a greater energy-saving effect than NY's model.

energy-saving＝省エネ　énergy［エナヂー］

4 わが社の製品の処理速度は、他社のよりもはるかに速いですよ。

Our processing speed is much faster than the others'.

5 この製品は50代の女性に人気があります。

This model is popular with women in their 50s.

50s＝fifties［フィフティーズ］

6 たいていのコンビニで、この製品を販売しています。

Most convenience stores sell this product.

❗ sell の主語は、店・商品なども可。「この本は売れている」は This book is selling well.

7 ご注文は100個からお受けいたします。

We can take orders for 100 or more.

100 or more＝100以上

8 ご提案の価格はどのくらいですか？

☞ **How much would your proposal cost?**

9 見積もりをください。

Please give us an estimate of the cost.

10 200箱まとめて購入した場合の割引は、どのくらいになりますか？

If we buy 200 cartons, how much of a discount would you give us?   carton＝カートン（箱の単位）

11 値引きしていただけますか？

Can you give us a discount?

❗「7％割引いたします」は We can offer 7 percent off.

12 本社に問い合わせてみます。

I'll contact the head office.

13 わが社にご提示いただける一番安い価格は？

What's the best price you can offer to us?

14 カートン全部で1万ドルではいかがでしょう？

How about the whole carton for 10,000 dollars?

15 それはよい話ですね。

That's nice to know.

🟰 That sounds good.

16 この条件は受け入れられませんね。

These terms are unacceptable.

terms＝（契約上の）条件、条項

17 実に有意義な商談でした。

It was really a fruitful meeting, wasn't it?

❗「前向きに検討します」は We'll think about it.／We'll see what we can do.

3 ビジネス会話
退社・残業・接待

CD1 Track 87

1 今日、早退してもよろしいですか？
Is it okay if I leave early today?

2 打ち合わせに行って直帰します。
I'm going straight home from the meeting.

3 お先に失礼します。
I'm leaving now. See you tomorrow.

4 今日、残業できますか？
Can you stay late today?

5 必要であれば、残業も気になりません。
If necessary, I'm not reluctant to work overtime.
reluctant＝気乗りしない　work overtime＝残業する

6 することが山ほどある！　今日は残業だ。
I've got so much to do! I have to work overtime today.
洒落で Lucky you.「それはよかったね」「いいなあ」と言って励ましても楽しい。

7 貧乏ヒマなしだね。
No rest for the wicked.
the wicked＝悪人　英語では「悪人ヒマなし」という表現に。

8 今日はもう終わりにしよう。
Let's call it a day.
＝ Let's finish up.

9 ちょうど仕事が終わったところ。

I just got off work.

= I've just finished work.

10 終わった！ 今日は定時で帰れるよ。

All done!　I'll leave the office at the regular time today.

11 今日は忙しかったね。

☞ **It's been a long day.**

= We've worked hard today.

12 今夜、接待だ。

I'm entertaining clients tonight.

entertain＝もてなす、接待する　client＝顧客、取引先

13 接待するのに、よい場所を知りませんか？

Do you know a good place to entertain my clients?

14 駅のそばの、あの高級料亭はどうかな？

How about the classy Japanese-style restaurant near the station?

15 個室を予約しておきました。

I reserved a private room.

16 彼女は気が利くね。

She knows just what's needed.

❗「何が必要なのか、ちゃんとわかっている」の意味。

17 これも仕事のうちですから。

It's part of the job.

= All in the line of duty.

退社・残業・接待

ビジネス会話

4 | オフィスでの会話

給料のこと

CD2 Track 1

1 給料日が待ち遠しいなあ。

I can hardly wait for payday.

2 昇給したんだ！

I got a raise!

ráise[レイズ]　get a raise＝給料が上がる

3 給料、大幅にカットされちゃった。

My salary was cut drastically.

4 給料は毎月25日に振り込まれます。

My salary is deposited in my bank account on the 25th of every month.

deposit＝振り込む

5 私の給料では、新車を買う余裕なんてない。

I can't afford a new car on my salary.

❗「安月給でさ」は I work for peanuts.　＊peanutsは、「安月給」の意。

6 毎日サービス残業だよ。

I work overtime without pay every day.

❗「サービス残業」は work overtime without pay「支払いなしで残業する」で表す。

7 彼がどうして私の倍の給料をもらっているのか、わからないわ。

I don't understand why his salary is twice what mine is.

8 冬のボーナス、思ったよりも少なかった。

👉 My winter bonus was smaller than I expected.

～ than I expected＝予想していたよりも～

4 オフィスでの会話
昇進・異動

1 斉藤さんが昇進するって聞いたよ。
I heard Ms. Saito is getting promoted.

2 彼、出世コースにのったね。
He's on the road to success.

> road to success は「成功への道」という意味。

3 年功序列は時代遅れだ。
Seniority roles are becoming outdated.

seniority＝年功序列

4 うちは能力主義だよ。
At our company, salary is based on competence.

competence＝能力

5 この調子でいけば、君は昇給するよ。
You keep this up and you're going to get a raise.

6 このままだと君、降格になるぞ。
At this rate, you'll probably be demoted.

be demoted＝昇格させられる

7 役職についたけど、給料はそのままだよ。
I got a new post, but it's a dry promotion.

dry promotion＝(昇給なしの)役職だけの昇進

8 異動願いを出したんだ。
I put in a transfer request.

transfer＝転任、転勤

9 異動、決まった？

Have you been reassigned?

rèassign [リアサイン]

10 来週、人事異動が発表されるんだ。

Personnel reassignments will be announced next week.

personnel reassignment＝人事異動

11 私、異動になったら辞めます。

If you try to transfer me, I'll quit.

12 次はどんなポストにつくの？

Do you have any idea where you'll be posted next?

13 4月1日付けでソウルに転勤になりました。

☞ **I'll be relocated to Seoul as of April 1st.**

relocate＝異動させる、配置転換させる　as of ～＝～時点で

14 彼、東京本社に転勤になるんだ。

He's being transferred to the head office in Tokyo.

ニューヨーク支社 the New York branch

15 中国へ転勤なんて、夢にも思わなかったな。

China is the last place I expected to be transferred to.

16 仕事の引き継ぎをしなければ。

☞ **I have to train my replacement.**

replacement＝後継者、代わりの人

17 彼は単身赴任中なんだよ。

He's on an unaccompanied assignment.

unaccompanied＝同伴者のいない

4 オフィスでの会話
転職

1 最近、転職する人が多いよね。

Recently, more people have been changing jobs, haven't they?

change jobs＝転職する

2 転職を考えているの？

☞ **Are you thinking of changing jobs?**

❗「今の仕事がイヤなら転職すれば？」は If you're not happy, why don't you change jobs?

3 転職するなら今のうちだよ。求人広告を見ると、「40歳まで」というのが多いからね。

Well I guess it's now or never. Most of the ads stipulate a need for someone "under 40."

4 給料のいい仕事がしたいよ。

I want to find a well-paying job.

5 もっとやりがいのある仕事がしたい。

I want something more challenging.

6 リスクは高いけど、小さな会社に転職するつもり。

I'm going to take the risk and change to a smaller company.

7 手に職がないから、誰も雇ってくれない。

Nobody will hire me. I'm not qualified for anything.

be qualified for ～＝～の能力がある、資格がある

8 定年の65歳までいるつもり。

I'm staying until I retire at 65.

retire＝退職する　＊ここでは年齢を加えて「定年」の意味をはっきりさせている。

4 オフィスでの会話
上司・同僚のこと

1 私の上司はやさしくて頼りがいもあって、有能なの。

My boss is kind, reliable and efficient.

reliable＝頼りがいのある　efficient＝有能な

2 僕の上司は、いろいろうるさくて。

My boss is pretty demanding.

demanding＝(人が)要求・注文が多い、厳しい

3 今度の上司は、頭は切れるし、ユーモアのセンスもあるね。

Our new boss has a really sharp mind and a great sense of humor.

4 上司は、心の温かい人なの。あんな人が父親だったらいいのになあ。

The boss is a very warm-hearted person. I wish he were my father.

5 うちの上司は、細かいことは気にしないよ。

Our boss generally lets small things slide.

slide＝放っておく、(問題に)触れない

6 あら探しばかりする上司なんだ。

☞ **My boss keeps busy finding fault.**

7 あの部長、部下の面倒見がいいね。

The manager takes good care of his people.

8 彼は支社へ異動になっちゃったんだ。

He got transferred to the branch office.

9 彼って誠実だよね。
He's faithful.

faithful＝誠実な、信頼できる、義務を遂行する

10 彼って頭の回転が速いし、よく働くね。
He's really smart, and he works hard.

11 彼女、なかなかのやり手ですね。
She's a go-getter.

go-getter＝やり手、すご腕

12 あの子、ちょっと新鮮だよね。
She's just like a breath of fresh air.

❗ 気になる人や、興味をもった人について言う表現。

13 彼って、どうしてあんなに頑固なの？
Why is he so bullheaded?

bullheaded＝(筋が通らないほど)頑固な、強情な

14 彼はいつも上司にゴマをすっている。
He's always sucking up to his boss.

suck up to ～＝～にゴマをする、～の機嫌をとる

15 彼って、いつも上司の言いなり。
He's always at his boss's feet.

be at ～ feet＝～の言いなりだ、～にこびている

16 彼は、積極的で誠実だ。
He's outgoing and honest.

17 彼女の笑顔、明るくてなごむわ。
She has a bright, friendly smile.

18 田中さん、先週、中国人との交渉がうまくいったらしいよ。
I hear Ms. Tanaka negotiated with the Chinese successfully last week.

19 彼は私を目の敵にしている。
☞ **He has it in for me.**

have it in for ～=～に悪意を抱いている、～に難癖をつける

20 彼にはとてもつき合いきれない。
He's a difficult guy to get along with.

21 あの子、男の前ではブリっ子よね。
She acts cute in front of the guys.

22 彼女、ボスのお気に入りね。
She's the boss's favorite.

23 えこひいきよね。
That's not fair.

❗「不公平だ」という表現。

24 彼女は控えめで礼儀正しい人ね。
She's modest and smart.

25 彼はハンサムで仕事もできる。
He's handsome and competent.

26 彼は今までで最高の同僚だと思う。
I think he's the best co-worker I've ever had.

4 オフィスでの会話
給湯室でのおしゃべり

1 今朝、メイクした？
Did you apply makeup this morning?

2 朝、ギリギリまで寝ちゃって。
I slept until the last minute this morning.

3 ストッキング、伝線しているわよ。
☞ **There's a run in your pantyhose.**
  ❗ Oh. Thank you for telling me. 「本当だ。教えてくれてありがとう」

4 髪、切った？
Did you get a haircut?

5 その服、似合ってるね。
You look great in your clothes.

6 バーゲンで半額だったの。
I bought it at half-price at a sale.

7 貧血気味なの？ 少し顔色が悪いけど。
Do you have anemia? You look a little pale.
  anémia ［アニーミア］＝貧血(症)

8 生理痛がひどくて。
☞ **I have terrible menstrual pain.**
  menstrual pain＝生理痛

9 ダイエット、うまくいってる？

How is your diet going?

How is ～ going? ＝～はどのように進展していますか？

10 どうやってダイエットに成功したのか教えて。

Tell us. How were you able to succeed in your diet?

11 ダイエットする必要ないわよ。全然、ぜい肉なんかついてないじゃない。

You don't have to go on a diet. There's not an ounce of fat on you.

12 彼女は評判がいいね。

Everybody speaks highly of her.

13 同僚の田中くんと、つきあっているらしいよ。

I hear she's seeing Mr. Tanaka, one of her colleagues.

❗「そのうわさ本当かな？」は Can the rumor be true? 「それは大うそだよ」は That's totally untrue.

14 彼、ついに部長に昇格するらしいよ。

I hear he's finally going to be promoted to manager.

15 彼、子どもができたって聞いた？

Did you hear he had a baby?

16 うわさをすれば、何とやら。

☞ **Speak of the devil (and he appears).**

Talk ❗直訳は「悪魔の話をすれば（悪魔が現れる）」。

17 たった今、あなたのうわさをしていたの。

We were just talking about you.

18 彼氏ができたの。

☞ **I'm seeing someone.**

I'm seeing 〜. =〜と交際している

19 昨日、圭介とデートしたの。

I made a date with Keisuke yesterday.

20 初めてのデートで、ドキドキしっぱなしだったわ。

My heart was racing the whole time on our first date.

21 まあ、もうすぐ40歳だし、今しかチャンスないもん。

Well, I'm pushing 40 and I won't have another opportunity when I'm older.

22 彼女、今年の6月に結婚だってさ。

I heard she's getting married in June.

23 婚約指輪、高そうなのもらってた。

The engagement ring she got looks expensive.

24 もう、3年も彼氏がいないのよね。

I've been without a boyfriend for over three years.

25 男性はやっぱり、女性らしい子が好きよね。

Men like women who are feminine after all.

feminine =女らしい、やさしい　＊「男らしい、力強い」は masculine

26 あの2人どうして、別れたの？

Why did they break up?

split up

4 オフィスでの会話
住まい・家族のこと

1 マイホームを建てたんだって？
You became a homeowner, didn't you?

become a homeowner＝マイホームを持つ

2 二世帯住宅にしたよ。
We built a two-family home.

two-family home＝二世帯住宅

3 父の介護が必要でね。
I have to take care of my father.

4 ボーナスは全部、ローンの支払いに回されてしまうだろうな。
I'm afraid all of my bonus will go toward paying off my loan.

5 銀行に住宅ローンを断られちゃったよ。
The bank turned me down for a housing loan.

6 来年で住宅ローンが払い終わる。
We'll pay off our mortgage next year.

mórtgage ［モーギッジ］＝（抵当権付き）住宅ローン

7 妻は専業主婦です。
My wife is a homemaker.

homemaker＝主婦　＊housewife より一般的。

8 うちは共稼ぎなんです。
We have a double income.

9 女房のほうが稼いでいるよ。

My wife is the bigger breadwinner.

breadwinner＝稼ぎ手、大黒柱

10 夫は育児には協力的なの。

My husband helps with childcare.

childcare＝育児

11 うちは5人家族。

We're a family of five.

❗「何人家族ですか」は How many are there in your family?

12 3歳の娘がいるんだ。

I have a three-year-old daughter.

❗year を複数形にしないこと。

13 三世代の同居なんです。

Three generations live under one roof.

14 彼の親ばかぶりは、相当なものだ。

He's a doting father.

doting＝溺愛する

15 夫とは別居中なの。

My husband and I are separated.

16 離婚して、今一人暮らし。

I got divorced and live alone now.

17 自宅で、主人の母の介護をしています。

I take care of my husband's mother at home.

オフィスでの会話

住まい・家族のこと

4 | オフィスでの会話
ちょっと一杯

CD2 Track 7

1 今日はビール日和だね。
It's beer weather today, isn't it?

2 ちょっと一杯やろうか。
☞ Let's have a drink or two.
= Let's go for a drink.　＊Let's go drinking. と言うと、「徹底的に飲もう」といったニュアンスに。

3 軽く飲みに行かない？
Are you in the mood for a drink?
❗「もう1軒行こうか」は Let's hit another bar.

4 飲みに行きたいのは、ヤマヤマなんだけど…。
I wish I could go out for a drink tonight, but ...

5 9時までに帰らないと、ヨメさんに殺される。
My wife will kill me if I don't get home by 9:00.

6 <u>忘年会</u>、いつにする？
When are we going to have a <u>year-end party</u>?
🔄 新年会 New Year('s) party／歓迎会 welcome party／送別会 farewell party

7 誰か、幹事やってくれる人いる？
Are there any volunteers to be the organizers?
organizer＝(会の)幹事、世話役

8 彼は宴会部長だね。
He's a party animal.
party animal＝パーティが大好きな人

4 オフィスでの会話

グチはよそうよ

1 厳しい営業ノルマには、うんざりだよ。
I'm fed up with tough sales quotas.

quota＝(販売などの)ノルマ

2 カリカリするなよ！
Don't be so up-tight!

3 もう耐えられないよ。
☞ **I can't stand it.**

stand＝がまんする、辛抱する

4 もう仕事をやめたいよ。
I want to quit this job.

5 彼、かなり酒グセ悪いね。
He really has a drinking problem.

≡ He's a mean drunk.

6 グチはよそうよ。
Let's stop whining.

whine＝グチをこぼす

7 お酒の席で、仕事の話はイヤだわ。
I don't like discussing business over drinks.

8 グチをこぼしたくなったら、いつでも聞いてあげるよ。
If you ever need someone to talk about anything, I'll always be happy to listen.

5 つき合う、恋愛
恋バナに花が咲く

1 今日、デートなんだ。
I'm going out today.

go out＝デートする

2 どっちが告白したの？
Who made the first move?

❗「彼がデートに誘ってくれたの！」は He asked me out!

3 彼、恥ずかしがって、手も握ってくれないのよ。
He's too shy and doesn't even hold my hand.

4 じゃあ、あなたから仕向けたら？
Then, you should lead him to do so?

5 奇跡が起きたわ。プロポーズされた。
☞ **The impossible happened. I was proposed to.**

impossible＝起こりえないこと、あり得ないようなこと

6 彼といるとラクなの。
I'm so comfortable when I'm with him.

comfortable＝くつろいだ、気楽な

7 彼女、去年会ったときは結婚しないと言っていたのに。
She said she wasn't going to get married when we met last year.

8 彼女、どうしてそんなに急に気持ちが変わったのかな。
I wonder why she suddenly had a change of heart.

9 だって彼女、運命の相手とゴールインするんだもの。

As long as she's going to marry Mr. Right.

Mr.Right＝理想の男性、ふさわしい相手　＊「理想の女性」なら Ms. Right

10 うらやましい！

I'm jealous!

11 私は生涯独身だわ。

I'm going to stay single for the rest of my life.

12 私、男っぽい性格に見えるのかな？

Maybe I seem to be like a tomboy?

tomboy＝おてんば娘

13 彼のケータイがつながらないの。

I can't get him on the cell phone.

14 男の人って移り気なのかも。

The man might be temperamental.

temperamental＝移り気な、気まぐれな

15 私たち、いろいろなことがあったのよ。

We've had plenty of drama.

16 彼のことが忘れられない。

I can't get over him.

get over ～＝～を忘れる、あきらめる

17 今ではいい思い出。

It's now just a good memory.

5 | つき合う、恋愛
好き、恋をする

1 気になる人がいるんだ。
There's someone I like.

2 ひと目惚れなんだ。
It's love at first sight.

love at first sight＝ひと目惚れ

3 初恋なんだ。
This is the first time I've been in love.

＝ I've never been in love before.

4 こんな気持ちは初めてだよ。
I've never felt this way before.

5 恋をしているんだ。
I'm in love.

6 恋に落ちたよ。
I've fallen in love.

7 彼のことを考えると、胸が苦しくなるの。
Just the thought of him fills me with an unbearable longing.

unbearable＝耐えられない　longing＝あこがれ

8 片思いって、せつないね。
One-sided love is kind of sad.

9 彼に告白しちゃおうかな。

☞ **Maybe I'll tell him how I feel (about him).**

10 もしよかったら、私と出かけない？

I'm just kind of wondering if you'd maybe go out with me.

I'm just kind of wondering if ～＝もしよければどうかな　＊人を誘うときのソフトな表現。

11 一緒に行きたいところがあるんだ。

There's a place I'd like to take you (to).

12 デートしない？

Let's go on a date.

❗「ありがとう。うれしい」は Thank you. I'm glad. 「考えとく」は I'll think about it.

13 そのうち、ランチでもどう？

Want to go to lunch sometime?

❗ Do you を省略することで、よりフランクな言い方になる。

14 今度、食事に誘ってもいいかな。

Let me treat you to dinner sometime.

treat＝ごちそうする

15 年下には興味ないの。

I'm not interested in people younger than me.

16 つき合っている人はいる？

☞ **Are you seeing anyone?**

❗「誰かと定期的に会っている？」の意味。Do you have a boyfriend? より、こなれた感じ。

17 あなたのこと、もっと知りたいの。

I'd like to get to know you better.

5 つき合う、恋愛

好き、恋をする

18 あなたに夢中なの。
☞ **I'm crazy about you.**
　　🟰 I have a crush on you.

19 あなたしか見えない。
I only have eyes for you.
　　have eyes for ～ = ～に関心がある

20 あなたのことが頭から離れない。
I can't get you off my mind.

21 いつも君のことを考えているよ。
You're always on my mind.

22 君に恋しちゃったみたい。
I think I'm falling in love with you.
　　🟰 I think I'm crushing on you.

23 あなたのこと、友達としか思えない。
I can only think of you as just a friend.
　　❗「友達でいたい」は I'd rather just be friends.

24 私も前からあなたが好きだったの。
I've liked you for a long time, too.

25 友達から始めましょう。
Let's just start out as friends.

26 悪いけど、つき合っている人がいるんだ。
Sorry, I'm already seeing someone.

5 つき合う、恋愛
デートする

1 家まで車で迎えに行くよ。
I'll come pick you up in my car.

2 遅れてごめん。待った？
Sorry, I'm late. Have you been waiting long?

3 ううん、私も今、来たところ。
No, I just got here myself.

4 どこか行きたいところ、ある？
Is there any place you'd like to go (to)?

5 今日は、家でDVDでも見てのんびりしようか。
Let's just take it easy and watch a DVD at home today.

6 手、つないでいい？
Can I hold your hand?

7 恥ずかしいってば。
I'm mortified.

mortified＝恥ずかしい、きまり悪い

8 ねぇ、あんまりくっつかないで。
Hey, stop clinging to me.

cling to ～＝～にぴったり寄り添う

9 あなたのそういうところ、好き。
☞ **That's what I like about you.**

10 その新しい服、かわいいね。
You look <u>sweet</u> in your new dress.
good／nice／pretty

11 君のハンカチ、いいにおいがする。
Your handkerchief smells sweet.
❗「香水つけたんだ」と返すなら I put perfume on it.

12 君といると幸せだなって思ってさ。
I'm thinking how happy I am with you.

13 誕生日、いつだったっけ？
When is your birthday again?
❗一度聞いたけれど忘れてしまったときは again をつけるとよい。

14 つき合ってから、もう3年たつね。
☞ **We've been going out for three years.**

15 怒ってる君もかわいいよ。
You're so cute when you're mad.

16 たまには温泉にでも連れていってよ。
Take me out to a hot spring resort once in a while.
once in a while=たまには

17 ごめん。来月まで忙しいんだ。
Sorry honey. I'll be busy until next month.
❗honey は、恋人や夫・妻など、愛する人への呼びかけの語。

18 話しすぎて、もうこんな時間になっちゃった。

We talked so much that we didn't notice the time.

19 本当に今日は楽しかったね。

Time flies when you're having fun.

time flies＝時がたつのは早い

20 もう少し一緒にいたいな。

I want to stay with you a little longer.

a little longer＝もう少し長い時間

21 門限が10時なの。

My curfew is 10:00.

curfew＝門限

22 1時間も過ぎちゃってる。

I'm already late by an hour.

23 うちの父、すごく怖いから、今日は帰るわ。

My father is going to have a fit, so I'm going home for today.

have a fit＝激怒する

24 車で送ろうか？

☞ **Do you need a lift?**

lift＝車に乗せていくこと

25 車で送ってくれてありがとう。

Thank you for driving me.

26 今度、いつ会える？

When can I see you again?

27 あなたのこと、いつも思っているから。

My thoughts always go out to you.

28 もう遅いし、1人で帰りたくないな。

It's getting late. I don't wanna go home alone.

29 家まで送っていこうか？

Would you like me to see you home?

see (人) home＝人を家まで送る

30 ちょっと寄っていかない？

Why don't you stop by for a little while?

stop by＝(立ち)寄る

31 あなたの部屋に来るなんて、思ってもみなかったわ。

I never thought of coming to your place.

32 泊まっていきたいな。

I'd rather stay here (tonight).

33 今夜、泊まっていい？

Can I stay over at your place tonight?

34 君を抱きたい。

I want to make love to you.

35 今夜は最高の夜だった。

I had a wonderful night tonight.

= It's one of the happiest nights of my life.

5 | つき合う、恋愛

けんかをする

1 話があるの。
We need to talk.

2 今すぐ来てくれない?
I need you right away.

right away=すぐに、ただちに

3 機嫌、悪いね。
You're out of sorts.

be out of sorts=機嫌が悪い

4 昨日の夜、ずっと電話通じなかったけど?
Your phone was off all last night.

off=(スイッチが)切れて/(機能が)停止して　❗「何してたの?」は What were you doing?

5 大きなお世話だよ。
☞ **Mind your own business.**

6 言い訳なんて聞きたくない!
I don't want to hear any excuses!

7 みんな、笑いごとじゃないのよ。
Not cool guys.

guys=みんな、君たち　*話し相手が男性でも女性でも使える。

8 もういい加減にして。
Stop doing that.

❗ that は、相手がやっていることや言っていることで、自分を不快にさせていることを指す。

185

5 つき合う、恋愛

けんかをする

9 どうしていつもそうなの？
Why are you always like that?

10 どうしろって言うんだよ。
What am I supposed to do?
be supposed to 〜＝〜することになっている、〜しなければならない

11 勝手に人のケータイを見るなよ！
Stop looking at my phone without my permission!

12 何をそんなにむきになっているの？
Why are you so persistent?
persistent＝しつこい、頑固な

13 その態度、腹がたつ。
Your attitude is making me angry.

14 今さらごまかそうとしないでよ。
It's too late to try to whitewash what you did.
whitewash＝体裁を取り繕う

15 そういうしつこいところがイヤ。
I don't care for that kind of nosy behavior.
nosy＝おせっかいな

16 わかって欲しい。
I'm hoping you understand this.

17 あなたの気持ちがもうわからない！
I don't know how you feel about me anymore!
not 〜 anymore＝もはや〜ない、これ以上〜ない

5 | つき合う、恋愛

仲直りをする

1 まだ怒ってる？

Are you still upset with me?

❗「僕が悪かった」は Sorry. It's my fault.

2 さっきは言いすぎた。

Sorry about what I said earlier.

❗「そのせいで私たちの関係が悪くなることはないわ」は This isn't exactly a deal-breaker.

3 仲直りしようよ。

I want to make up with you.

❗「キスして仲直りしよう」と言う場合は It's time to kiss and make up.

4 やり直さない？

👉 Can't we give it another chance?

= Do you want to give it another try?

5 よりを戻そう。

Let's get back together.

6 捨てられたかと思った。

I thought you skipped out on me.

skip out on (人)＝(人)を置き去りにする、(人)を置いて出て行く

7 君から電話は返ってこないだろうと思ってた。

I thought you wouldn't return my calls.

return some one's call＝折り返し電話をかける

8 これから、君に埋め合わせをするつもり。

I'm going to try to make it up to you.

make it up to (人)＝(人)に対して埋め合わせをする

5 | つき合う、恋愛
失恋、別れ話をする

CD2 Track 14

1 あなたの顔なんて、もう二度と見たくない。
I never want to see your face again.

2 あなたには、もう、うんざり。
☞ **I've had it with you.**
　　＝ I'm fed up with you.

3 もう信じられないよ。
I can't trust you anymore.

4 私の前から消えて！
Get away from me!

5 あなたには、これ以上ついていけない。
I can't keep up with you anymore.
　　keep up with ～ = ～についていく

6 このままだと、お互いにとってよくないよ。
Going on like this is no good for either of us.

7 私たち、もう会うべきじゃないと思う。
I don't think we should see each other anymore.

8 私たち、しばらく距離を置いたほうがいいと思う。
I think we need some time apart.
　　＝ Let's keep our distance for a while.

9 彼に1人になりたいって言ったの。

I told him I needed space.

space=自由、束縛のないこと

10 1人になって考えたいの。

I need time alone to think.

= I want to be by myself to think for a while.

11 しばらくそっとしておいて。

Leave me alone for a while.

leave (人) alone=(人)を放っておく　for a while=しばらくの間

12 ほかに好きな人ができた。

☞ **I've fallen in love with someone else.**

13 うそだと言ってよ。

Tell me you're lying.

lie=うそをつく　＊lie→lying の語形変化に注意。

14 もう僕たち、別れるべきだと思う。

I think we should break up.

15 別れるなんて言わないで。

Don't say you want to split up.

split up=別れる

16 もう終わりだね。

We're finished.

= It's over (between us).

17 別れましょう。

I think we need to end this.

= Let's break up.

5 つき合う、恋愛

失恋、別れ話をする

18 僕たちの関係は冷めたんだ。
Things have cooled down between us.
≡ Where has our love gone?

19 私たち、いつからこうなっちゃったのかな。
How did this happen to us?
≡ When did we get like this?

20 部屋の鍵、置いていくね。
I'm leaving you the key.

21 部屋の鍵、返してくれる？
Can I have my key back?

22 もう取り返しがつかないよ。
There's no getting over something like this.
≡ What is done cannot be undone.

23 何を言っても無駄みたいだね。
☞ **There's nothing I can say that will change things.**

24 あなたが遠く感じる。
It's like you're a million miles away.
be a million miles away＝百万マイルと遠くにいる

25 もう一度だけチャンスをくれないか？
Couldn't you just give me one more chance?
❗「よくそんなことが言えるわね」は How can you say that?

26 今までありがとう。
Thanks for everything you've done.

5 つき合う、恋愛
プロポーズ・結婚

CD2 Track 15

1 結婚してください。
Will you marry me?
> ❗ 「はい」は（Yes) I will.「少し考えさせて」は I need time to think about it.

2 何があっても一緒にいよう。
Whatever happens, we'll be together.

3 あなたと一緒に残りの人生を過ごしたい。
I want to spend the rest of my life with you.

4 君以外、考えられない。
☞ I can't think of anyone but you.
but ～＝～以外に、～を除いて

5 私にはあなたしかいないの。
You're the only one for me.

6 あなたのいない人生なんて意味がない！
Without you, life has no meaning!

7 君を見た瞬間、君となら幸せになれると思ったんだ。
The second that I saw you, I knew we could be great together.

8 妊娠したみたいなの。
I think I'm pregnant.
be pregnant＝妊娠している

つき合う、恋愛 / プロポーズ・結婚

9 僕にとって、何よりも大切なのは君だ。

You're more important to me than anything else in the world.

10 一緒に幸せな家庭を築こう。

Let's have a happy family together.

11 結婚なんて、まだ心の準備ができていないよ。

I still don't feel ready to be married.

12 一生、君を守るよ。

I will always protect you.

「君を幸せにする」は I promise I'll make you happy.

13 君には不自由はさせないよ。

I'll put you on easy street.

put (人) on easy street=(人) に何不自由ない生活をさせる

14 浮気は絶対にしないでね。

Promise me, no screwing around.

screw around=浮気する 「誓うよ」は I give you my word.

15 どんな式にしたい？

What kind of wedding do you want?

16 こじんまりとした式がいいわ。

I'd like to have a small wedding.

17 新婚旅行はパリがいいな。

I want to go to Paris on our honeymoon.

Part 3 オフタイムの会話

1 レジャー、娯楽 ……… 194
2 ドライブ ……… 208
3 美容院、ジム、エステ … 216
4 ショッピング ……… 228
5 外食 ……… 240
6 飲み会、カラオケ ……… 252
7 招待、訪問、パーティ ……… 260

1 映画に行く

レジャー、娯楽

CD2 Track 16

1. 映画に行かない？
   How about going to a movie?
   = Let's go see a movie.

2. 今、何を上映しているの？
   What's <u>showing</u> now?
   on／playing

3. ケータイで、映画のスケジュールを調べてみるよ。
   I'll check movie schedules with my cell phone.

4. どんな映画が見たい？
   What kind of movie do you want to see?

5. それ、どこでやってるの？
   Where's the movie playing?

6. 主演は誰？
   Who's starring in the movie?
   star＝主演する

7. その映画って、どんな話？
   What's that movie about?

8. 実話に基づいているんだ。
   It's based on a true story.
   be based on ～＝～に基づいている

9 僕が好きそうな映画だ。

That sounds like the type of movie I would like.

10 僕の見たいタイプの映画じゃないな。

It doesn't strike me as my kind of movie.

strike (A) as (B)＝(A)に(B)という印象を与える

11 評判はいいよ。

☞ **It's been getting good reviews.**

12 次の上映は何時？

What time is the next showing?

13 映画が始まるまで、20分あるよ。

Twenty minutes till the movie.

14 誰かと一緒に映画を見るのは、久しぶりだな。

It's the first time in a while that I've watched a movie with someone.

15 もっと前の席にしようよ。

Let's sit closer up front.

16 飲み物とポップコーンを買ってくる。

I'm going to get some drink and popcorn.

17 あの人の頭でよく見えない。

That person is blocking my view.

≡ That person is in my way.

1 レジャー、娯楽

映画の感想

CD2 Track 17

1 すごくよかったね。久しぶりに、映画を見て泣いたよ。

It was marvelous. For the first time in so long, I cried at a movie.

2 すごく感動した。

☞ **It really moved me.**

move＝感動させる　affected

3 感動で胸がつまったよ。

I got a catch in the throat.

💡 catch は「つかえ、引っかかり」で、全体で「言葉に詰まるほど感動した」ということ。

4 今まで見た中で、最高の映画の一つだ。

This is one of the best films I've ever seen.

5 アカデミー賞にノミネートされているんだよ。

It received an Oscar nomination.

💡 Oscar は、アカデミー賞受賞者に与えられる黄金のトロフィー。

6 まあまあよかったね。

☞ **The movie was A-OK.**

A-OK [エイ オウケイ] ＝まあまあいい、平均よりやや上の　＝ It was an all-right movie.

7 ストーリーはよかったけど、配役がいまいちだったな。

The story was good, but the casting was not that great.

8 原作とは全然違ったね。

The movie was completely different from the original book.

be different from ～＝～と異なる、違う

9 あの監督の映画は、いつもハッピーエンドだね。

The director always chooses the happy ending.

10 話の筋が複雑すぎて、ついていけなかった。

The plot of the movie was too complicated for me to follow.

11 結末が意外だったよね。

☞ **The ending of the film was quite unexpected.**

12 彼の映画は、どれも似たり寄ったりだな。

His films are all almost alike.

13 すごく面白そうに思えたのに、期待外れだったね。

I thought it would be a lot of fun, but it was a letdown.

letdown＝期待外れ

14 とても退屈で、期待外れだった。

It was very dull and disappointing.

disappointing＝がっかりさせる

15 この映画、ちっともよくなかった。

I was totally unimpressed with this movie.

16 心底がっかりした。

It frustrated me enormously.

frustrate＝失望させる

17 あの映画を2時間も我慢して見る人はいないよ。

Maybe no one can stand to watch the movie for two hours.

stand to 〜＝〜するのを我慢する、〜することに耐えている

1 レジャー、娯楽

観劇に行く

1 チケット売り場はどこですか？
Where's the box office?

box office＝チケット売り場

2 今晩のチケットは、まだありますか？
Do you have any tickets left for tonight?

3 完売です。
It's sold out.

sold out＝売り切れ

4 いつのチケットならありますか？
☞ **For when do you have tickets?**

5 平日の昼の公演なら、いくつか席がございます。
We have some seats available for the weekday matinee performance.

màtinée [マトゥネイ] ＝昼の公演

6 電話予約はできますか？
Can I make my reservation by phone?

7 ネットでチケットを予約しました。
I booked tickets online.

book＝予約する

8 スタンバイ・チケットはありますか？
Do you have standby tickets?

💡 スタンバイチケットは、キャンセル待ちのチケットのこと。

9 S席はいくらですか？

How much are the <u>special seats</u>?

S seats／seats in the S section

10 なるべく見やすい席がいいんですが。

I'd prefer seats with a good view of the stage.

11 座席表で見ると、席はどこになりますか？

Where's the seat according to the seating chart?

according to ～＝～によると　seating chart＝座席表

12 前から5列目の席です。

It's the seat on the 5th row from the front.

row＝列

13 立見席でもかまいません。

I wouldn't mind standing room.

standing room＝（劇場・競技場などの）立ち見席

14 入口でチケットを見せるんだって。

You'll need to show your ticket at the entrance.

15 開場は何時なの？

What time do the doors open?

16 開演は午後6時だ。

The curtain goes up at 6 p.m.

17 このミュージカルのチケット、やっと手に入れたんだ。

I managed to get tickets for this musical.

manage to ～＝どうにか～する

レジャー、娯楽

観劇に行く

18 すごくいい席だね。
We have great seats, don't we?

19 英語のセリフが聞き取れない。
I can't catch the English lines.

catch＝聞き取る　line＝台詞

20 ストーリーを読んでおけばよかったな。
I should've read up on the storyline.

21 配役がいいね！
What a fine cast!

22 本場のミュージカルは華やかだね！
Real musicals are glamorous!

glamorous＝華やかな、活気のある

23 迫力ある演技だね。
☞ **It's an impressive performance.**

🍃 迫真の realistic／熱のこもった impassioned／渋い low-keyed／素人っぽい amateurish

24 やっぱり、ライブの演奏は楽しいね！
Live performances are entertaining.

live ［ライブ］

25 ライブのほうが迫力あるなあ。
Live performances are more powerful.

26 この曲大好き！
I love this tune!

tune＝曲

1 レジャー、娯楽

美術館に行く

1 芸術の秋だね。美術館へでも行く？
Autumn is the best season for art. Why don't we go to a museum or something?

2 国立美術館で、ピカソ展やってるよ。
☞ **They're putting on the Pablo Picasso exhibition at the national gallery.**

3 入館料は、いくらですか？
How much is the admission (fee)?

admission＝入場料、入館料

4 この美術館のパンフレットはありますか？
Do you have a brochure for this museum?

brochúre [ブロウシャ]＝パンフレット

5 まず、特別展示を見ようよ。
Let's start with the special exhibit.

🔄 常設展示 permanent exhibit

6 どこも行列だらけ。うんざりしてきた。
Wherever I go, there are lines. I'm getting tired of it.

7 これは誰の作品？
Whose work is this?

💡「いつ頃の作品？」は When was this work done?

8 現代芸術は、理解するのが難しい。
Contemporary art is difficult to understand.

1 レジャー、娯楽

スポーツ観戦をする

1 ナイターに行こうよ。
Let's go watch a night game.
💡 「ナイター」は和製英語。Let's go to a baseball game tonight. で表すこともできる。

2 地元チームのファンなんだ。
I'm a fan of the local team.
local＝地元の

3 野球は見るだけ、やるのはサッカーだな。
Baseball is fun to watch and soccer is good to do.

4 日本の野球より、メジャー・リーグが好きだな。
I like Major League baseball better than Japanese baseball.

5 4対2で、ZYチームがリードしてる。
The ZY team leads by 4 to 2.

6 接戦だ。
☞ It's a close game.
🔃 引き分け a tie／圧勝 am overwhelming victory

7 ついに同点だ。
The game is finally tied.

8 ZYチームが逆転したよ。
The ZY team came from behind and won the game.
come from behind＝追い上げる、逆転する

9 ACチームが勝てば、優勝だ。

The AC team can take the pennant if they win this game.

10 劇的なサヨナラホームランだったね！

It was a dramatic game-winning home run!

11 ACチームが先制点を入れた。

The AC team scored the first goal.

12 どっちが勝ってる？

☞ **Which side is winning?**

13 今、5対3で日本が勝ってるよ。

Right now, the score is 5 to 3 and Japan is winning.

14 ロスタイムは何分？

How many minutes of injury time do they have?

injury time＝(サッカーなどの)ロスタイム

15 残り10秒！

Ten seconds left!

16 延長戦にもつれ込んだぞ。

They're going to play overtime.

💡 野球の場合は go[run] into extra innings「延長回に入る」

17 オリンピックとワールドカップの開催中は、いつも寝不足だ。

I don't get enough sleep during the Olympic Games and the World Cup.

1 レジャー、娯楽

遊園地へ行く

1 まず、最初は何に乗りたい？
What do you want to ride first?

2 ここ、新しい観覧車ができたんだって。
They have a new Ferris wheel here.

Ferris wheel＝観覧車

3 それに乗るには、列に並ばないと。
We need to stand in line to ride it.

4 2時間待ちだって。
☞ **They say there'll be a two-hour wait.**

🟰 We'll have to wait for two hours.

5 ジェットコースターに乗りたい。
I want to ride the roller coaster.

roller coaster＝ジェットコースター

6 勘弁してよ、高所恐怖症なんだから。
It's impossible for me because I have acrophobia.

acrophobia＝高所恐怖症　I'm afraid of heights.

7 お化け屋敷、入った？
Did you go into the haunted house?

háunted [ホーンティッド]

8 ああ、怖かった！
Wow, that was scary!

1 レジャー、娯楽

海に行く

1 どこの海に行く？
Which beach are we going to?

2 今日は波がよくないな。
The surf's not very good today.

3 クロールできる？
Can you do the crawl?
→ 平泳ぎ breaststroke／背泳ぎ backstroke／バタフライ butterfly

4 ねえ、あの岩場まで競争しようよ。
Come on, I'll race you to those rocks.

5 日陰にいるよ。日焼けしたくないから。
I'm going to stay in the shade. I don't want to get a suntan.

6 この辺りでは何が釣れますか？
What can you catch around here?
❗「釣れますか」は Are they biting?／Can you catch anything?

7 今日は魚の食いつきが悪い。
The fish aren't biting today.

8 こんな大物を釣ったのは初めてだよ。
This is the first time I've caught anything this big.

1 | レジャー、娯楽

登山やスキーを楽しむ

CD2 Track 23

1 登山口で落ち合おう。
Let's meet at the trailhead.

trailhead＝登山道の起点、登山口

2 この坂、きついね。
This slope is very steep, isn't it?

3 霧が晴れてきましたね。
The fog is clearing.

4 頂上まで、あと一息！
☞ **We're almost at the top.**

summit

5 スキーには最高の天気だね。
It's perfect weather for skiing, isn't it?

6 レンタルのスノーボードはありますか？
Do you have snowboards available for rent?

7 スノーボードは初めて？
Is this your first time to snowboard?

8 どっちのコースに行く？
Which run shall we go on?

run＝(スキーなどの)コース

1 レジャー、娯楽

ゴルフをする

1 ちょっと、打ちっ放しに行ってくる。
I'm going to the driving range now.

driving range＝打ちっぱなしのゴルフ練習場

2 彼女、いいスイングするね。
She's got a good swing.

3 彼、パットがうまいね。
He's a good putter.

4 ここは5番アイアンでいこう。
I'll use the five iron here.

💡「5番アイアン」は fifth iron ではなく（number）five iron。

5 ラインが読めない。
I can't read the green.

6 ボールがバンカーから出ない。
I can't get a ball out of the bunker.

7 パーを逃した！
I missed a par!

💡 ボギーは bogey、パーは par、バーディーは birdie、イーグルは eagle。

8 90たたいちゃった。
I shot a 90.

💡「スコアはどうでした？」は What did you shoot?

2 | ドライブ

車で出かける

1 海までドライブなんてどう？

How about driving to the beach?

> 「ドライブに行こう」は Let's go for a drive. drive の代わりに ride や spin も可。

2 本当にいい天気！　絶好のドライブ日和だね。

What a beautiful day! It's perfect weather for driving.

3 何時に迎えに行けばいい？

What time do you want me to pick you up?

4 明日、車を使っていい？

Is it OK if I use your car tomorrow?

5 運転は僕に任せてよ。

Leave the driving to me.

6 シートベルトは締めた？

Did you buckle up?

⊜ Did you fasten your seatbelt?

7 免許証、忘れないでよ。

Don't forget your driver's license.

driver's license＝運転免許証

8 エンジンをかけて。さあ、出発！

Start the engine. Okay, let's get going!

9 エアコンつけてくれる？

Turn on the air conditioner, please.

10 はい、これ、ドライブにぴったりのCD。

Here's a CD I recommend for driving.

11 窓を開けていい？

Can I roll down the window?

＝ Can I open the window?

12 こら！ おとなしくしなさい！

Hey! Settle down back there!

❗ 後部座席にいる子どもに対して言う表現。

13 外に顔を出さないで！

Don't stick your head out of the window!

14 ジュースはシートに置かないで。カップホルダーに戻してよ。

Don't leave your juice on the seat.　Put it back in the cup holder.

15 運転に集中させてくれよ。

Please let me focus on driving.

16 次のサービスエリアで休憩しよう。

☞ **Let's take a break at the next rest area.**

17 車に酔ったみたいだ。

I guess I got carsick.

2 ドライブ

運転する

1 前の車、のろのろ運転だなあ。

The car in front of us is crawling.

crawl＝ゆっくり進む

2 追い越し車線に行こう。

Let's get into the passing lane.

passing lane＝追い越し車線　＊「走行車線」は driving lane / running lane。

3 飛ばしすぎじゃない？

☞ **You're driving too fast, aren't you?**

4 わかった。スピード落とすよ。

All right. I'll slow down.

5 車間距離をとってね。

Don't tailgate, please.

tailgate＝ぴったりついて走る

6 スピード違反の取り締まりが行われている。

There's a speed-trap.

7 左車線の流れは、今のところ順調だ。

For now, traffic is flowing freely in the left lane.

traffic＝交通（量）

8 この道、違うんじゃない？

☞ **Are we going the wrong way?**

9 迷ったみたい。

I think we got lost.

10 後ろに地図はある?

Do you see a map back there?

⚠️ 「あるよ。はい、これ」は Yeah, here you go.

11 道は合っているよ。

We're on the right road.

right＝正しい

12 カーナビによれば、あっちだって。

The navigation system says it's that way.

navigation system＝カーナビ

13 あそこの交差点を右折して。

Turn right at that intersection.

Make a right

14 一方通行だ。

It's a one-way street.

⚠️ 二車線は two-lane road

15 さっきの道を左に曲がるべきだったんだ。

☞ **We were supposed to turn left back there.**

16 Uターンしよう。

Let's turn around.

🟰 Let's do a U turn.

17 運転代わってもらえる? 疲れてきた。

Could you take over the wheel? I'm getting tired.

2 ドライブ

運転する

18 いいよ。車を寄せて。
All right. Pull over.

19 ストップ！ サイドブレーキが、かかったままだよ。
Stop! You forgot to release your handbrake.
「ブレーキをかける」は put on the brake

20 ごめん。君の車を運転するのに、慣れていなくて。
I'm sorry. I'm not used to driving your car.

21 車の流れがずいぶんゆっくりだ。
The traffic is just creeping along.
Creep＝ゆっくり動く 「渋滞でのろのろ運転だ」は Traffic is inching along.

22 高速に乗ろう。
Let's get on the expressway.
「高速を降りる」は get off the expressway

23 見て！ いい景色だ。
Look! Isn't the view fantastic?
What a magnificent view!「絶景だね！」

24 急停車しないでよ！
Don't make such a sudden stop!

25 あと少しで到着するよ。10分で浜辺に着くかな。
We're almost there. We'll be at the beach in ten minutes.

26 着いたよ。車から降りなさい。
We're here, hop out of the car.
Here we are

212

2 | ドライブ
ガソリンスタンドで

CD2 Track 27

1 ガソリンが少なくなってきた。
We're running out of gas.

= We're low on gas.

2 古い車は燃費が悪いね。
An old car eats a lot of gas.

3 あっ、あそこにガソリンスタンドがある。
Look, there's a gas station.

gas station＝ガソリンスタンド

4 セルフ式のガソリンスタンドだ。
It's a self-service gas station.

5 レギュラーを満タンで。
☞ **Fill it up with regular, please.**

her ＊車や船などの乗り物は女性扱いすることがある。　⚠ ハイオクは high octane／premium

6 灰皿を空にしましょうか？
May I clean the ashtray?

ashtray＝灰皿

7 リッター120円は、安いね。
A hundred and twenty yen per liter is reasonable.

8 空気圧を見てもらえますか。
Can you check the tire pressure?

tire pressure＝空気圧

2 ドライブ
交通渋滞・トラブル

1 車をぶつけちゃった！
I had a car crash!

2 事故かなんか、あったんだよ。
There must have been an accident or something.

3 パトカーが来ているみたい。
It looks like there's a police car.

police car＝パトカー

4 赤く点滅している光が見えるよ。
I see some flashing red lights.

5 渋滞に、はまったな！
☞ **We're stuck in a traffic jam!**

= We're stuck in traffic.

6 少なくとも、1時間はトイレには行けないよ。
You won't be able to go to the restroom for at least an hour.

bathroom

7 左車線は流れているよ。
The left lane is moving faster.

8 どこか、半ドアじゃない？
I'm afraid one of the doors isn't closed properly.

❗「半ドア」は「ドアがしっかりと閉まっていない」と表す。

9 室内灯がついたままだ。
The car lamp stays on.

10 うわっ、タイヤがパンクした！
Oh, no! We got a flat tire!
　　　　　　　　　　　　　blowout

11 直せる？
Can you fix it?

12 ヘッドライトを消し忘れちゃった。
I forgot to turn off the headlights.

13 バッテリーが上がっちゃうよ。
☞ **The battery's going to go dead.**
　　　💡「バッテリーを充電する」は recharge one's battery

14 この辺で駐車するのは無理だ。
Parking's impossible around here.

15 ここに駐車すると、レッカー移動されるかも。
If we park here, we run the chance of having the car towed away.　　run the chance of 〜＝〜の恐れがある

16 また、駐車違反しちゃった！
I got another parking ticket!
　　　　　💡ticketには「交通違反の切符」という意味もある。

17 止まりなさい。スピード違反です。
Pull over. You were speeding.

3 フィットネスクラブ

美容院、ジム、エステ

1 月会費はおいくらですか？

How much is the monthly membership fee?

monthly membership fee＝月会費

2 一般会員は月４０００円からです。

From 4,000 yen for a regular member.

3 今ならキャンペーン中につき、入会金無料です。

There is no initiation fee now because of a special campaign.

initiation fee＝入会金

4 入会するわ。

I'd like to join this club.

5 レッスンは週１回、毎週水曜日です。

The class is given once a week every Wednesday.

6 次のレッスンの申し込みをしなければ。

I need to sign up for the next lesson.

sign up for ～＝～に受講登録する、～に名前を登録する

7 途中解約は可能ですか？

Is it possible to cancel halfway through the contract?

cancel the contract＝解約する

8 講師は、テレビでおなじみの、あの佐藤先生です。

The lecturer is Mr. Sato, a famous teacher on TV.

9 ジムに入ろうと思っているんだ。

I'm thinking of joining a gym.

10 どこか、おすすめのジムはありますか？

Is there any place you recommend to work out?
recommend＝勧める　work out＝運動する

11 そのジムは、隣の駅前にあるんだ。

The gym is located in front of the next station.
be located ～＝～に位置している、～にある

12 まず、基礎体力の測定を行います。

First, let me check your basic physical ability.

13 事前に健康診断を受けてください。

Please have a health check up in advance.

in advance＝前もって

14 これがお客様のトレーニングメニューです。

This is your training plan.

15 おなかが出てきたのが気になって。

I'm worried about my big belly.

belly＝腹、腹部

16 最近、全然運動をしていないんです。

☞ **Recently, I haven't been getting any exercise.**

exercise＝運動

17 最近、体力の衰えを感じています。

I don't have as much energy as I used to.

＝ I've been getting weaker recently.

3 美容院、ジム、エステ フィットネスクラブ

18 腰痛には腹筋が効果的です。
Sit-ups will work for your backache.
_{sit-ups＝腹筋(運動)　backache＝腰痛}

19 少し筋肉を強化する必要がありますね。
You need to build up your muscles a little.
múscle［マスル］＝筋肉

20 以前に、これをやったことはありますか？
☞ Ever done this before?
💡 冒頭の Have you が省略された形で、話し言葉でよく使われる。

21 もっと穏やかな運動がいいわ。
I'd like to do a less strenuous workout.
strenuous＝きつい

22 腰からまっすぐ背中を伸ばして。
Straight up from your hip.

23 腕をこんな風に回して。
Circle your arms like this.
circle＝円を描くように回す

24 いろいろな動かし方があるんですよ。
We have a lot of moves.

25 脚がつっちゃった。
☞ I got a cramp in my leg.
get a cram in one's leg＝脚がつる

26 無理しないほうがいいですよ。
You'd better not strain yourself.
strain oneself＝精一杯動かす、働かせる

27 私、反射神経が悪いのよ。

I have bad hand-eye coordination.

> hand-eye coordinationは、もともと「手と目の協調」という意味。「反射神経」のこと。

28 心拍数はいくつになっていますか？

What is your pulse?

pulse＝（1分間の）心拍数

29 カロリー消費量を記録してください。

Please record your calorie consumption.

30 クロールで1日に3000メートル泳ぐのが、あなたの目標です。

Your target is swimming the crawl for 3,000 meters each day.

31 あとでクールダウンします。

I'll cool down later.

32 サウナに入ろう。

Let's take a sauna.

sáuna [サーナ]

33 運動後のジャグジーが楽しみなんだ。

I'm looking forward to the Jacuzzi after working out.

Jacúzzi [ジャクージ]

34 最近、ジムをさぼりがちなんだ。

Lately, I haven't been going to the gym very often.

35 私、少しやせたかしら？

Have I lost any weight?

3 美容院、ジム、エステ

美容院

1 今日はどうなさいますか？
How would you like your hair done today?

2 このような髪型にしていただけますか？
Could you do my hair like this?

3 このモデルのようなカットにしてください。
Could you cut my hair like this model's?

4 流行の髪型にしたいです。
I'd like the "in" style.

in＝はやっている

5 カットとパーマをお願いします。
I'd like a cut and a perm.

6 全体に少しだけ短くカットしてください。
Can you cut it a little shorter all around?

7 髪が多いので、軽くしてください。
Could you thin my hair because it's too bulky?

thin＝間引く　bulky＝量が多い

8 前髪はどうされますか？
How would you like your bangs cut?

bangs＝前髪

9 眉のところで揃えてください。

I'd like straight bangs just over the eyebrows.

10 髪を染めたいのですが。

☞ **I want my hair dyed.**

> 「白髪を染めたい」という場合は I'd like to dye my gray hair.

11 毛先を整えて、枝毛を切るくらいでいかがでしょう。

I suggest we trim it and cut off the split ends.

cut off the split ends＝枝毛を切る

12 前回のパーマで髪が傷んでいますね。

Your hair seems damaged from your last perm.

13 サイドをふわっとさせてください。

Can you make both sides look kind of puffy?

puffy＝ふわっと

14 くせっ毛を矯正したいのですが。

I'd like to relax my frizzy hair.

frizzy＝縮れた

15 ストレートパーマはいかがでしょうか？

How about getting a straight perm?

16 真ん中で分けてください。

Please part my hair in the middle.

part＝分ける　　サイド（横）で on one side

17 エクステでボリュームを出しましょう。

Let's put in extensions to give your hair more volume.

extension＝拡張、つけ毛

3 フェイシャルケア

美容院、ジム、エステ

1 フェイシャルエステを試してみない？
Want to try a facial?

facial＝フェイシャルエステ、顔のお手入れ

2 私のフェイシャルエステの担当者を紹介しようか？
I can introduce my facialist to you.

3 どんなところが気になりますか？
What concerns you?

4 顔のしわが気になっちゃって。
I'm worried about my facial wrinkles.

5 顔のシミを消したいです。
I want my facial liver spots removed.

liver spot＝肌のシミ

6 肌に吹き出物ができちゃって。
My skin is breaking out.

break out＝吹き出物が出る

7 おでこに、しわが出てるの。
I've got frown lines.

frown linesは、年齢とともに増えてくる「しわ」のことを指す。

8 目じりのしわを取りたいんです。
I'd like to unwrinkle my crow's feet.

crow's feet＝目じりのしわ

9 肌がたるんできてしまって。

My skin's sagging.

sag=たるむ、下がる

10 肌荒れがひどくて。

I have a rough skin.

rough=ざらざらした

11 顔のマッサージをお願いします。

Could you give me a facial massage?

12 顔のマッサージは気分をほぐし、肌や顔の筋肉に刺激を与えるんですよ。

A facial massage relaxes you and stimulates your skin and facial muscles. stimulàte [スティミュレイト]=刺激する

13 ふだん、どのようなケアをされていますか？

What's your regular skin care regimen like?

regimen [レジメン]=治療法　＊「洗顔だけです」は I usually just wash my face.

14 週に1回、パックをします。

I do a pack once a week.

15 お肌のタイプをお調べしたいのですが。

I'd like to check your skin type.

16 私は、かなり敏感肌なんです。

I have ultra sensitive skin.

🔊 脂性肌 oil skin

17 眉毛がだいぶ伸びていますね。

You have bushman eyebrows.

bushman=生い茂っている

18 この石けんはお肌のきめを整えてくれます。

This soap can improve the skin's texture.

19 XYZの化粧品はありますか？

Do you have XYZ cosmetics?

20 色落ちしにくい口紅が欲しいのですが。

I want a lipstick which doesn't come off.

come off＝色が落ちる

21 ファンデーションを選んでいただけませんか？

Would you choose a good foundation for me?

foundátion ［ファウンデイション］

22 クリームタイプとパウダータイプのファンデーションがあります。

We have cream and powder foundations.

23 乾燥肌ですので、クリーム・ファンデーションをお勧めします。

As you have dry skin, I recommend cream foundation.

24 試してみてもいいですか？

Could I try some on?

25 こちらのオイルを使ってマッサージをしますね。

I'll give you a massage with this oil.

26 はい、終わりました。

We're done now.

3 ネイルサロン

美容院、ジム、エステ

1 爪の手入れをしていただきたいのですが。
☞ **I'd like to have my nails done.**

2 甘皮のお手入れが必要ですよ。
You need to take care of your cuticles.

take care of ～＝～の手入れをする

3 ネイルアートをお願いできますか？
Could you put nail-art on my nails?

4 マニキュアをお願いします。
I'd like a manicure.

5 派手すぎず、肌になじむ色がいいです。
Something that's not too flashy and that matches my skin.

6 また、爪が割れちゃったんです。
I broke my nail again.

7 爪を健康で美しく保つ方法を教えてください。
Please tell me how to keep nails healthy and beautiful.

8 ジェルを無理にはがそうとすると、爪に負担がかかります。
If you try to force the gel off, you'll damage your nails.

3 リラクゼーション、エステ

美容院、ジム、エステ

CD2 Track 33

1 足がむくみやすくて。

My feet get swollen easily.

swollen＝(足が)むくむ

2 血行をよくするにはフットスパがいいよ。

Taking a foot spa helps your blood circulation.

blood circulation＝血行

3 あそこのスパでは、ボディースクラブができるよ。

That spa has a body scrub on the menu.

4 ここのスパは、泥パックが有名なの。

Mudpacks are now in vogue at this spa.

vogue＝流行、人気

5 リラックスするには、どのアロマオイルがいいですか？

Which aroma oil will help you relax?

6 西洋では古くからアロマセラピーが行われてきました。

Aromatherapy has been practiced in the West since ancient times.

the West＝西洋

7 リフレクソロジーは、減量にも効果があります。

Reflexology can help you lose weight.

8 腰のあたりを念入りにマッサージしてください。

Please massage around my waist a lot.

9 肩がひどく凝っていますね。

You have very stiff shoulders.

stiff＝凝っている

10 冷え性で悩んでいます。

☞ **I have bad circulation.**

❗「血行が悪い」ということ。「冷え性だ」は I'm sensitive to cold.

11 気持ちがいいです。

It feels good.

12 少しくすぐったいです。

It tickles a little.

tickle＝くすぐったい　❗「痛っ！ そこ、痛みます」は Ouch! It hurts there.

13 もう少し強くもんでください。

Please massage harder.

14 体がほぐれてきました。

I feel the tension leaving my body.

15 仰向けに寝ていただけますか？

Would you lie on your back?

lie on one's back＝仰向けに寝る　＊「うつ伏せに」は on one's stomach。

16 おなかの贅肉をとりたいのですが。

I'd like you to get rid of some of the fat around my waist.

17 90分の全身コースにします。

A ninety minute whole body massage, please.

4 ショッピング

買い物に行く

1. 買い物につきあってくれる？
   Would you please go shopping with me?

2. あの店はバーゲン中です。
   ☞ **There's a sale at that store.**

3. ウインドウショッピングに行かない？
   Do you want to go window-shopping?

4. お気に入りのお店を教えてください。
   Tell me your favorite store, please.

5. よく、衝動買いをするの。
   I often buy something on impulse.

   buy ~ on impulse＝~を衝動買いする

6. 近くに薬局はありますか？
   Is there a drugstore near here?

7. 雑貨は100円ショップで買おう。
   Let's buy some things at the 100-yen shop.

8. すぐ近くに、コンビニがオープンしたよ。
   A new convenience store has opened nearby.

   ❶「コンビニ」は和製英語。

4 ショッピング

店内で

1 何をお見せいたしましょうか？
What can I show you?

2 ちょっと見ているだけです。
I'm just looking.

3 これの在庫はありますか？
Do you have this in stock?

stock＝在庫

4 新聞でセールの広告を見たのですが。
I saw a sales ad in the paper.

ad＝advertisement＝広告

5 セール品はありますか？
Anything on sale?

6 どれも、いつもの30パーセント引きです。
Everything is 30 percent off the regular price.

7 主人にあげるものを探しているんです。
I'm looking for something for my husband.

8 手に取ってもいいですか？
Can I pick it up?

店内で

9 これは、今、流行りなんですよ。
This is in fashion now.

be in fashion＝流行っている

10 こちらは最新モデルです。
Here are the latest styles.

latest＝最新の

11 見本を持ってまいります。
I'll bring the samples.

sample＝見本、サンプル

12 すみません、それは品切れです。
Sorry, we don't have it in stock.

13 取り寄せてもらえますか？
Could you order it for me?

14 どの商品が一番人気ですか？
Which items are the most popular?

15 どちらが安いですか？
Which is cheaper?

16 どちらがお好みですか？
Which one would you like?

17 両方とも好き。
I like both.

4 ショッピング
洋服を買う

1 ジャケットを探しています。
I'm looking for a jacket.

2 このジャケットはおいくらですか？
How much is this jacket?

3 今、バーゲン中なので50ドルです。
It's on sale now, for just 50 dollars.

4 色がいいわね。
The color is right.

5 これ、あなたに似合うと思う。
I think this looks good on you.

6 あなたにお似合いですよ。
It looks nice on you.

7 試着してもいいかしら？
May I try it on?

try on＝試着する

8 どうぞ。試着室はあちらです。
Sure. The fitting room is over there.

fitting room＝試着室

洋服を買う

9 いかがですか?
How is it?

10 こちらはいかがですか?
How do you like this one?

11 ぴったりだわ。
This fits perfectly.
> 「ワンサイズ大きい[小さい] ものはありますか?」は Do you have this in one size larger [smaller]?

12 これにします。
I'll take this.

13 ジーンズはありますか?
Do you have jeans?

14 あいにく、ジーンズは扱っておりません。
I'm sorry, we don't have jeans.

15 もう少し安いものはありませんか?
Do you have something a bit less expensive?

16 デザインや色などは、お決まりですか?
Do you have a particular design or color in mind?

17 ええっと、特に何も決めていません。
Well, nothing in particular.

18 この白いストライプの薄茶色のシャツはいかがでしょう？

How about this light brown shirt with white stripes?

light＝薄い色の　stripe＝ストライプ

19 明るい色のネクタイを何本か見せてください。

Please show me some bright ties.

bright＝明るい色

20 この柄はあまり好みではないです。

I don't care for this pattern.

pattern＝柄

21 ちょっと派手ですね。

It's a little loud.

loud＝派手な

22 もう少し、地味なほうが好きです。

I prefer something more conservative.

conservative＝地味な

23 寸法を取らせていただきます。

Let me take your measurements.

measurement＝寸法

24 どこかきついところはございますか？

Is there any place where it feels tight?

tight＝きつい

25 ウエスト回りをゆったりとさせたいです。

I want plenty of room around the waist.

plenty of ～＝たくさんの～　room＝余白、余裕

26 袖丈はいかがでしょうか？

What about the length of the sleeves?

sleeve＝袖

4 ショッピング

洋服を買う

4 ショッピング

アクセサリー、小物を買う

1 真珠のネックレスを見せてください。
Please show me some pearl necklaces.
pearl＝パール、真珠

2 ずいぶん、高いんですね。
Quite expensive, isn't it?
expensive＝高い

3 こちらは天然真珠です。
These are natural pearls.
養殖の cultured／人工の artificial

4 ショーウインドウの、あのバッグを見せてください。
Please let me see that bag in the showcase.
showcase＝ショーウインドウ

5 今、どんな靴が人気ですか？
What kind of shoes are in now?

6 黒のブーツが一番人気です。
Black boots are the most popular.

7 フォーマルな席にはどの帽子がいいですか？
Which hat is for formal occasions?

8 このスカーフは秋の定番アイテムです。
This scarf is a good item for autumn.
good item＝定番

4 ショッピング

家電品を買う

1 このパソコンについて、少し教えてもらえますか？

Could you tell me a little about this computer?

2 これは新型ですか？

Is this a new model?

> 最新型 the latest model／旧型 an old model

3 こちらは、これまでの製品よりも機能が充実しています。

It has improved features over the previous one.

4 今のところ、残り3台しかございません。

We have only three models available at the moment.

5 取り置きしておいてくれますか？

Could you hold one for me?

6 配送日は指定できますか？

Can I specify the date of delivery?

7 ほかの店も見てみます。

I'm going to check some other stores.

8 検討してみます。

I'll think about it.

> 「また来ます」は I'll come back later.

4 ショッピング

支払い

1 支払いはどこですか？
Where can I pay for this?

2 おいくらですか？
How much?

3 お釣りです。
Here's your change.

change＝お釣り

4 お支払いは、いかがいたしますか？
How would you like to pay (for this)?

I'd like to pay by cash(credit card).「現金（カード）で支払います」などと答えよう。

5 お支払いは現金ですか、カードですか？
Will that be cash or charge?

charge＝カードによる支払い

6 クレジットカードで支払えますか？
Do you accept credit cards?

Can I pay for this with my credit card?

7 いくらになりますか？
How much will that be?

8 分割払いはできますか？
Do you have an installment plan?

9 消費税込みで4200円です。

It comes to 4,200 yen including tax.

10 今朝、この割引券をもらいました。

I got this discount ticket this morning.

discount ticket＝割引券

11 プレゼント用に包んでいただけますか？

☞ **Will you gift-wrap it?**

gift-wrap＝プレゼント用に包む

12 あちらにラッピングカウンターがございます。

There's the gift-wrap counter over there.

13 1つずつ包んでくださいますか？

Can you wrap them individually?

individually＝1つずつ

14 ラッピング代に100円かかります。

There's a 100-yen wrapping charge.

wrapping charge＝ラッピング代

15 箱と袋のどちらになさいますか？

Which would you like, a box or a bag?

16 簡単な包装で結構です。

Simple wrapping would be okey.

17 1万円以上お買い上げいただくと、無料で配送いたします。

We offer free shipping on orders over 10,000 yen.

offer＝申し出る　shipping＝配送

4 ショッピング

通販、ネットショッピング

1 通販カタログが送られてきたわ。

A mail order catalog has arrived.

mail order catalog＝通販カタログ

2 結構いいものがあるね。

There are some pretty good items.

3 しかも、お店で買うより安いわ。

And they're less expensive than in the stores.

less expensive than ～＝～より安い

4 本はもっぱら、ネットで購入しています。

I mainly buy books on the Net.

buy ～ on the Net＝～をネットで購入する

5 送料が無料なんだ。

There's no shipping charge.

shipping charge＝送料

6 注文後、2日で届くよ。

It will reach us two days after we order.

7 1週間以内なら注文をキャンセルできるよ。

You can cancel your order within a week.

within ～＝～以内で

8 料金代引きでお願いします。

Please make the order COD.

COD＝cash on delivery＝料金代引き、着払い

4 ショッピング
クレーム

1 お釣りが間違っているみたいなのですが。
I think you gave me the wrong change.

2 計算が間違っていませんか？
I think you've got the figures wrong.

3 この生地、傷んでいました。
This cloth was damaged.

> 食品などの場合は go bad を使って、The meat has gone bad. のように表す。

4 1つ上のサイズに替えられますか？
Can you exchange it for the next size up?

> 「取り替えてもらえますか？」は Can you exchange this?

5 コップが粉々になっていました。
The glass was already broken.

6 これ、ぼろぼろの茶色の紙で包装されていました。
This package was tied up in tattered brown paper.

tattered＝ぼろぼろの

7 思っていたものと違いました。
It was different from what I expected.

8 返品したいのですが。
☞ **I'd like to return it.**

5 外食
ファストフードで

1 チーズバーガーとコーラのMを2つずつください。
I'd like two cheeseburgers and two medium Cokes each.

2 こちらでお召し上がりですか、お持ち帰りですか?
For here or to go?

3 テイクアウトします。袋に入れてもらえますか?
To go, please. Could you put this in a bag?

> 「テイクアウト」は to go が一般的。

4 店内で食べます。
For here.

5 ご注文は以上でしょうか?
Will that be all?

6 クーポン券でお願いします。
Here are my coupons.

coupon=クーポン券

7 Bセットをお願いします。
I'll have the B meal.

8 マスタードは抜きで。
Hold the mustard.

hold ~=~を抜きにする

5 外食

レストランに行く

1 今日、外で食事しませんか?

What do you say to eating out today?

What do you say to 〜ing? = 〜するのはいかがですか?

2 新宿のおしゃれなレストランを知っているんだ。

I know a fancy restaurant in Shinjuku.

fancy = おしゃれな、しゃれた

3 雰囲気がいいから、きっと気に入るよ。

I hope you like the good atmosphere.

💡「明日の7時から予約できるかな?」は I'd like to make a table reservation for 7:00.

4 今から予約できる?

Can you reserve a table now?

5 ここのレストランのステーキは、街で一番といわれています。

The steaks in this restaurant are said to be the best in town.

be said to 〜 = 〜といわれている

6 定休日は月曜日です。

They are closed every Monday.

7 明日、予約を入れておきます。

☞ **I'll make a reservation tomorrow.**

make a reservation = 予約する

8 あのお寿司屋さんに行ったことある?

Have you ever been to that sushi bar?

💡 カウンターのある店は bar で表す。

5 外食

レストランに行く

9 トロが最高だよ！
Their toro is the best.

10 手ごろな料金のお店がいいな。
I hope to go to a reasonable restaurant.

11 2人ですが、席はありますか？
Do you have an open table for two?
= For two, please.

12 別々のテーブルに分かれてもいいのですが。
We don't mind being seated separately.

13 満席でございます。
All the seats are taken.
= No tables are available.

14 7時に予約を入れてあります。
I have a reservation at 7:00.

15 お客様の予約は夜8時になっておりますが。
Our reservation list says your reservation is at 8 p.m.
= Your reservation is for 8 p.m.

16 すぐにご案内できます。
We can prepare two tables for you immediately.
「2つのテーブルが用意できます」の意味。

17 相席かカウンターでもかまいません。
☞ **I don't mind sharing a table or sitting at a counter.**
share a table＝相席する

18 あいにく、禁煙席は満席です。

We're sorry, but none of the non-smoking tables are available.

19 喫煙席なら、あいていますか？

Are smoking tables available now?

20 少々、お待ちいただけますか？

Would you please wait a moment?

21 どのくらい待ちますか？

How long is the wait?

> 「10分程お待ちいただきます」は It'll take about 10 minutes.

22 バーでお待ちください。

Please wait at the bar.

> 「バーで待ちます」は We'll wait at the bar.

23 この席からは街の夜景が見えないね。

We can't enjoy the night view of the city from here.

24 先に食券をお求めください。

Please purchase the meal tickets first.

purchase＝買う

25 お好きな席にどうぞ。

You can sit wherever you like.

26 席を移りますか？

Would you like to change tables?

5 外食

レストランに行く

5 外食

料理を注文する

1
メニューを見せていただけますか？
May I have a menu, please?

2
郷土料理のようなものはありますか？
Could you recommend me some <u>traditional dishes</u>?   local specialties

3
ご注文はお決まりですか？
Can I have your order?

4
これをお願いします。
I'll have this one.

💡 メニューを指さしながら使う表現。

5
本日のおすすめをください。
I'll have today's special.

6
私も同じものをお願いします。
Same here.

7
今日のランチは何ですか？
What's today's lunch?

8
何かおすすめはありますか？
What do you recommend?

9 フィッシュ&チップスがおすすめです。
I recommend fish and chips.

10 何が一緒についてきますか？
What comes with it?

11 コーンスープとサラダをお願いします。
I'll have corn soup and salad.

12 注文したものが、まだきません。
☞ **I haven't gotten my order yet.**

> ❗ 「お調べいたします」は Let me check.

13 ローストビーフをいただきたいのですが。
We'd like to order roast beef.

14 これは注文したものと違います。
This is not what I ordered.

15 サラダは頼んでいません。
I didn't order salad.

16 注文をキャンセルできますか？
May I cancel my order?

17 すみませんが、注文を変更できますか？
Excuse me. Can I change my order?

料理を注文する

5 | 外食
希望を伝える

1 量を少なめにしてください。
Please make it a small portion.

portion＝量

2 追加で注文をしたいのですが。
I want to order something else.

3 お子様用のイスをお持ちしますか？
Would you like a booster seat?

booster seat＝補助イスで、イスの上に乗せる子ども用のイス

4 冷房が強すぎます。弱くなりませんか？
The air-conditioning is too cold. Could you turn it down?

air-conditioning＝空調

5 ただいま、弱めます。
I'll turn it down right away.

↻ 強めます up

6 暖房をもっと強くしていただけますか？
Please turn the heat up.

7 おしぼりをいただけますか。
Can I have a hand towel?

8 このステーキ、生だ。ミディアムとお願いしたのに。
This steak is too rare. I ordered medium.

9 もう少し、火を通してきます。
We'll cook it some more.

10 卵アレルギーなんです。
I have an egg allergy.

　　　　　　　　　　　　　　　　＝ I'm allergic to eggs.

11 お皿が汚れています。別のお皿に取り替えてください。
This plate is not clean. Could I have another plate?

12 パスタが冷めています。
My pasta is cold.

13 フォークがありません。
I didn't get a fork.

14 シェアしたいので、お皿をいただけますか？
We'll share. Will you bring an extra plate?

15 ローストビーフと魚をシェアなさいますか？
How about sharing roast beef and fish?

How about 〜 ing? =〜してはいかがですか？

16 時間がないので、急いでいただけますか？
I have to leave soon. Could you hurry up?

17 すぐにお持ちできると思います。
I think you can have it soon.

5 外食
食事を楽しむ

1 塩を取っていただけますか？
Would you please pass me the salt?

❗ Would you please ~? を使うとていねいな表現になる。

2 コショウ、いる？
Do you want the pepper?

3 お水を1杯いただけますか？
May I have a glass of water?

4 スープをこぼしてしまいました。
I spilled my soup.

5 ひと口、味見させて。
Can I try this?

❗ 料理中に「味見させて」と言うときは、Let me have a bite. ／Let me taste it.

6 ビールをもう1杯ください。
I'd like another beer, please.

7 これをもう1皿お願いします。
Could you give me another plate of this?

8 量が多すぎて食べられません。
It's more than I can eat.

9 いいにおい！

It smells good!

10 これは大好物なんだ。

This is my favorite food.

> 「これ、苦手なんだ」は This is my least favorite food.

11 とても楽しい食事でした。

I enjoyed the dinner very much.

12 こんなおいしい料理、食べたことないよ。

I've never had such delicious dishes.

have never 過去分詞＝（今までに）〜したことがない

13 僕もそれを頼めばよかったな。

I should've ordered that, too.

should have 過去分詞＝〜しておくべきだった

14 こんなに辛いとは思わなかった。

Didn't think it would be this spicy.

spicy＝辛い、香辛料の効いた

15 この店、味が落ちたね。

The food here isn't as good as it used to be.

16 残ったものを持ち帰りたいのですが。

I'd like to take the leftovers home.

leftover＝料理の残り

17 持ち帰り用の袋をもらえますか？

Can I have a doggie bag?

5 外食
ドリンク、デザートを注文する

CD2 Track 47

1 料理に合うワインをお願いします。
You can bring any wine with the meal.

meal＝食事

2 デザートはあとで注文します。
I'll order dessert later.

later＝あとで

3 コーヒーはお食事とご一緒に、それともデザートとご一緒になさいますか？
Do you want coffee with the meal or with dessert?

4 食後でお願いします。
After, please.

💡 after the meal を短くした表現。

5 コーヒーを持ってきてください。
Bring me some coffee, please.

bring＝持ってくる

6 僕はミルクティにする。
I want to have milk tea.

7 私は何もいりません。
☞ **Nothing for me, thanks.**

8 デザートはやめておくよ。ダイエット中なんだ。
I'll skip dessert. I'm on a diet.

💡 「カロリー控えめのデザートはありますか？」は Do you have any low-calorie desserts?

5 | 外食
支払いをする

1 レジはどこですか？
Where's the cashier?

2 お会計が違っているようです。
I think the check is wrong.

3 これは何の料金ですか？
What's this amount for?

4 すみません。すぐに訂正いたします。
I'm sorry. I'll correct it at once.

at once=すぐに、速やかに

5 こちらが正しいお釣りになります。
Here's the correct change.

6 このお店、カードは使えないって。
They say this restaurant doesn't take credit cards.

7 割り勘にしよう。
Let's split the bill.

≡ Let's go Dutch

8 私に払わせてください。
☞ **Let me take care of the bill.**

≡ I'll get the check./This is my treat.

6 飲み会、カラオケ

居酒屋で

CD2 Track 49

1 今夜、飲みに行こうよ。
☞ **Let's go for a drink tonight.**
　　　　　　　　　　　🟰 Let's go have a drink.

2 どんな店がいい？
What kind of place do you want to go to?

3 いつもの店にしよう。
Let's go to the usual place.
　　　usual place＝いつもの場所、お決まりの場所

4 飲み放題の店がいいよ。
I'd like an all-you-can-drink tavern.
　　　all-you-can-drink＝飲み放題の　＊「食べ放題の」は all-you-can-eat

5 飲み物だけ、先に頼もうか？
How about just ordering drinks first?

6 とりあえず、ビールから始めよう！
☞ **Let's start off with a beer!**
　　　start off with ～＝～で始める

7 日本酒党なんだ。
I have a liking for sake.
　　　have a liking[taste] for ～＝～好き、～を愛好する

8 冷えるから熱燗にしよう。
Let's get some atsukan, as we feel chilly.
　　　chilly＝ぞくぞくする、寒い

9 チューハイがいいな。

I'd like a chuhai.

10 ちょっとメニューを見てから決めよう。

I'm just going to look over the menu and think about it.

look over ～ =～にひと通り目を通す

11 ボトルで頼む？

Ask for a bottle?

ask for ～ =～を頼む、～を求める

12 つまみは何にする？

What kind of snacks do you want to have?

snack =つまみ

13 乾杯しよう！

Let's toast!

💡 「乾杯！」は Cheers!

14 今日はとことん飲むぞ。

We should drink to our hearts' content.

till we drop

15 今日は僕のおごりだから。

It's my treat today.

treat =もてなし、おごり

16 割り勘でいきましょう。

Let's go fifty-fifty on the bill.

halves

17 お勘定、お願いします。

Check, please.

check =勘定

6 飲み会、カラオケ

居酒屋で

6 飲み会、カラオケ

バーで

1 何にいたしましょうか？
What can I get you?

2 ハイボールをお願いします。
I'd like a highball, please.

3 レモンを絞って入れますか？
Shall I squeeze the lemon juice?

4 次は少し強めのお酒にしようかな。
I'd rather a little bit stronger liquor next time.

5 バーボンの水割りを。
A bourbon whiskey and water, please.

whiskey and water＝水割り　＊「ロックで」は on the rocks

6 スコッチのストレートをダブルで。
Give me a double Scotch (whiskey), straight up, please.　❗ アルコール飲料の「シングル」は single、「ダブル」は double。

7 おすすめのカクテルはありますか？
Can you recommend any cocktail?

8 ドライマティーニはいかがでしょう？
How about a dry martini?

dry＝(酒が)辛口の

6 飲み会、カラオケ

飲み会、合コン

1 よく来てくれたね。
Thank you for coming.

2 楽しんでる？
Are you having fun?

3 すっかり盛り上がってるね。
It's a lively party.

lively＝活気のある

4 退屈そうだね。
You seem to be dull.

dull＝つまらない、退屈な

5 飲み会はちょっと苦手なんです。
I'm not too fond of parties.

not too ～＝あまり～でない　be fond of ～＝～が好きだ

6 おっ！　かわいい子がそろってる！
Wow, full of good-looking girls here.

7 好みのタイプはいる？
Did you find your type?

8 彼は年収が高そうにみえます。
He seems to earn millions a year.

9. がっかり！
What a bummer!

10. 自己紹介をさせてください。
May I introduce myself?

introduce＝紹介する

11. どんな仕事をしているの？
What do you do?

occupation＝職業

12. 電話番号を教えて。
Can I have your phone number?

13. 今、彼氏はいるの？
Do you have a steady boyfriend?

steady＝決まった

14. もっと君のことを知りたいな。
I'd like to get to know you better.

15. このあと、踊りに行こう。
Let's go dancing after this.

go dancing＝踊りに行く

16. 今夜、一緒に過ごさない？
Why don't we hang out tonight?

hang out＝つるむ、付き合う

17. 昨日の合コンで彼女をゲットしたよ。
I got a new girlfriend at the match (making) party yesterday.

「合コン」は match (making) party／joint party

6 飲み会、カラオケ

カラオケ

1 カラオケに行かない？
Why don't we go to karaoke?

2 君から歌って！
Would you sing first, please?

3 どの曲にしようかな？
Which songs should I pick?

pick＝選ぶ

4 それは僕の持ち歌だよ。
It's my repertoire.

repertoire＝レパートリー、持ち歌

5 キーが合わないよ。
This isn't my key.

6 音を下げてくれる？
☞ **Could you turn the sound down a few notches?**

notch＝段階、階級

7 デュエットしようよ。
Why don't we sing a duet?

sing a duet＝デュエットする

8 音痴なんだ。
I have no ear for music.

🟰 I'm a terrible singer.

257

6 飲み会、カラオケ
飲みすぎ、二日酔い

CD2 Track 53

1 飲みすぎて、頭がもうろうとしていた。
My mind was in a haze after drinking so much.
haze＝もや、かすみ

2 昨日、友達とワインを3本も空けたよ。
My friends and I drank three bottles of wine last night.

3 大酒飲みだね。
You're a die-hard drinker.
die-hard＝筋金入りの

4 どうしてそんなに飲めるの？
How can you drink so much?

5 うちの家系はみんな酒豪なんだ。
Everyone in my family can hold their liquor.
hold one's liquor＝酒に強い

6 もう1杯どう？
How about another round?
another round of drinks を省略した形。

7 ほろ酔い気分だ。
I feel a little tipsy.
tipsy＝ほろ酔いの

8 かなり酔っ払った。
I'm loaded.

9 もう十分飲んだだろう。
You've had enough.

10 あんなに飲むんじゃなかった。
☞ **I shouldn't have drunk that much.**

11 むかむかする。
I'm feeling sick.

12 酔っ払っているようだね。
You look drunk.

13 彼は昨夜、飲みすぎたに違いない。
He must have drank too much last night.

must have 過去分詞＝～したに違いない

14 ワインの飲みすぎでふらふらだった。
I was groggy from too much wine.

groggy＝足元がふらつく、意識がもうろうとした

15 お酒くさいよ。
You smell like alcohol.

16 ひどい二日酔いだ。
I have a horrible hangover.

hangover＝二日酔い

17 今、禁酒してるんだ。
I'm on the wagon now.

on the wagon＝禁酒して　　❗「僕は下戸なんだ」は I don't drink.

7 招待、訪問、パーティ

自宅に招待する

1 今度の金曜日にパーティを開きます。
I'm having a party on Friday.

2 何のパーティですか？
What's the occasion?

occasion＝特別な行事、記念

3 ぜひ、いらしてください。
I'd love you to come over.

❗「行けたらいいのですが（行けない）」は I wish I could.

4 わが家でお茶でもいかが？
How about having tea in my house?

5 次の土曜日、わが家の夕食にご招待したくてお電話しました。
I called to invite you to dinner in my house next Saturday.

6 ご都合はいかがですか？
☞ **Would it be convenient for you?**

❗ be convenient の主語は you(人)ではなく it。

7 この辺の地理に詳しいですか？
Are you familiar with our area?

≒ Do you know our area?

8 グーグルで探していきます。
I can access it with Google.

7 招待、訪問、パーティ
知人宅を訪問する

1 今週末、お宅へうかがってもよろしいですか?
Can I come over to your house this weekend?
💡「ええ、どうぞお越しください」は Sure. Be my guest.

2 娘が風邪をひいてしまって、お宅にうかがえなくなりました。
I'm sorry to tell you I can't come over because my daughter has caught a cold.

3 予定より早く着きました。
We've arrived earlier than scheduled.
💡「予定より5分遅れそうです」は We'll get there five minutes behind schedule.

4 橋本と申します。まり子さんにお目にかかりたいのですが。
I'm Hashimoto, and I'd like to see Mariko, please.

5 通りかかったので、彼女に会いに寄らせていただきました。
I was just passing by, so I've dropped in to see her.
pass by=通り過ぎる　drop in=立ち寄る

6 近所まで来たものですから。
We're just in the neighborhood.
neighborhood=近所

7 突然お訪ねしてごめんなさい。
We're sorry to drop in on you.
drop in on(人)=予告もなしに(人)を訪ねる

8 どうぞ、おかまいなく。
☞ **Please don't trouble yourself.**

7 | 招待、訪問、パーティ

CD2 Track 56

お客様を迎える

1 いらっしゃい。
We're so glad you came.
> 直訳は「来てくださってうれしいです」。

2 ようこそ、おいでくださいました。
It's nice to see you again.
> 直訳は「またお目にかかれてうれしいです」。

3 さあ、お上がりください。
Come in, please.
> 「ブラウンさんがいらしたわよ」は Mr. Brown is here.

4 コートをお預かりしましょうか?
May I take your coat?

5 楽になさって。
☞ Make yourself at home.
> 「ゆっくりして」は Make yourself comfortable. 「どうぞ座って」は Have a seat.

6 何かお飲みになる?
Would you like something to drink?
> 「飲み物でもお持ちしましょう」は Can I get you something to drink?

7 ご親切に。
That's very sweet of you.

8 ゆっくりできる?
Can you stay long?
> 「しばらくゆっくりできる?」といったニュアンスなら Can you stay for a while?

9 迷いませんでした？
You weren't lost, were you?

10 三咲さんも、もうすぐ着きます。
Misaki is arriving soon, too.

11 これ、お土産です。
Here's a gift for you.

12 何かしら？
What is it?

13 ケーキだから、冷蔵庫に入れておいて。
It's a cake. Keep it in the fridge.

14 みんなで食べようと思って。
☞ **We're all going to eat it.**

15 お手洗いをお借りできますか？
Can I use the bathroom?

16 何か手伝いましょうか？
How can I help you?

17 来る途中に、素敵な雑貨屋さんを見かけました。
I saw a fancy variety store on my way here.

7 招待、訪問、パーティ
家の中を案内する

1 家の中を案内するわ。
I want to show you the house.

2 まあ、素敵。
Oh, it's gorgeous.

3 すばらしいお宅ですね。
You have a beautiful home.

4 素敵なところですね。
☞ **You have a wonderful place.**

5 外の眺めがいいですね。
You have a gorgeous view.

6 緑が多くていいですね。
You have lots of trees.

7 居心地がいいわ。
It's nice and cozy.

8 この家は、自分でデザインしたのよ。
I designed our own house.

9 日当たりがとてもいいの。
The room is sunny.

= The room gets a lot of sunshine.

10 もう少し広ければいいんだけどね。
I wish it was a little larger.

「ちょっと狭いでしょ」と言いたいときに使う。

11 洗面所はここです。
This is the bathroom.

12 使いやすそうなキッチンね。
It looks like a well-planned kitchen.

13 去年、家全体をリフォームしたの。
We renovated the entire house last year.

renovate＝リフォームする（大規模の場合） ＊模様替えや家具の買い換え程度なら remodel。

14 オール電化なんです。
Everything is electric.

15 太陽光発電です。
It's solar-powered.

16 新しいライフスタイルね。
It's a new lifestyle.

17 光熱費がとても助かっているわ。
I can save on lighting and heating expenses.

lighting and heating expenses＝光熱費

7 家族を紹介する

招待、訪問、パーティ

1 家族を紹介するわ。
☞ **Let me introduce my family.**

2 こちらは夫の太郎です。
This is my husband, Taro.

3 うちには、息子と娘、それにペットの犬が1匹います。
We have a son, a daughter and a dog.

4 息子さんは娘と同じ年齢だわ。
He's the same age as my daughter.
= He's as old as my daughter.

5 次男はサッカーチームに入っているの。
My second son is on the soccer team.

6 息子さんはおいくつですか?
How old is your son?

7 ごきょうだいは?
Do you have any siblings?
sibling=(男女問わず)きょうだい = Do you have any brothers or sisters?

8 ひとりっ子です。
I'm an only child.
= I don't have any brothers or sisters.

9 兄が1人と妹が1人います。

I have an elder brother and a younger sister.

10 お兄さんとは仲がいいのですか？

Are you on good terms with your brother?

11 ご長男ですか？

Are you the oldest son?

> 💡「きょうだいの中で何番目？」は What's your birth order?

12 ご両親はどちらにお住まいですか？

Where do your parents live?

13 人には、母親似だといわれます。

People say I resemble my mother.

resemble＝〜に似ている

14 生まれはどちらですか？

Where were you from originally?

15 生まれも育ちもサンディエゴなんです。

☞ **I was born and grew up in San Diego.**

16 あなたの故郷はどんなところですか？

What's your hometown like?

17 人口7万人で、静かないいところですよ。

It's a nice quiet place with a population of 70,000.

---

7 招待、訪問、パーティ　家族を紹介する

18 どのくらいの頻度で帰省しますか？

How often do you go back home?

💡 「年に 3 回くらいです」と答えるなら About three times a year.

19 日本に来てどのくらいですか？

How long have you been in Japan?

20 何とお呼びすればいいかしら？

👉 What should I call you?

21 ブレンダと呼んでください。

Please call me Brenda.

22 日本での生活はいかがですか？

How do you like living in Japan?

💡 「こちらでの生活を楽しんでいますか？」は Are you having a good time here?

23 1人でいらしているのですか？

Are you here by yourself?

24 家族が恋しくはないですか？

Do you miss your family?

miss＝〜が恋しい、〜がいなくて寂しい

25 どのような関係のお仕事をされているのですか？

What line of business are you in?

💡 シンプルに「ご職業は？」と尋ねる場合は What do you do?

26 どこかにお勤めですか？

Do you work for a company?

7 招待、訪問、パーティ
料理を楽しむ

1 今夜は庭でバーベキューをしようよ。
Let's have a barbecue in the yard tonight.
BBQ

2 きのう釣った魚を焼こう。
Let's grill some fish I caught yesterday.

3 お酒は何にする？
What would you like to drink?

4 おかわりはいかがですか？
Would you like another helping?
helping＝(食べ物の) 1杯、一盛り

5 お肉をもう1切れ、いただけますか？
Can I have another piece of meat?

6 苦手な食べ物はありますか？
Is there any food you don't like?

7 食べ物に好き嫌いはありません。
I'm not particular about food.

8 デザートは私が持っていくわ。
I'll bring the dessert for you.

9 嫌いな物は残してください。

Please leave what you don't like.

leave＝残す、放っておく

10 奥さんの手料理、最高ですね。

☞ **Your wife's cooking is amazing.**

11 お世辞でもうれしいわ。

Thank you for your compliments.

compliment＝賛辞、ほめ言葉

12 毎日こんなおいしい食事ができて、幸せですね。

You are lucky to have such a delicious meal every day.

13 幸せ太りするのも、無理ないですね。

It's natural for you to gain weight from happiness.

gain weight＝体重が増える、太る

14 コーヒーはあちらのソファでいただきましょうか？

Shall we sit on the sofa over there and have coffee?

15 カフェイン抜きのコーヒーはいかがですか？

Do you have decaffeinated coffee?

decáffeinàted [ディーカフィネイティド]　＊decaf [ディーカフ] と略すことも。

16 抹茶もご用意できますよ。

We can serve green tea.

offer

17 わが家で茶道をお披露目しましょうか？

Shall I show you the tea ceremony at home?

7 招待、訪問、パーティ

おいとまする

1 くつろげましたか？
Were you comfortable enough?

2 とても楽しかったです。
I had a wonderful time.

3 こちらこそ楽しかったです。
It's been our pleasure.

4 今晩は最高でした。
It was a lovely evening.

5 本当に楽しいパーティでした。
It was a great party.

6 そろそろ失礼します。
I'll be leaving now.
= I'm off. ／I've got to run.　＊ていねいに言うと Could you excuse me, please?

7 お招きいただいて、ありがとうございました。
Thank you for having me over.

8 次回は、わが家へお越しください。
Hope to see you at my house next time.

7 招待、訪問、パーティ
いろいろなパーティ

1 クリスマスは家族と過ごしました。
I spent the Christmas holidays with my family.
Christmas holiday＝クリスマス休暇

2 最近では、日本でもハロウィーンパーティが開かれるようになってきたね。
Halloween parties are becoming more popular in Japan these days.

3 女子会で盛り上がったわ。
Our girl's-night-out was fun.
girl's-night-out＝女子会

4 彼女にサプライズパーティはどう？
How about giving her a surprise party?
surprise party＝サプライズパーティ

5 年末年始は、忘年会や新年会やらで胃腸を休める暇がありません。
I have no time to give my stomach a rest because of end-of-the-year and New Year's parties.
stomach＝お腹、胃腸

6 次の日曜日は、河原でバーベキュー大会だよ。
We're having a barbecue party on the riverside next Sunday.

7 最近、ファミレスでお誕生日会をするママたちが多いのよ。
Many mothers hold birthday parties at family restaurants these days.

8 欧米では、ホームパーティが頻繁に開かれているようですね。
It seems to me that Westerners often have parties at home.

Part 4 話題別の会話

1. 趣味、娯楽 …… 274
2. ファッション、グルメ … 292
3. 美容、健康 …… 300
4. パソコン、携帯 …… 304
5. エコ、環境 …… 320
6. 結婚、育児、教育 …… 324
7. 政治、経済、宗教 …… 338
8. 日本文化 …… 344

1 趣味、娯楽

趣味について

1 趣味は何ですか？
What are your interests?

= What are your hobbies?

2 暇なときは、何をしていますか？
What do you (like to) do in your free time?

これも、趣味をたずねたいときに使える表現。

3 これといった趣味がないんですよ。
I don't have any hobbies in particular.

4 何をやっても長続きしないんだ。
I never do anything for very long.

= I never stick with a hobby.

5 下手の横好きだよ。
I love it, although I'm not good at it at all.

6 趣味と実益を兼ねているんだ。
I do it for fun and profit.

business and pleasure

7 まだまだ初心者なんだ。
I'm still just a beginner.

8 歳をとってから始めたんです。
I started it when I was already old.

9 最近、陶芸を始めたんだ。

I recently started doing ceramic art.

　making ceramics

10 月に1回、陶芸教室に通ってるんだ。

I go to a ceramic art school once a month.

11 茶道を習っています。

I practice the tea ceremony.

12 アロマセラピストの資格を取ろうと思っています。

I'm trying to get qualified as an aroma therapist.

13 中国語を習うのに、どこかによい教室を知りませんか？

Are there any good places where I can study Chinese?

14 古本屋めぐりは楽しいですよ。

It's fun to go around browsing the used bookstores.

15 暇さえあれば骨董屋めぐりをしています。

I go shopping for antiques whenever I have free time.

16 彼はオーディオマニアだよ。

He's a serious audiophile.

　ビデオマニア videophile

17 盆栽は奥が深いよ。

Bonsai is steeped in tradition.

　Bonsai is a deep tradition. / The art of bonsai is profound.

趣味、娯楽 1

趣味について

1 趣味、娯楽

音楽

1 いつも、どんな音楽を聴いていますか？
What kind of music do you usually listen to?

2 そうだな、パンクとヘビメタ以外は何でも聴くよ。
☞ **Well, just about anything except punk and heavy metal.**

3 Jポップは、あまり聴かないな。
I don't really listen to Japanese pop.

4 レゲエのことなら、彼に聞いたらいいよ。
When it comes to reggae, you should talk to him.
it comes to ～＝～のことなら

5 僕はクラシックよりジャズが好き。
I prefer jazz over classical.
prefer ～ over (to) …＝…より～を好む

6 デビュー以来、ずっと彼女のファンなんだ。
I've been a fan of her since she debuted.

7 彼女の曲、僕には全部同じに聞こえるんだけど。
Her music all sounds the same to me.

8 その曲、iTunesでダウンロードしたよ。
I downloaded that song from iTunes.

9 彼の新しいCDはおすすめだよ。

I recommend his new CD.

10 何か楽器ができますか？

Can you play any instruments?

instrument＝楽器

11 子どもの頃、ピアノを習っていたんだ。

I used to take piano lessons when I was a child.

12 彼は、ギターだけじゃなくてドラムもできるんだよ。

He not only can play the guitar but also the drums.

just

13 君がフルートを吹くなんて意外だな。

☞ **I didn't expect you to play the flute.**

14 何歳からバイオリンをやっているの？

How old were you when you started to play the violin?

15 何か楽器が弾けるといいよね。

It would be nice to be able to play a musical instrument.

16 楽譜が読めないんだ。

I can't read music (scores).

17 地域のオーケストラで演奏しているんだ。

I play with a community orchestra.

❗「バンドを組んでいるんだ」は I'm in a band.

1 趣味、娯楽

音楽

1 趣味、娯楽

絵画

1 どんな絵が好きですか？
What kind of pictures do you like?

画家 artists

2 水彩画を描くのが好きです。
I like to paint in watercolors.

watercolors＝水彩画　油絵 oil

3 自分でも描くの？
Do you yourself paint?

4 油絵を勉強しているところです。
I'm studying oil painting.

oil painting＝油絵

5 いつもスケッチブックを持ち歩いているんだ。
I always have a sketchbook with me.

6 人物画は描いたことがないな。
I've never drawn a portrait.

7 よく画廊に立ち寄ります。
I often drop by an art gallery.

8 昔から絵は苦手なんだ。
I've never been good at drawing.

1 写真

趣味、娯楽

1 写真を撮るのは楽しいよ。

Taking pictures is really fun.

2 どこへ行くにも、お気に入りのカメラを持っていくんだ。

I carry my favorite camera with me wherever I go.

3 娘が生まれて、一眼レフのカメラを買いました。

I bought an SLR camera after my daughter was born.

SLR=single-lens reflex=一眼レフ

4 この写真は、どこで撮ったの？

Where did you take this photo?

↩ いつ When

5 この写真を引き伸ばそうか。

Let's have this photo blown up.

blow up=引き伸ばす、拡大する

6 ちょっとピンボケだね。

It's a little out of focus.

= It's not focused.

7 写真をブログにアップしておくよ。

I'll post the pictures on my blog.

post=（インターネットなどに情報を）掲載する、投稿する

8 なかなか気に入った写真が撮れないんだ。

I never seem to be able to take pictures I like.

1 | 趣味、娯楽

読書

1 好きな作家は誰ですか？
Who's your favorite author?

2 1か月に何冊くらい本を読みますか？
How many books do you read in a month?

3 ずっと、雑誌以外は読んでいないな。
I haven't read anything but magazines for a long time.

4 いつもネットで本の情報を得ているんだ。
I usually get information about books from the Internet.

5 買ったのに読んでいない本がたくさんあります。
There are a lot of books that I've bought but never read.

6 この本はよく売れているらしいね。
I hear this book is selling well.

on the best-seller list

7 この本、読み始めたら止まらないよ。
This book is a page-turner.

❗ page-turner には「ページめくり機」の意味がある。「息もつけないほど面白い本」を表す。

8 一気に読んでしまったよ。
I couldn't put it down.

❗「途中で置くことができなかった」という意味。　= It was unputdownable.

1 ガーデニング

趣味、娯楽

1 最近、妻が庭いじりに夢中で。

My wife has been bitten by the gardening bug.
be bitten by ～＝～に夢中

2 バラを植えています。

I'm planting roses.

❗「来年はたくさんのバラが咲くよ」は Many roses will bloom next year.

3 種から育てるより、苗を買ったほうがずっとラクだね。

Buying seedlings is a lot easier than growing plants from seeds.
seedling＝苗、苗木

4 卵の殻は肥料として使えるよ。

You can use egg shells as fertilizer.
egg shell＝卵の殻　fertilizer＝肥料

5 ベランダ園芸も人気があるよね。

Balcony gardening is popular, too.

6 自分で育てたものを食べたことはありますか？

Have you eaten things you've grown yourself?

7 プチトマトは比較的、簡単にできるよ。

It's relatively easy to grow cherry tomatoes.

8 うちで育てたハーブを料理に使っています。

We cook with the herbs we grow at home.

エクササイズ、スポーツ

1 趣味、娯楽

CD3 Track 7

1 週1回、ジムで汗を流しています。
☞ **I work out once a week at the gym.**

2 どんなトレーニングをしているの？
What kind of workout do you do?

3 たいてい、ウエイト・トレーニングをしているんだ。
I mostly use the free weights.

free weights＝ウエイト・トレーニング

4 見てくれよ、このムキムキな体！
Take a look at this muscular body!

múscular ［マスキュラー］

5 寝る前に、腹筋と腕立てふせをするんだ。
I do sit-ups and push-ups before bed.

sit-ups＝腹筋 / push-ups＝腕立てふせ

6 通販であのマシンを買ったんだ。
I bought that machine through mail order.

mail order＝通販

7 2か月で、あと3キロ落としたいなあ。
I'd like to lose three more kilos in two months.

8 もっと運動しなきゃ。
I really need to exercise more.

9 少なくとも、週2回は走ろうと思っています。
I try to jog at least twice a week.

10 週末は泳ぐことにしています。
I usually <u>swim</u> on weekends.

go swimming

11 起きたら、まずジョギングをするんだ。
I start the day by jogging.

12 どんよりした曇り空の日でも、走ると気分がよくなるよ。
Jogging makes me feel great, even on a gloomy day.

13 ジョギングより、ウォーキングが流行っていますね。
Jogging is out and walking is in.

14 ウォーキングは長寿の秘訣だよ。
Walking is a key to your longevity.

longevity＝長生き、長寿

15 ヨガの何にひかれたの？
☞ **What drew you to yoga?**

draw A to B＝AをBに引き寄せる　⊜ Why do you like yoga?

16 心身ともにリフレッシュできるんだ。
I feel refreshed in body and spirit.

17 1日に30分くらい瞑想します。
I meditate for about 30 minutes a day.

趣味、娯楽

エクササイズ、スポーツ

趣味、娯楽 / エクササイズ、スポーツ

18 オーストラリアに潜りに行ったよ。
I went to Australia to do some diving.

19 彼はサーフィンに夢中なんだ。
He's nuts about surfing.

be nuts about ～＝～に夢中

20 いつか、ハワイで波乗りしたいな。
I want to surf in Hawaii one day.

21 今シーズン、スノーボードは5回目だ。
This is my fifth time snowboarding this season.

22 まだスノーボードにはまっているの？
☞ **Are you still into snowboarding?**

23 休日はゴルフだね。
I go golfing on my days off.

24 山歩きする人が増えていますね。
More people are enjoying hiking in the mountains.

25 登山歴10年です。
I've been climbing mountains for ten years.

hiking in the mountains

26 スポーツは、するより見るほうが好きです。
☞ **I prefer to watch rather than play sports.**

1 趣味、娯楽

釣り

1 釣りのことなら、彼は誰よりも詳しいよ。
☞ **When it comes to fishing, nobody knows more than him.**

2 彼は週末、必ず釣りに行くんだ。
He always goes fishing on weekends.

3 彼女、釣りにはまっているんだって？
Is she a dedicated angler?

dedicated＝熱心な　angler＝釣り人、釣り師

4 釣りをしたことはありますか？
Have you ever tried fishing?

5 ルアーとフライをやります。
I do lure and fly-fishing.

6 釣った魚は、自分でさばくんだ。
I catch fish and clean them myself.

clean＝(魚を)さばく

7 アユ釣りが解禁になったよ。
Open season on ayu is here.

＝ The ayu season has opened.

8 友達に、いい釣り場を教えてもらったんだ。
My friend told me where the great fishing spots are.

1 趣味、娯楽

映画

1 コメディーは好きですか？
Do you like comedies?
> 「どんな映画が好き？」は What kind of films do you like?

2 映画はどのくらい見る？
How often do you watch movies?

3 僕たち、映画の好みが似ているね。
☞ **We have similar tastes in movies.**

4 ハリウッド映画は見飽きちゃった。
I've seen enough of Hollywood movies.

5 ティム・バートン監督の映画が好きです。
I like films directed by Tim Burton.
> direct＝(映画を)監督する

6 ジョニー・デップの映画はほとんど見ました。
I've seen almost all of Johnny Depp's movies.
> almost all of ～＝～のほとんどすべて

7 その映画は、大げさではなく10回くらい見ました。
I've seen the film about ten times, and I'm not exaggerating.

8 ホラー映画は苦手です。
I don't care for horror movies.
> ↪ アクション action / 戦争 war / ドキュメンタリー documentary

9 映画はたいてい、テレビで見るんだ。

I usually just watch movies on TV.

10 それほど映画好きではありません。

I'm not much of a movie fan.

11 この映画、もう見た?

Have you seen this movie yet?

⚠️ 「もう見た」は I've seen that already. 「まだ見ていない」はNo, not yet.

12 あの映画、ものすごくよかった。今まで見た中で最高の映画だと思うよ。

That movie blew me away! I think it's the best film I've ever seen before. blow (人) away=(人)を感動させる

13 誰が出ているの?

Who's in it?

⚠️ 「主演は誰?」は Who's starring in the movie?

14 監督は誰?

Who directed it?

15 封切りはいつですか?

☞ **When will it be released?**

16 映画館に行ってまで、その映画を見ようとは思わないな。

I won't go out to a theater and see the movie.

17 DVDが出るまで待とうよ。

Let's wait for it to come out on DVD.

⚠️ 「その映画のDVDはいつ出るの?」は When does the movie come out on DVD?

1 趣味、娯楽

ペット

1 ペットを飼いたいと思いますか？
Do you like to keep pets?

keep＝飼う

2 あなたは犬派？　猫派？
Are you a dog person or a cat person?

「犬派」と答えるなら I prefer dogs.

3 ペットを飼おうと思っているんだ。
I'm thinking about getting a pet.

= I want to get a pet.

4 室内で飼えるペットがいいな。
The best pet for me is one I can keep indoors.

5 ペットは人生を豊かにしてくれるよ。
Pets enrich our lives.

6 ミニチュアダックスフントを買ったんだ。
I bought a miniature dachshund.

7 血統書付きだよ。
He came with a pedigree.

pedigree＝血統書

8 犬の散歩、1日に何回してる？
How many times a day do you walk your dog?

9 おたくの犬、どこでグルーミングしてる？

Where do you have your dog groomed?

10 避妊手術しなきゃ。

She'll be spayed.

> オスの場合は He'll be neutered. と言う。「去勢してもらった」は We got our dog fixed.

11 年に1度の定期健診は欠かさない。

I make sure to take him for a checkup every year.

checkup＝検査、健康診断

12 犬に服を着せていますか？

Do you put clothes on your dog?

＝ Do you dress your dog?

13 ペットに山ほどお金を使う飼い主が、たくさんいますね。

A lot of pet owners spend tons of money on their pets.

14 子猫を分けてもらったんだ。

I got a kitten from a new litter.

> litter は「（動物の）一腹の子」の意味。from a new litter で、「一度に生まれた何匹かの中から」。

15 猫の名前は何というの？

What do you call your cat?

16 うちの猫、僕の膝の上で丸くなるのが好きなんだ。

My cat likes to curl up on my lap.

17 うちの猫はトイレを覚えないんだ。

My cat doesn't know where to poop.

poop＝ウンチをする

1 ゲーム

趣味、娯楽

CD3 Track 11

1 オンラインゲームに、はまっているんだ。

I'm hooked on online games.

be hooked on 〜 = 〜にはまる、〜に夢中になる

2 朝の4時までゲームをやっちゃった。

I was up till four in the morning playing games. 「4時間やりっ放しだった」は I was playing for four hours straight.

3 一度やり始めると、途中でやめられないんだよ。

I can't quit in the middle of the game once I start playing.

quit = やめる

4 しょっちゅう、セーブし忘れるんだよな。

I always forget to save my data.

5 来月、新作のゲームが出るらしいよ。

I heard a new game is coming out next month.

6 学習系のゲームが好き。

I prefer games that combine play with study.

7 ゲームはほとんどしないな。

I hardly ever play video games.

「ゲームはまったくしない」は I don't play video games at all.

8 ゲームは子どもには悪影響だよ。

Video games have a harmful influence on children.

1 趣味、娯楽

旅行

1 少しでもまとまった休みが取れると、たいてい旅行に行きます。

Whenever I can spare some time off, I pretty much go on trips.
_{take}

2 外国を旅したら、地元の人と触れ合うのが好きなんです。

When I travel abroad, I like to interact with the locals.
interact＝交流する

3 これまで、あまり旅行はしなかったな。

I wasn't a big traveler in my lifetime.

4 国内旅行には、よく行っていますか?

Have you traveled much within Japan?

5 旅行はやっぱり、食べ物がおいしくないとね!

☞ **If the food isn't good on a trip, what's the point?**

6 子どもを連れて旅行するのは大変だよ。

It's a lot of trouble traveling with the children.

7 その国を旅行するのが、ずっと僕の夢だったんだ。

It has always been my dream to travel in the country.

8 宇宙旅行は、もはや実現不可能な夢ではないよ。

Space travel is no longer an impossible dream.
no longer ～＝もはや～でない

2 ファッション、グルメ

ファッションセンス

1 服のセンスいいね。
You have good taste in clothes.

2 それ、いいね。
It's stunning.

stunning＝とても魅力的な、美しい

3 流行には気をつかっているの。
I'm really up on fashion.

up on fashion＝流行に敏感な

4 おしゃれでいたいの。
I really like to stay in fashion.

5 私はファッションセンスないから。
I have no style or sense of fashion.

6 いつも、服はどうやって選んでいる？
How do you usually pick your clothes out?

7 どれとどれが合うのか、考えるのよ。
I just think about what matches what.

8 どうしたら、センスを磨けるかな？
How can I develop a sense of style?

develop＝発展させる、発達させる

9 てっとり早いのは、ブランド物を揃えることね。

The easiest way is to keep buying designer outfits. ❗「最も簡単な方法は、ブランド物を買い続けることだ」の意味。

10 お金が続かないよ。

I'm going to be broke.

broke＝一文なしで、破産して

11 この色なら、誰にでも合うわ。

This color would look good on everybody.

12 着てみると、思ったよりいいね。

☞ **It looks better on me than I thought.**

13 馬子にも衣装だね。

Clothes make the man.

＝ Fine feathers make fine birds. / The tailor makes the man.

14 これは本当におしゃれね。

This is genuine style.

genuine＝本物の

15 彼女の服はいつもセンスいいよね。

☞ **She always dresses really well.**

16 彼女、雑誌で最新ファッションをチェックしているのよ。

She checks the latest fashions in the fashion magazines.

17 彼のファッションセンスは、ちょっと変わっているね。

His fashion sense is a little odd.

odd＝奇妙な、変わった

2 ファッション、グルメ
TPOに合わせて

CD3 Track 14

1 この服は、やりすぎかな？
Do you think this is too much?

2 これは、ちょっと地味すぎるよね？
This is a bit too simple, isn't it?

3 ネクタイとシャツが合っていないよ。
☞ **Your tie doesn't go with your shirt.**

go with 〜＝〜とよく合う

4 今日はラフな服装でいいよ。
You don't need to dress up today.

5 職場にふさわしい服を着なきゃ。
You have to wear the right clothes in the office.

6 このパンツは、私の好みじゃない。
These pants are not really my thing.

taste ＊「自分の好み、タイプ」の意味。

7 新しい服、よく似合っているよ。
You look so cool in your new clothes.

cool＝素敵、かっこいい

8 あなたの着こなしは最高ね。
The way you dress is so fabulous.

fabulous＝すばらしい、魅力的である

9 あなたは、タキシードがよく似合うわ。

You look handsome in a tux.

tux＝タキシード

10 この縦ボタンのコート、かわいい！

This coat with the vertical buttonholes is so cute!

vertical＝垂直の、縦の

11 このスカート、かわいいでしょう。

☞ **Don't you think this skirt is adorable?**

adorable＝とてもかわいい、魅力的である

12 このスカーフを、首に巻いてごらんよ。

Drape this scarf around your neck.

drape＝ゆったり垂らして掛ける

13 このジャケットを上から羽織ってみたら？

How about wearing this jacket over it?

14 あのパンツに合う靴がいるわね。

I have to get shoes to match those pants.

15 この靴は、毎日、磨かないといけないわね。

These shoes need to be polished every day.

16 海へ行くならサンダルがいるわね。

We need flip-flops for the beach.

flip-flop＝かかと部とつま先部のない平底のサンダル

17 キラキラしたのがいいな。

I like shiny and sparkling things.

shiny and sparkling＝(ラメなどが付いて)キラキラした

2 | ファッション、グルメ
ファッションカタログ

1 これはオタクっぽいかな？
This looks nerdy?

nerdy＝オタクっぽい

2 このジャケット、使えそう。
This jacket might come in handy.

come in handy＝役に立つ

3 ここの服は、よくある若者の服って感じね。
They have natural street fashion here.

street fashion＝（街でよく見かける）若者ファッション

4 それステキ！　私に合うかな？
I love that! Will that fit me?

5 これ、絶対に流行るよね。
☞ This will be a sensation.

sensation＝大評判のもの

6 半額になっているよ。
It's 50 percent off.

7 これは前払いかな？
Is this prepaid?

prepay＝前払いをする

8 10パーセントのキャッシュバックがあるよ。
We'll get 10 percent cash back.

2 | ファッション、グルメ
話題のブランド

1 これ、流行ってるよね。
This is in.
be in＝流行っている ＊「流行おくれ」は be out

2 どこのブランド？
What's the label?
label＝ブランド

3 ブランドものじゃないよ。
This dress is by no one.
❗ ここでの one は「デザイナー」を指す。

4 このピンヒール、ちょっとキツイ。
These stilettos are a little tight.
stiletto＝細くて高いヒールの靴、ピンヒール

5 女の子にはたまらないアイテムよね。
Thousands of girls would kill for this item.
kill for 〜＝〜のためなら何でもする、〜が欲しくてたまらない

6 おしゃれを取るか、実用性を取るかね。
Which do I need, style or utility?
utility＝実用性、有用性

7 今シーズンのMarc Jacobsのバッグは、どこも売り切れね。
The new Marc Jacobs designer bags for this season are sold out everywhere.

8 今、このブランドは人気だからね。
This brand is hot right now.
hot＝よく売れている、人気のある

2 ファッション、グルメ

食べ物の好み

CD3 Track 17

1 食べ物で好き嫌いはある？
Do you have likes and dislikes about food?

2 納豆以外なら何でも食べられる。
I can eat anything except natto.

⚠️ 「ほとんど何でも食べる」は I eat almost anything.

3 2日に1度はラーメンを食べてる。
I eat ramen once every two days.

⚠️ 「ラーメン」は Chinese noodles に置き換えてもよい。

4 ラーメン大好き人間だよね。
☞ **You have a passion for ramen.**

have a passion for 〜 ＝ 〜が大好きだ、〜に目がない

5 私はファストフードばっかり。
I'm a fast-food person.

6 おでんのおいしい季節じゃない？
Doesn't oden taste great at this time of year?

7 家庭料理が一番よ。
Home cooked meals are the best.

8 彼、典型的なグルメだね。
He is a typical gourmet.

gourmét ［グーメイ］＝食通、美食家

2 ファッション、グルメ
グルメブーム

1 グルメブームだよね。
There's a real gourmet boom.

2 雑誌でグルメ特集をやっているよ。
This magazine has a special on food.

3 スイーツは、どれが人気?
Which dessert is popular?

4 甘いものには目がないのよ。
I can't resist sweet things.

= I'm partial to sweet things.

5 ネットで注文できるかなあ?
☞ **Could I order them online?**

6 この焼肉屋さん、おすすめ。
I recommend this yakiniku restaurant.

recommend=推薦する、すすめる

7 2500円で食べ放題なんだよ。
They have an all-you-can-eat special for 2,500 yen.

all you can eat=食べ放題の

8 あの店では、本場の讃岐うどんが食べられるよ。
That restaurant serves genuine Sanuki udon.

3 | 美容、健康

お気に入りの化粧品

1 化粧品は、どんなものを使っている？

What kind of cosmetics do you use?

❗ メーカーを尋ねる場合は Which cosmetics brand do you use?

2 このパック、家でエステ気分を味わえるのよ。

This facial mask makes me feel like I'm at a beauty salon.

facial mask＝顔用パック

3 これって乾燥肌用？

Is this for dry skin?

↪ 脂性肌 oily skin

4 試してみていい？

☞ **Can I try it on?**

5 ベタつかないね。

That's not oily.

6 肌がしっとりするの。

It makes my skin moist.

7 小じわにもいいのよ。

It's good for fine wrinkles.

wrinkle＝シワ

8 5歳若返ったみたい。

I feel like I'm five years younger.

feel like 〜＝〜のような気がする

3 お肌の悩み

美容、健康

1 最近、肌がカサカサなの。

Recently, my skin has started drying out.

dry out＝乾燥してカサカサになる

2 こんなところにシミが…。

I found a blemish here.

blemish＝シミ

3 このシワ、何とかならないかしら？

☞ **Can't I do anything to smooth this wrinkle?**

smooth＝平らにする、シワをのばす

4 顔がひどくむくんじゃって。

My face is badly swollen.

swollen＝むくんだ、はれ上がった

5 吹き出物が、なかなか治らないの。

These pimples don't go away easily.

pimple＝吹き出もの、にきび

6 お肌の曲がり角って、何歳のこと？

At what age does our skin start showing signs of aging?   ＝ When is the turning point for our skin?

7 髪が傷んでるの。

My hair is damaged.

8 帰宅したら、すぐに化粧を落とすようにしているの。

I take off my makeup as soon as I get home.

take ～ off＝～を取り除く

3 ダイエット、健康

美容、健康

1 最近、贅肉がついていやだわ。
I'm worried recently about excess weight.

→ おなかの周りの贅肉 excess weight around the waist

2 甘いものの誘惑には勝てない！
I can't resist eating sweet things!

3 あの人気のダイエット法をやってみたら？
Try that popular diet.

4 食べたものを記録するの？
Do I keep a record of what I eat?

5 体重を毎日グラフに記録しているの。
I record my weight on a chart every day.

chart＝グラフ

6 あなたはいつもスリムね。
You always look slim.

look ～＝～に見える

7 バランスのいい食事をとるように心がけています。
I try to eat a well-balanced diet.

diet＝食、食生活

8 炭水化物を控えてカロリー計算をしているの。
I'm cutting down on carbs and counting calories.

carb＝carbohydrate＝炭水化物

9 いつも疲れ知らずだね。

You never get tired.

10 サプリメントが効いているのかもね。

The supplements might be working.

work＝効き目がある

11 健康オタクだね。

☞ **You're very health conscious.**

~-conscious＝〜に強く関心がある

12 健康第一だよ。

There's nothing more valuable than good health.

13 マルチビタミン剤がおすすめです。

Why don't you try multivitamins?

14 腰痛に効くサプリメントはある？

Are there supplements for lower-back pain?

lower-back pain＝腰痛

15 薬よりも運動のほうがいいよ。

Working out is better than medicine.

work out＝運動する

16 食事では摂れない栄養を補うために、サプリメントを飲んでいるの。

I take supplements to make up for the lack of nutrients in my food.

17 40歳を過ぎたら、体調管理が大切だね。

After 40, taking proper care of your body is important.

4 パソコン、携帯

パソコンを使う

1 最新式のパソコンなんだ。

I got the latest computer.

latest＝一番新しい、最新式の

2 ノートとデスクトップの両方を持っているよ。

I have both a laptop and a desktop computer.

laptop＝ノートパソコン

3 デスクトップは古い機種なんだ。

My desktop is an old model.

model＝型、機種

4 パソコンは、今や仕事に欠かせない。

We can't really do any work without a computer anymore.

5 パソコンは難しいな。

Computers are difficult to use.

6 まだ、勉強中なんです。

I've still got a lot to learn.

7 パソコンは、かなり得意なんでしょう？

You're pretty good on the computer, aren't you?

pretty＝かなり

8 このパソコンの使い方を教えてもらえませんか？

Would you mind showing me how to use this computer?

9 データ保存の仕方を覚えましょう。

Let's learn how to store the data.

store＝保存する

10 あっ、まだ電源は切らないで！

☞ **Oh, don't turn it off yet!**

⚠ 「電源を入れる」は turn it on.

11 リターンキーを押して、プログラムを終了する前にファイルを保存してください。

Please press the return key and save the file before you close the program.

save＝保存する

12 このソフトは使いやすいよ。

This software is easy to use.

software＝ソフト

13 このソフトでPDF文書を加工できるんだ。

This software can manage and process your PDF documents.

process＝処理する　⚠ PDFは portable document formatの略。

14 ほとんどの報告書は、PDF形式で手に入るからね。

Almost every report is available in PDF format.

15 経理ソフトって、何て便利なんだ。

Accounting software really makes things easy.

accounting software＝経理ソフト

16 画像を取り込んで、印刷してよ。

Scan a picture into the computer and print it out.

scan＝取り込む　picture＝画像

17 圧縮されたファイルを解凍する必要があるね。

You have to unpack the compressed file.

unpack＝解凍する　compress＝圧縮する

4 パソコン、携帯
パソコンのトラブル

1 キーを押しまちがえちゃった。
I pressed the wrong key.

2 このデスクトップ、だんだん動作が遅くなってきている。
This desktop is getting slower.

3 ノートパソコンがフリーズした！
☞ **My laptop froze!**

freeze＝凍る、(コンピュータなどが)動かなくなる

4 ファイルが開かないんだ。
I can't open the file.

5 大事なファイルに上書きしちゃった。
I overwrote an important file.

overwrite＝上書きする

6 データが、全部消えちゃったみたい。
It seems I've lost all my data.

❗日本語ではデータが「消える」と言うが、英語ではデータを「失う」＝ lose で表現する。

7 このファイル、ウイルスに感染しているかも。
This file may be infected with a virus.

be infected with a virus＝ウイルスに感染している

8 ウイルスソフトは何を使っている？
What antivirus software do you use?

àntivírus [アンティヴァイラス]

9 ウイルスバスターをかけたほうがいいよ。

You should run a virus buster.

10 パソコンを初期化しなくちゃ。

I have to initialize the computer.

initialize＝初期化する

11 このソフトは互換性がないよ。

This software isn't compatible with it.

be compatible with ～＝～と互換性がある

12 このディスクは、もういっぱいだ。

This disk is already full.

13 ハードディスクの容量不足だね。

There isn't any space left on the hard disk.

＝ The hard disk lacks capacity.

14 不要なデータは消して。

Delete the garbage data.

garbage data＝不要なデータ　＊garbage には「生ごみ、がらくた」の意味がある。

15 バックアップを取り忘れた。

I forgot to back it up.

16 バッテリーが少なくなっているよ。

The battery is running low.

17 問題が解決しない場合は、サポートサービスに問い合わせて。

If the problem persists, contact the support service.

persist＝続く

4 ネット検索

パソコン、携帯

1 インターネットの接続の仕方を教えてもらえる？

Would you show me how to hook up the Internet?

hook up ～=～に接続する、つなぐ

2 ネットにアクセスするには、パスワードを入力して。

Enter your password to access the Net.

3 アクセスできると、ブラウザーが立ち上がるよ。

If you can access it, your browser will start up.

start up=立ちあがる、起動する

4 好きな単語を検索してみて。

Try to search for your favorite words.

search for ～=～を検索する

5 検索キーワードは何を入れたらいいかな。

What search keyword should I enter?

search keyword=検索語

6 キーワードは、「イタリアン」「銀座」と入れてみて。

Enter the keywords "Italian," and "Ginza."

7 そのキーワードでは、ヒットしないよ。

I get no hits with that keyword.

8 このサイト、ブックマークしておこう。

I'll bookmark this site.

9 検索履歴は削除しておいたほうがいいよ。

You'd better erase the browser history.

10 どんなサイトをよく見るの？

What kind of websites do you often look at?

website＝サイト

11 旅行や観光のサイトをよくチェックするよ。

I often visit sites on traveling and sightseeing.

12 ネット通販も、いつも利用しているよ。

I also use the Internet all the time for shopping.

13 このサイトを使えば、割引きされるらしいね。

I heard I can get a discount on this website.

discount＝割引

14 車もネットで探したんだ。

I also found a car on the Internet.

15 今度、ホームページを開設するんだ。

I'm going to set up a homepage.

set up ～＝～を開設する

16 君のホームページのURLを教えて。

Please tell me your URL.

17 ブログを始めたんだ。

I started my own blog.

18 今日はブログを更新しなくちゃ。
☞ **I have to update my blog today.**

19 このリンクをたどれば、彼のブログへつながるよ。
Follow this link, and you'll go to his blog.

❗「リンクを張る」は provide a link と言う。

20 僕のブログ、炎上しちゃった。
☞ **My blog is in a flame war.**

flame war＝ののしり合い

21 掲示板への書き込みは、一時中止だ。
Posting a message on an online discussion board is a temporary halt.

halt＝中止、休止

22 海外の友達とチャットするのが、毎週末の楽しみだよ。
I enjoy chatting with my friends outside Japan online every weekend.

23 フェイスブックで、大学時代の友人と連絡がとれたよ。
I was able to resume contact with my friends from college through Facebook.

24 スポーツ解説者の山田徹のツイッター、すごく面白いよ。
Sports commentator Toru Yamada's twitter is really interesting.

25 ツイッターでつぶやくのが日課なんだ。
Tweeting has become a daily activity.

daily activity＝日課

26 ツイッターやフェイスブックで世界が広がったよ。
Twitter and Facebook have really broadened my world.

4 | パソコン、携帯
メールをする

1 メールって、本当に手軽だね。
E-mail is really easy to use.

2 1時間に一度はメールチェックしてる。
I routinely check my e-mail once an hour.

routinely＝日常的に

3 1月10日付けのメール、受け取ったよ。
I received your e-mail of January 10.

4 でも、文字化けしてた。
But it was garbled.

garble＝文字が化ける

5 詳しいことはメールして。
Please send me an e-mail with the details.

details＝詳しいこと、詳細

6 その写真を添付したメールを送るよ。
I'll send you an e-mail with the photo.

7 このメールを関係者に転送してくれる？
Could you forward the e-mail to the people concerned?

people concerned＝関係者

8 心当たりのないメールは開かないように。
Don't open any e-mails unless you're expecting them.

311

4 パソコン、携帯

携帯電話

1 それ、新しいケータイ？
Did you get a new cell phone?

2 機種変更したんだ。
I replaced my cell phone with another model.
replace A with B＝AをBと取り替える

3 お得な料金プランだった。
There was an inexpensive rate plan.
rate plan＝料金プラン

4 ケータイの料金プランは、わかりにくいね。
Cell phone rate plans are hard to understand.

5 ケータイ番号は変わらないよね？
You don't have to change your cell phone number, do you?

6 ケータイのアドレスを教えてくれる？
Would you give me your cell phone address?

7 赤外線通信でアドレスを交換しよう。
I'd like to exchange addresses with the infrared function.
infrared function＝赤外線機能

8 会社の住所をケータイにメールするよ。
I'll text you our address.
text＝携帯メールを送る

9 僕のケータイには、いろいろな機能がついているんだ。

My cell phone has various functions.

10 まだ、使いこなせていないけど。

☞ **I'm not used to using it yet.**

be used to ～ ing=～することに慣れている

11 へえ、ケータイでテレビが見れるんだ。

Wow, you can watch TV on your cell phone.

12 ケータイでブログも更新できるよ。

I can also update my blog <u>with</u> my cell phone.

from

13 写真は、デジカメと同じくらい、きれいに撮れるんだ。

It takes about the same quality of picture as a digital camera.

the same ～ as ...=…と同様の～

14 あなたのケータイで僕の写真を撮ってよ。

Take my picture with your cell phone.

15 あとで僕のケータイにメールを送って。

Please e-mail it to my cell phone later.

16 写メールして送るね。

I'll take a photo on my cell phone camera and send it.

17 僕のケータイには、余計な機能はついていないよ。

My cell phone doesn't have any unnecessary functions.

18 ケータイは、電話とメールができれば十分。

Any cell phone will do, as long as I can make calls and send e-mail.

will do＝十分である、足りる

19 お年寄りにはシンプルなほうが使いやすいね。

Simple cell phones are better for the elderly.

the elderly＝高齢者

20 なんてかわいい待ち受けなんだ！

Your wallpaper is so cute!

wallpaper＝待ち受け画面　＊idle screen / stand-by displayとも言う。

21 着メロは、何にしてるの？

☞ **What is your ringtone melody?**

ringtone melody＝着メロ

22 ケータイの飾りはオリジナルなんだ。

The decoration on my cell phone is my original design.

23 その曲を、ケータイにダウンロードしよう。

I'll download the music onto my cell phone.

download A onto B＝AをBにダウンロードする

24 準備ができたら、ケータイを鳴らして。

Give me a ring when you're ready.

Ring me

25 ケータイを落としちゃった。

I've lost my cell phone.

26 住所録がパーだ。

My address list is gone.

ruined

4 | パソコン、携帯

圏外エリア

1 電話が切れちゃった。ごめん。

Sorry, my cell phone got cut off.

2 ここは電波がよくないんだ。

The reception isn't good here.

reception＝受信

3 地下だから圏外だ。

My cell phone is out of service now because I'm in the basement.

out of service＝(サービス)圏外

4 アンテナが3本立っているよ。

They are three bars showing on the screen.

bar＝棒　＊ここでは「アンテナ」の意味。

5 最近は、どこでも電波が入る。

Cell phones can get a good reception anywhere these days.

6 ケータイのバッテリーが切れた。

The battery of my cell phone is dead.

7 どこでケータイを充電したらいいかな？

☞ **Where should I recharge my cell phone battery?**

8 僕の充電器を使いなよ。

Go ahead and use my power adapter.

battery charger

4 パソコン、携帯

携帯電話のマナー

1 ケータイを買ってよ。
Please buy me a cell phone.

2 まだ早いよ。
You're not old enough.

3 ちゃんと、マナーを守るから。
I have good manners.

4 学校で許可されていないだろう。
You're not allowed to use a cell phone at school.
be allowed to ～=～することが許可されている

5 ケータイはマナーモードにしておいて。
☞ **Keep your cell phone on vibration mode.**
silent

6 会議中に着メロが鳴っちゃった。
My ringtone sounded during the meeting.

7 病院ではケータイはオフにしなさい。
Turn your cell phone off in the hospital.
keep

8 電車の中ではケータイで話さないで。
Don't talk on your cell phone in the train.

4 スマートフォン、タブレットコンピュータ

パソコン、携帯

1. スマートフォンがブームだね。
   Smartphones are booming.

   boom＝人気が出る、ブームがわく

2. まだiPadを持っていないんだ。
   I haven't got an iPad yet.

   ❗ iPadは、タブレットコンピュータ（tablet computer）の一種。

3. ちょっとやってみて。とても便利だよ。
   Try it. It's very convenient.

4. パスワードを入力して、OKをタップしてみて。
   Enter the password and tap OK.

   tap＝軽くたたく、打つ

5. ページをめくってごらん。
   Flick the page.

   flick＝すばやくページを動かす、めくる

6. 次は縮小して。
   Next, pinch-in the page.

   ❗ pinch-in は、縮小するときに使う指でつまむ操作のこと。拡大する場合は pinch-out

7. 写真を大きくするには、ダブルタップだよ。
   Double-tap the picture to enlarge it.

   ❗ double-tap は、画面を2回連続して軽くたたくこと。

8. スクリーンの上の黒い部分をタップすると、ツールバーが出るよ。
   Tap in the black area near the top of the screen to display the toolbar.

9 iPadをパソコンにつないでごらん。

Connect your iPad to your computer.

10 Wi-Fiにつながっているよ。

You're connected to a Wi-Fi network.

11 iPadって、本当に使えそうだね。

The iPad seems to be useful.

「使える」は useful で表す。

12 アプリの数もハンパじゃないしね。

☞ **There are a large number of apps as well.**

app＝application＝アプリケーション

13 おまけに定番アプリの多くは無料なんだ。

What's more, most of the must-have apps are free. must-have＝必需品の、なくてはならない　free＝無料の、ただの

14 iPadにはブルートゥースのヘッドセットもつなげるよ。

You can connect a Bluetooth headset to an iPad.

15 スマートフォンでフィナンシャル・タイムズが購読できるんだ。

I can subscribe to the Financial Times with my smart phone. subscribe to ～＝～を定期購読する

16 「自炊」というのはね。本を自分で電子書籍に加工することだよ。

What does Jisui mean? It means self-digitalization of paper books into e-books.

17 アマゾンが電子書籍リーダーのキンドルを値下げしたね。

Amazon cut the price on its Kindle electronic reader. cut the price on ～＝～を値下げする

4 パソコン、携帯
デジタル家電

1 マルチメディアソフトの普及で、ビデオテープはまったくの時代遅れだね。

Video tapes were rendered obsolete by the spread of multimedia applications. render＝～の状態にする　obsolete＝時代遅れの

2 この番組をハードディスクに録画できる？

Can you record this show on a hard-disk recorder?

3 このテレビはマルチメディア機能は搭載していないよ。

This TV set doesn't support multimedia functions.

4 このDVDプレーヤーは、自然な色を再現してくれるよ。

This DVD player reproduces natural colors.

reproduce＝再生する、再現する

5 DVDは、音声も字幕も英語で見ているんだ。

I watch a DVD in English with English subtitles. captions

6 片面2層DVDの容量は、8.5GBです。

The capacity of a single-sided DVD is 8.5 GB.

capacity＝容量

7 音楽はもっぱらiPodで聴いている。

☞ **I listen to music only on my iPod.**

8 これからはみんな、パソコンを家電製品みたいな感覚で買うんだろうな。

In the future, people will buy PCs the same way they buy household appliances. household appliance＝家電製品

5 エコ、環境
環境にいいこと

1 今日はゴミの日だ。
It's garbage (collection) day today.

2 ゴミはちゃんと分別しなきゃ。
You should separate the trash.

3 新聞紙をリサイクルに出したいんだけど。
I'd like to take a stack of old newspapers out for recycling.
a stack of ～=積み重ねられたひと山の～、多量の～

4 古新聞の回収は行われているのかな？
Do they collect old newspapers?

5 段ボール箱もリサイクルしなくちゃ。
We have to recycle the cardboard boxes too.
cardboard box=段ボール箱

6 環境にいいことを何かやっていますか？
☞ **What do you do for the environment?**
environment=環境

7 重曹と酢を使って、エコ掃除をしています。
I do eco-friendly cleaning with baking soda and vinegar.
baking soda=重曹　vinegar=酢

8 省エネに努めています。
I try to save energy.
save energy=エネルギーを節約する　＊「省エネ」は energy saving

5 エコ、環境
環境問題

1 大気を汚染しているのは、自動車の排気ガスだよ。

Automobile exhaust is causing air pollution.

automobile exhaust＝自動車の排気ガス　air pollution＝大気汚染

2 大気汚染は深刻な地球規模の問題だ。

☞ **Air pollution is a serious global problem.**

3 その銅像の腐食の原因は酸性雨だよ。

The decay of the bronze statue is due to acid rain.

due to ～＝～が原因で、～によって　acid rain＝酸性雨

4 環境破壊に、反対の声が上がっています。

Voices are being raised against all this environmental destruction.

destruction＝破壊

5 もっと環境を大切にしたほうがいいですね。

We should place more value on the environment.

place much value on ～＝～を重視する

6 地球温暖化問題は、迅速な対応が求められています。

Global warming problems call for quick action.

7 政府は、太陽エネルギーの有効活用を考えているようだね。

The government is considering making use of solar energy.

8 あの新しいエネルギー政策は、環境面で安全だと思うよ。

I think the new recycling policy is environmentally safe.

environmentally＝環境面で

5 エコ、環境

自然災害

1 あっ、また地震だ!
Oh, it's an earthquake again!

earthquake＝地震

2 ここは地震が多いんだ。
This is a quake-prone area.

〜-prone＝〜しやすい

3 震度4ぐらいだね。
☞ **Maybe the earthquake intensity is 4.**

4 地震による津波が心配です。
I'm afraid the earthquake will generate a tsunami.

5 津波が発生しました。
A tsunami has struck.

hit／swept

6 たった今、警報が解除されたよ。
Just now, a tsunami warning was canceled.

warning＝警報

7 この雨がやまないと、洪水になる。
If it goes on raining, we're going to have a flood.

flood［フラッド］＝洪水

8 土石流は山火事のあとに発生します。
Avalanches occur after mountain fires.

avalanche＝土石流　occur＝生じる

9 梅雨時には、集中豪雨に気をつけなければなりません。

We should watch out for torrential rains in the rainy season.

torrential rain＝集中豪雨

10 去年の夏は、台風の影響で休みの計画がよく変わった。

Typhoons often affected our vacation plans last summer.

affect＝影響を及ぼす

11 日本は自然災害の多い国だね。

There are a lot of natural disasters in Japan.

natural disaster＝自然災害

12 不幸は続けて起こらないよ。

Lightning never strikes twice in the same place.

「雷は同じところに二度は落ちない」の意味。

13 停電だ！

It's a blackout!

blackout＝停電

14 昨年は異常な冷夏だった。

It was exceptionally cold last summer.

exceptionally＝異常に

15 異常気象により、米は10年ぶりの凶作となりました。

The rice crop was the worst in ten years as a result of unusual weather.

rice crop＝稲作

16 長期予報によると、暖冬だそうだ。

The long-range forecast says we'll have a mild winter.

mild winter＝暖冬

17 地球温暖化の影響かな。

I wonder if it's an influence of global warming.

6 結婚、育児、教育

結婚する

1 彼女、今度の秋に結婚するのよ。
She's getting married next fall.

get married＝結婚する

2 もうすぐご結婚と伺い、とてもうれしく思っています。
We're so happy to hear that you're getting married soon.

be happy to hear (that) 〜＝〜と聞いてうれしい

3 婚約おめでとう！
Congratulations on your engagement!

4 お似合いのカップルね。
You'll make a great couple.

5 ご主人になる人は幸せよね。
Her husband is so lucky!

6 彼女と知り合ったきっかけは？
How did you get to know her?

get to 〜＝〜するようになる

7 披露宴にきてくれる？
Could you attend my wedding reception?

attend＝出席する

8 結婚祝いには、何が欲しい？
What do you want as a wedding gift?

9 ハネムーンは、どこへ行くの？
Where are you going on your honeymoon?

10 ご結婚されていますか？
Are you married?

11 誰かいい人を紹介して！
Please introduce me to someone nice.

12 ご結婚してどのくらいですか？
How long have you been married?

13 プロポーズの言葉は何だったの？
☞ **What did he say when he proposed to you?**

14 「生涯をかけてあなたを守ります」だったわ。
He said, "I'll protect you as long as I live."

as long as 〜＝〜のかぎり、〜の間(は)

15 彼は、その言葉を守っている？
Is he as good as his word?

as good as 〜＝〜に忠実な

16 結婚記念日はいつですか？
When's your wedding anniversary?

17 その日は、素敵なレストランで夕食をとることにしています。
We plan to have a dinner at a lovely restaurant on the same day.

6 結婚、育児、教育

結婚生活

1 彼、新婚ホヤホヤなの。
He just got married.

is newlywed

2 幸せそうね。うらやましい！
He looks so happy. He's lucky!

3 結婚生活はどうですか？
How do you like being married?

4 まあまあ、ふつうよ。
I can't complain. It's OK.

❗ can't complain は「不満は言えない」ということ。

5 彼は完全に尻に敷かれちゃったよ。
He's completely henpecked.

henpeck＝(妻が夫を)尻に敷く

6 倦怠期なの。
We got bored of being married.

with each other

7 私たち2人とも、再婚なの。
This is the second time for both of us to get married.

8 前の夫は浪費家で。
My ex-husband was a big spender.

↪ 前の妻 ex-wife

9 主人とはケンカが絶えなかったの。
I often quarreled with my husband.

quárrel［クウォレル］＝口げんかをする

10 赤ちゃんはまだ？
Aren't you going to have a child?

11 主人はとても赤ちゃんを欲しがっているわ。
My husband is desperate to have a child.

desperate to ～＝～したくてたまらない

12 でも、私はまだ産む決心がつかないの。
But I haven't decided to have a baby yet.

13 専業主婦には、なりたくないわ。
I don't want to be a housewife.

14 結婚後も仕事を続けたいの。
I'd like to continue working after marriage.

15 もちろん、家事は分担ね。
Of course, we'll share the housework.

housework＝家事

16 彼は、バツイチよ。
He's been married once before.

「かつて1度結婚していた」ということ。

17 独身生活を謳歌しています。
He's making the most of being single.

make the most of ～＝～を最大限に生かす

6 結婚、育児、教育

結婚生活

6 結婚、育児、教育

離婚の危機

1 あなたたち、うまくいっているの？
How's being married going?

2 もう、だめみたい。
👉 **It seems our marriage is in crisis.**

in crisis＝危機的な

3 何がいけないの？
What's the problem?

4 彼が、浮気しているのよ。
He's cheating on me.

cheat on（人）＝（人）を裏切って浮気をする

5 離婚をするしかないわ。
I have to divorce him.

❗「慰謝料を払わなければならない」は I have to pay alimony.

6 よくある離婚の原因ね。
It's a frequent cause of divorce.

7 でも、離婚届けはまだ出していないの。
We haven't filed for divorce yet.

file for a divorce＝離婚届を出す

8 子どものために我慢するしかないかも。
I may have to stay in this marriage for our children's sake.

for ～'s sake＝～のために

6 妊娠・出産

結婚、育児、教育

1 子どもができたんだって？
Are you going to be a mother?

💡「予定日はいつ？」は When are you due?

2 今、3か月なの。
I'm three months pregnant.

pregnant＝妊娠している

3 予定日は3月3日頃よ。
The baby is due around March 3.

4 来年、初めての子どもが生まれるんだ。
We're expecting our first child next year.

5 父親になるって、どんな気持ち？
How do you feel about becoming a father?

6 生まれたら、知らせてね。
Let me know when you have your baby.

7 彼女、つわりがひどくて。
She's suffering from bad morning sickness.

morning sickness＝つわり

8 先生に電話して！ 陣痛が始まったみたい。
Call the doctor！ I think I'm in labor.

in labor＝分娩中で、陣痛発作中で　＊医学用語で「子宮収縮、陣痛」は contraction

9 破水したわ。

My water broke.

10 ご出産おめでとうございます！

Congratulations on the new baby!

11 女の子ですよ。

It's a girl.

12 母子ともに健康です。

Both mother and child are doing well.

13 娘は身長が50cmで、体重は3400グラムだったのよ。

My daughter was 50 centimeters long and weighed 3,400 grams. ❗乳児の身長には tall よりも long を使う。

14 安産だったのよ。

☞ **I had an easy labor.**

🔄 難産 hard labor

15 目はお父さん似で、口元はお母さんに似ていますね。

She's got her father's eyes and her mother's mouth.

16 産休はどのくらい？

How long will your maternity leave be?

maternity leave＝産休

17 育児休暇と合わせて1年半よ。

It'll be one year and a half, including childcare leave. include [インクルード] ＝含む　childcare leave＝育児休暇

6 結婚、育児、教育

子育て

1 母乳で育てているの。
I'm a breast-feeder.

breast-feeder＝母乳で育てる人

2 多くのママが紙オムツを使っているわ。
Many mothers use disposable diapers.

disposable diaper＝紙オムツ

3 彼がオムツを替えてくれるから、助かるわ。
It's nice of him to change diapers.

⚠️ 「パンツ型おむつ」は huggies

4 赤ちゃんをお風呂に入れるのは、彼の役目なの。
It's his job to bathe our baby.

give our baby a bath

5 彼、寝不足でイラつき気味だわ。
He got irritated by a lack of sleep.

6 赤ちゃんの夜泣きがひどいのよ。
Our baby cries a lot at night.

7 昨日の夜、ひきつけを起こしたの。
Our baby had a convulsion last night.

convulsion＝けいれん、ひきつけ

8 赤ちゃんがひどい高熱だわ。
Our baby has a very high fever.

結婚、育児、教育 / 子育て

9 もう、首はすわったの？
Does she already hold up her head?

10 ハイハイをし始めたところ。
☞ **She's just begun crawling.**
crawling＝ハイハイ、はい歩き

11 1日中、目が離せないわ。
I have to keep my eyes on her all day long.

12 何でも口に入れちゃうのよ。
She puts everything into her mouth.

13 奥様、少しノイローゼ気味じゃない？
Your wife is slightly neurotic, isn't she?
neurotic＝神経症の

14 彼女、育児に悩んでいるみたい。
She seems to be worried about child rearing.
child rearing＝育児

15 彼女、育児の手伝いが必要よ。
She needs help with childcare.

16 育児休暇が終わったら、すぐに仕事に戻るつもり。
After childcare leave, I'll soon return to work.

17 近頃は、保育所不足なんだって。
Day-care centers are in great demand these days.

6 結婚、育児、教育
子どもの教育

CD3 Track 39

1 英語は何歳から始めたらいいの？
☞ **What age is it best to start learning English?**

2 娘にはピアノの才能があるわ。
My daughter has a talent for the piano.

3 早期教育って必要なのかしら？
Do you think early-education is essential?

4 夫は息子の塾通いに反対なの。
My husband doesn't allow our son to go to cram school.

5 子どものうちは勉強より運動のほうが大事よ。
Exercise is more important than study in his childhood.

6 うちは放任主義なんだ。
We adopt a non-interference policy.
non-interference＝不干渉、放任

7 ＰＴＡの役員に指名されたわ。
I was chosen to be a PTA leader.
be chosen to be ～＝～に選ばれる

8 授業参観には、たくさんのお父さん方がいらしたわ。
A lot of fathers visited their children's classroom on parents' day.
parents' day＝授業参観日

6 | 結婚、育児、教育

子どものしつけ

CD3 Track 40

1 タロウ君は、いつも元気いっぱいね。
Taro has a lot of energy all the time.

2 お行儀が悪くて困っているの。
His bad manners trouble me.

3 親の言うことをきかないの。
He's a naughty boy.

naughty＝言うことをきかない、わんぱくな

4 反抗期かな？
☞ **Is he going through a rebellious period?**

rebellious＝反抗的な

5 マミは泣き虫なの。
Mami is a crybaby.

6 すごく人見知りなの。
She's really shy.

7 孫娘が6年生なんです。
My grand-daughter is in the sixth grade.

8 難しい年頃ですね。
She's at a sensitive age.

≡ She's at a difficult age.

9 先月、初潮を迎えたの。

She got her first period last month.

period＝生理、月経

10 いつまでも、子どもじゃないのよね。

She isn't a child anymore.

11 息子が登校拒否なんです。

My son refuses to go to school.

refúse［リフューズ］＝拒否する

12 彼は、学校でいじめられています。

He's being bullied at school.

bully＝いじめる

13 最近は、子どもたちが口ごたえばっかりするのよ。

☞ **These days, my children talk back to me all the time.**

talk back＝口ごたえをする、言い返す

14 子どもには、親に言いにくいことがあるはずよ。

Children have things they don't want to talk to their parents about.

15 それだけ成長した印よ。

It's a part of growing up.

grow up＝成長する

16 子どものしつけは、親の責任ね。

Parents have a responsibility to discipline their children.

discipline＝しつける

17 親としてのあり方を学ぶ必要があるわね。

We have to learn parenting skills.

parenting skill＝親としてのあり方

6 | 結婚、育児、教育
将来の進路

1 君は、そろそろ進路を考える時期だ。
You're old enough to start thinking about your path in life.

2 大学くらいは行っておいたほうがいいよ。
You should at least go to college.

3 このままでは、東大は難しいね。
You might not pass the entrance exam for the University of Tokyo at this rate.

4 彼女は、帰国子女としてこの大学に入学を許可されたのよ。
She was admitted to this university as a returnee.
retùrnée [リターニー]＝(海外滞在などからの)帰還者

5 大学進学は断念したわ。
I gave up getting a college education.

6 就職氷河期に仕事なんて見つからないよ。
It's difficult to get a job during this employment ice age.
employment ice age＝就職氷河期

7 いろいろな資格を取っておくべきだった。
I should've gotten various qualifications.

8 自分の好きな仕事をしなさい。
You should be what you want to be.

6 介護

結婚、育児、教育

1 祖父は、認知症の兆候があります。
My grandfather shows signs of dementia.
dementia＝認知症

2 5年間、母の介護をしています。
I've been taking care of my mother for five years.
looking after

3 1人で負担を抱え込まないで。
Don't carry the burden all by yourself.
burden＝負担、重荷

4 介護を分担することが重要よ。
It's important to share the care.

5 彼の奥さんは寝たきりなんだ。
He has a bedridden wife.
bedridden＝寝たきりの

6 最近、物忘れが激しくて。
I've recently been getting forgetful.

7 ぼけたくないな。
I don't want to go senile.
sénile「シーナイル」＝(年をとって)もうろくした、ぼけた

8 老後は老人ホームにお世話になるよ。
When I get old, I'll live in a nursing home.

7 選挙と政治

政治、経済、宗教

1 選挙期間は、いつも騒がしいな。
It's always noisy during election time.
election＝選挙

2 明日は投票日だね。
Tomorrow is the election day.

3 公民館が投票所だよ。
The community center is the polling place.
polling＝投票

4 誰に投票するか決めた？
Have you decided who you're voting for?
vote＝投票する

5 支持する政党がないんだ。
There's no political party I support.
political party＝政党

6 無党派層が増えているね。
The number of independents is increasing.
independents＝無党派層

7 国民の政治不信の反映だよ。
It reflects public distrust in politics.
distrust in politics＝政治不信

8 ほとんどの若者は、政治にはまったく興味がないね。
Most young people aren't interested in politics at all.

9 どの政党が勝つんだろう？

Which party will win the election?

10 今日の新聞によると、現内閣の支持率が下がっているんだって。

Today's paper says that the approval rate of the current cabinet is declining.
approval rate＝支持率　cabinet＝内閣

11 今度の総理大臣も、また辞任か。

The new prime minister will also be forced to resign.
resign＝辞任する

12 いわゆる、政治とカネの問題だね。

It's what we call a politics and money problem.

13 あの政治家は、違法な企業献金を受け取ったんだ。

That politician accepted illegal corporate donations.
illegal＝違法な　corporate donation＝企業献金

14 彼、汚職事件に関与しているらしいよ。

It appears that he was involved in the payoff scandal.
be involved in ～＝～に関係する　payoff scandal＝汚職事件

15 彼の政治生命も終わりだね。

☞ **It will end his political career.**

16 彼女は、行政改革で重要な役割を果たすだろう。

She's going to play an important role in the government reforms.
play a role＝役割を果たす　government reform＝行政改革

17 自民党は政権の座に長くありすぎた。

The Liberal Democratic Party of Japan has been in power far too long.
🔄 民主党 Democratic Party of Japan

7 政治、経済、宗教　選挙と政治

7 政治、経済、宗教
経済と金融

1 景気はどうですか？

How's business?

「状況はどのように進展していますか」「景気はどう？」といった意味で使われる。How goes it?も可。

2 日本はまだまだ景気が悪いね。

Japan's economy is still weak.

3 会社は倒産寸前だよ。

The company is on the brink of bankruptcy.

be on the brink of 〜＝〜の寸前である　bankruptcy＝倒産

4 失業率は依然高いままです。

The unemployment rate remains high.

unemployment rate＝失業率

5 消費者心理が冷え込んでいるね。

Consumer confidence has gone down.

consumer＝消費者

6 景気はいつ回復するんだろう？

When will the economy recover?

7 政府の景気対策に期待したいよ。

We hope the government's measures boost the economy.

8 特に減税を望みたいな。

We hope the government gives us a tax cut.

tax cut＝減税

9 政府が税法を改正するように願っているよ。

We want the government to amend the tax laws.
amend＝改正する　tax law＝税法

10 円高が進んでいるね。

☞ **The yen is appreciating against the dollar.**
appreciate＝値上がりする、相場が上がる

11 株価は下がり続けている。

Stock prices are dropping.
stock price＝株価

12 投資は何かやっている？

Are you invested in something?
invest＝投資する

13 株とFXを少しね。

I invest in stocks and forex a little.
stock＝株　forex＝foreign exchange＝外国為替

14 株で損しちゃった。

I lost money in the stock market.

15 FXはリスクが高すぎるよ。

The risks of forex investing are too high.

16 今は大恐慌以来、最大の金融危機です。

It's the largest financial shock since the Great Depression.
financial shock＝金融危機　Great Depression＝大恐慌

17 円ドル為替相場は、旅行者にどんな影響がありますか？

What effect does the yen-dollar exchange rate have on travelers?
effect＝影響　yen-dollar exchange rate＝円ドル為替相場

政治、経済、宗教 | 経済と金融

7 社会問題

政治、経済、宗教

1 東京の家賃は高い。

Rents in Tokyo are high.

rent＝家賃

2 社会福祉制度は、抜本的な改革が必要だ。

The social welfare system is in bad need of renovation. social welfare system＝社会福祉制度　renovation＝改革

3 近頃は就職難だ。

Nowadays jobs are hard to come by.

come by＝手に入れる

4 警察は、違法薬物を取り締まった。

The police clamped down on illegal drugs.

clamp down＝取り締まる　illegal drug＝違法薬物

5 日本は最近、自殺者が多い。

Japan's suicide rate has been very high recently.

suicide＝自殺

6 いじめが原因で自殺する子どももいます。

Bullying drives some kids to suicide.

bullying＝いじめ

7 所得格差の拡大が不公平感を生んでいます。

The expanding income disparities cause a sense of unfairness. expanding＝拡大　income＝所得　disparity＝格差、不均等

8 来年から新しい介護保険制度が始まります。

The new national elder-care insurance system starts next year.

7 政治、経済、宗教
宗教

1 日本では無宗教の人が多い。
Many Japanese have no religion.

2 私は無神論者なんです。
I'm an atheist.

atheist＝無神論者　❗「私は仏教徒です」は I'm a Buddhist.

3 彼女はキリスト教に入信した。
She become a Christian.

4 宗教上の理由で、お酒は飲みません。
☞ **I don't drink alcohol for religious reasons.**

5 神道は日本古来の宗教です。
Shinto is a native religion of Japan.

6 仏教には様々な宗派があります。
There are a lot of sects in Buddhism.

sect＝宗派

7 日本人には自然を敬う気持ちがあります。
Japanese have a great respect for nature.

8 政治と宗教の話は慎んだほうがいいよ。
You should avoid politics and religion.

avoid＝避ける

8 日本文化

食生活

1 天ぷら、刺身、寿司などが、和食の代表的なものです。

Tempura, sashimi and sushi are famous in Japanese cuisine.

cuisine [クイズィーン] =料理

2 和食を食べたことある？

Have you ever eaten Japanese food?

Japanese cuisine

3 食事をするときは、箸を使います。

Chopsticks are what we use to eat with.

chopsticks =箸　＊複数形で使う。

4 箸の使い方を教えてください。

How do I use chopsticks?

5 箸にはたくさんの作法があります。

There are a lot of rules for eating with chopsticks.

6 箸で食べ物を突き刺してはいけません。

☞ **You shouldn't stab food with your chopsticks.**

stab =突き刺す

7 和食では、バラエティに富んだ料理や郷土料理の数々を楽しめます。

Japanese cuisine offers a large variety of dishes and regional specialties.

8 来週の土曜日にすき焼きパーティをやるよ。

We're having a sukiyaki party next Saturday.

9 おにぎりは丸か三角の形をした、ごはんのボールみたいなものです。

Onigiri is a rice ball that's round or sometimes triangular shaped. ～shaped=～の形をした

10 おでんは寒い季節にぴったりの、日本の典型的な鍋料理だよ。

Oden is a typical Japanese hodgepodge suitable for colder seasons. hodgepodge=ごった煮

11 豆腐や味噌は健康食品として有名だね。

Tofu and miso are well-known as health food.

12 インスタントラーメンは日本人が発明したんだよ。

A Japanese invented instant noodles.

invent=発明する

13 寿司のネタで何が一番好き？

What kind of sushi do you like best?

14 寿司はサビ抜きにしてもらいたいです。

I'd like sushi without wasabi.

15 寿司は手で食べていいのよ。

You can eat sushi with your hands.

16 刺身はしょうゆを付けて食べて。

☞ **You dip sashimi in soy sauce before you eat it.** dip=浸す　soy sauce=醤油

17 天ぷらはポルトガル人によってもたらされたものです。

Tempura was brought to Japan by the Portuguese. Pòrtuguése[ポーチュギーズ]=ポルトガル人

8　日本文化

食生活

8 | 日本文化
ポップカルチャー

1 電化製品を探すなら秋葉原がいいよ。

Akihabara is the place to go if you're looking for electrical appliances. electrical appliance＝電化製品

2 秋葉原は東京の有名な電気街で、オタク文化の中心でもあるんだ。

Akihabara is Tokyo's famous electronics district and the center of the otaku world. district＝地域、場所

3 秋葉原は日本のカルチャーの発信地だ。

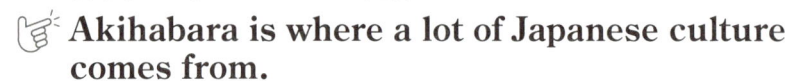

Akihabara is where a lot of Japanese culture comes from.

4 秋葉原出身のアイドルグループもいるよ。

There are some idol groups from Akihabara.

5 コスプレは、なりきりのコスチュームのことだよ。

Cosplay means costume plus role-play.

costume＝衣装

6 アニメキャラクターのコスプレは、海外でも人気です。

Cosplay of cartoon characters is getting popular outside of Japan.

7 マンガ喫茶ではマンガはもちろん、インターネットやテレビも楽しめるよ。

You can enjoy the Internet and TV in addition to manga at manga cafes.

8 アニメやマンガは、いまや日本を代表する文化だね。

Anime and manga developed as a form of typical Japanese culture. develop＝発展する

9 日本のマンガ文化には、世界中に多くのファンがいるんだ。

Japan's manga culture has legions of fans around the world.
legions of ～=たくさんの～

10 歴史も経営学も、マンガを通して学べるよ。

You can study history and business management through manga.

11 街にはキャラクターグッズがあふれています。

The towns are full of character goods.

12 『ドラえもん』がアニメ大使だって知ってた？

Did you know that *Doraemon* is the Anime Ambassador?
ambassador=大使

13 『ドラゴンボール』は、世界中で人気があるそうだね。

I hear *Dragonball* is popular all over the world.

14 そのアニメは外国でも放送されているんだ。

That anime is on the air even in other countries.
be on the air=放送されている

15 人気ドラマの原作は、ほとんどがマンガだよ。

The origin of most popular TV dramas was manga.
origin=起源、出所

16 テレビやマンガが原因で、学生たちはほとんど本を読まなくなったね。

Students don't read many books because of TV and comics.

17 カラオケはどの世代にも人気があります。

Karaoke is popular with all generations.
generation=世代

8 | 日本文化
伝統文化、伝統芸能

1 日本の伝統芸能について教えてくれませんか？

Would you tell me something about traditional performing arts in Japan?

2 文楽とは、日本独特の伝統的な人形劇のことをいいます。

Bunraku is a uniquely traditional Japanese puppet theater.

puppet theater＝人形劇

3 歌舞伎は派手なメークや衣装で、日本人にも外国人にも人気の高い演劇です。

Kabuki, with heavy makeup and colorful costumes, is a popular form of theater for Japanese and foreigners.

4 能は仮面をつけて演じられます。

Noh is performed with masks on.

5 神楽は神様に奉納する踊りのことだよ。

Kagura is a dance dedicated to the gods.

dedicate to ～＝～に奉納する

6 私は茶道にも華道にも興味はありません。

I'm not interested in the tea ceremony or flower arrangement.

tea ceremony＝茶道　flower arrangement＝華道

7 俳句は世界で最も短い詩です。

Haiku is the shortest form of poetry in the world.

8 俳句には季節を表す言葉、「季語」が必要です。

Haiku must have a seasonal word called "kigo."

seasonal＝季節の

9 「万葉集」は日本で最初の勅撰和歌集です。

"Manyoshu" is the first Japanese book of poems selected by the emperor.

emperor＝天皇

10 「源氏物語」は世界最古の長編小説といわれています。

"The Story of Genji" is said to be the oldest written epic in the world.

epic＝長編物語

11 彼は若者に人気の落語家なんだ。

He's a "rakugo" or funny story teller popular with young people.

12 漫才では、2人の芸人がおかしな会話を繰り広げて笑いを誘います。

"Manzai" is a comic duo which presents comedy routines and creates lots of laughter.

create laughter＝笑いを誘う

13 三味線は、3本の弦が張られた伝統楽器です。

"Shamisen" is a three-stringed traditional musical instrument.

three-stringed＝三弦の

14 笛や尺八のような管楽器は、竹でつくります。

Japanese wind instruments such as the "fue" or "shakuhachi" are made of bamboo.

15 柔道はオリンピックの種目にもなっている国際的なスポーツです。

Judo is an international as well as Olympic fighting sport.

fighting sport＝格闘技

16 相撲は日本の国技です。

Sumo is the national sport of Japan.

national sport＝国技

17 剣道では武士道の精神が大切です。

In kendo, the "bushido" spirit plays an important role.

play a role＝役割を果たす

8 日本文化

伝統文化、伝統芸能

8 日本文化 — 観光地

1 日光へ紅葉を見に行ってきたよ。
I went to see the autumn leaves in Nikko.

2 浅草には江戸情緒がたくさんあるよ。
☞ **Asakusa is brimming with the atmosphere of Edo.**
brim with ～＝～がたくさんある

3 東京の新名所といえば、スカイツリーだね。
The Sky Tree is the newest tourist attraction in Tokyo.

4 若者には、ディズニーリゾートのようなテーマパークが人気です。
Theme parks like Disney Resort are popular with young people.
theme [スィーム]

5 明日は、朝市に行こう。
Let's go to the morning bazaar tomorrow.
bazaar＝市場

6 温泉を体験してみたら？
☞ **How about trying out a hot spring resort?**
hot spring＝温泉　resort＝行楽地

7 カップルで温泉を楽しむ、貸し切り風呂が流行っているのよ。
Private hot spring baths are popular with couples.
be popular with ～＝～に人気がある

8 冬の露天風呂は最高ですよ。
There's nothing like enjoying an open-air bath in winter.

9 京都や奈良は、寺や神社の宝庫だね。

Kyoto and Nara are rich in temples and shrines.
be rich in ～=～の宝庫だ、～が豊富にある　shrine=神社

10 法隆寺は、世界で一番古い木造建築物だよ。

Horyuji Temple is the oldest wooden building in the world.
wooden=木造の

11 ここは金閣寺といって、1397年に建てられた寺なんだ。

This is called Kinkakuji-Temple, and it was built in 1397.

12 この仏像、国の重要文化財なんだって。

This Buddhist statue is an Important National Cultural Asset.

13 姫路城は国宝です。

Himeji Castle is a National Treasure.
National Treasure=国宝

14 ここは城跡です。

This is the site of a castle.
site=旧跡、古跡

15 当時は今ほどの技術はなかったろうに、素晴らしい建築だ。

It's such great architecture, considering the technology they had at the time.

16 自然を楽しむなら、北海道に行くべきだな。

You should visit Hokkaido if you want to enjoy nature.

17 知床は、世界遺産に登録されています。

Shiretoko is designated as a World Heritage Site.
World Heritage Site=世界遺産

8 日本文化

観光地

8 日本文化

日本の生活習慣

1 日本人はいろいろな場面でお辞儀をします。

Japanese bow in many different situations.

bow＝お辞儀をする

2 家には靴を脱いで上がります。

We remove our shoes before going into the house.

3 畳の上では正座するの？

Should we sit on the tatami mats Japanese-style with our buttocks on our ankles?

4 目上の人には敬語を使います。

We use polite expressions to elders.

polite＝ていねいな

5 麺類は音を立てて食べても大丈夫です。

We can make slurping sounds when we eat noodles.

slurp＝音を立てて食べる

6 近くの神社で合格祈願をしてきたよ。

I prayed for success on my entrance exam at the nearby shrine.

7 日本でチップは必要ありません。

We don't have a custom of tipping here in Japan.

8 不動産屋に支払う手数料と家主に払う敷金、礼金のようなものがあります。

You'll pay an agent's fee, deposit money and gift money to the house owner.

敷金や礼金は日本独特の習慣。

Part 5 場面別の会話

1 旅行 ………………… 354
2 公共の場所 ………………… 382
3 冠婚葬祭、年中行事 ……… 408

1 | 旅行
準備をする

1 来月は休みを取るよ。
I'll be taking a vacation next month.
take a vacation＝休暇を取る

2 どこで休暇を過ごすの？
Where are you spending your vacation?

3 ぜひ中国に行ってみたいな。
I'd love to go to China.

4 中国は何度目ですか？
How many times have you been to China?
how many times＝何回目

5 中国を訪れるのは、これが初めてなんだ。
This is my first visit to China.

6 予約係をお願いします。
Reservation desk, please.
reservation desk＝予約係

7 3月15日から5日間、部屋を取れますか？
☞ **Do you have a room available from March the 15 for five days?**
available＝利用（使用）できる

8 予算は1人につき、5泊で5万円です。
My budget is 50,000 yen per person for five nights.
per person＝1人につき

9 確認いたしますので、少々お待ちください。

Just a minute. I'll ask for you.

10 シングルですか、ダブルですか?

Would you like a single or a double?

> 「シングルルームを1泊だけ」の場合は A single room, please. For just one night.

11 禁煙の部屋をお願いします。

I'd like a non-smoking room, please.

12 何時までにチェックインすればいいですか?

How late can I check in?

13 3月15日の北京行き、JALの便を予約したいのですが。

I want to make a reservation for a JAL flight to Beijing on March 15.

14 エコノミークラスで、いくらですか?

How much does it cost for economy class?

15 旅行保険に加入していますか?

Do you have travel insurance?

16 この用紙に記入してください。

You'll need to fill in this form.

17 荷造りは、済んだ?

Have you finished packing yet?

1 旅行

空港で荷物を預ける

1 お預けの荷物はありますか？
Do you have any bags to check?

2 預ける荷物はありません。
I don't have any baggage to check.

> baggage「手荷物」は集合名詞なので、個々を表すときは bag。

3 預ける荷物はこれだけです。
This is the only bag I have to check in.

4 あなたのスーツケースは、2キロオーバーです。
Your suitcase is 2kg overweight.

5 スーツケースの中には、何が入っていますか？
What's in this suitcase?

6 洋服だけです。
Only clothes, nothing else.

7 この荷物は、機内に持ち込めますか？
Can I take this bag on the plane?

8 スーツケースを1つ、預けます。
I have a suitcase to check in.

9 手荷物の最大重量は？

How much hand baggage can I bring onboard?

carry-on baggage

10 これは機内に持ち込みます。

☞ **This is carry-on.**

carry-on＝機内持ち込み手荷物

11 手荷物検査にひっかかりました。

I didn't pass the security check.

12 アルコール飲料やたばこ、香水を持っていますか？

Do you have any alcoholic beverages, tobacco or perfume?

💡 税関でこう聞かれることも。

13 手荷物に小さなはさみが入っていますね。

You have small scissors in your hand baggage.

💡 「眉をカットするためのはさみです」は The're for cutting my eyebrows.

14 ナイフは一切、客室には持ち込めません。

You're not allowed to carry any kind of knife onboard.

allów [アラウ]＝許す

15 ナイフは、預ける荷物には入れることができたのですが。

You could have kept the knife in your checked baggage.

16 では、そのカッターナイフを放棄します。

I'll give up my utility knife, then.

17 これでは、超過料金をお支払いいただくことになります。

This will result in to an excess charge.

result in ～＝～という結果になる

1 旅行

搭乗手続きをする

1 フライト予約の確認をしたいのですが。
👉 **I'd like to reconfirm my reservation.**

2 お名前と便名をどうぞ。
Your name and flight number, please.

3 何か申告するものはありますか？
Do you have anything to declare?

declare＝申告する

4 何の書類が必要ですか？
What kind of documents will I need?

document＝書類

5 その便は時間通りです。
The flight is on schedule.

on schedule＝時間通りに、予定通りに

6 上海行きのJAL241便にチェックインしたいのですが。
I'd like to check in for JAL 241 to Shanghai.

7 これが航空券です。
Here's my ticket.

= Here you are.

8 パスポートをお見せください。
Please show me your passport.

9 入国記録カードを拝見したいのですが。
May I see your landing card, please?

10 お席は、通路側と窓側のどちらにいたしましょうか？
Would you like an aisle or a window seat?

áisle［アイル］＝通路側

11 通路側の席がいいです。
I'd like an aisle seat.

12 通路側は満席です。
All the aisle seats are full.

13 オンライン・チェックインシステムを導入する航空会社が増えてきましたね。
A growing number of airlines have introduced an online check-in system.

14 香港行きに乗り継ぎます。
I'll change planes to Hong Kong.

15 キャンセル待ちをしたいのですが。
Could you put me on the waiting list?

standby

16 列にお並びください。
Wait in line, please.

17 飛行機は定刻に出発しますか？
Will the plane take off as scheduled?

take off＝離陸する、出発する

搭乗手続きをする

18 ええ。予定通りです。
Yes. It's going to take off on time.
on time＝時間通りに

19 台風の影響で、すべての便が欠航です。
All the flights are canceled because of the typhoon.

20 再開の見通しは立っていないそうだ。
They say they still have no idea when normal flights will resume.
resume＝再開する

21 搭乗開始は何時からですか？
What time does boarding start?

22 搭乗は何番ゲートからですか？
From which gate do I board?

23 ご搭乗ありがとうございます。
Welcome aboard!

24 お土産、楽しみにしているよ。
I'm looking forward to the souvenirs.
sòuvenir [スーヴェニア]＝お土産

25 楽しい旅を！
☞ **Have a nice trip!**

26 お見送り、ありがとう。
Thank you for coming to see me off.
see（人）off ＝（人）を見送る

1 旅行

機内で

1 サインが消えるまで、シートベルトは締めたままでお願いします。

Please keep your seat belts fastened until the seat belt light is turned off. fasten＝締める　turn off＝消す

2 どうかなさいましたか？

☞ **Are you feeling okay?**

→ 気分が悪そうな人に声をかけるときの決まり文句。

3 すみませんが、シートベルトの締め方を教えてください。

Excuse me. Show me how to fasten my seat belt.

4 シートベルトをお締めになり、お手洗いの使用はご遠慮くださいませ。

Please fasten your seat belts, and kindly refrain from using the restrooms. refrain from ～＝～を控える、やめる

5 恐れ入りますが、もう一度シートベルトをお確かめくださいますようお願いします。

Please make certain your seat belt is fastened. make certain＝(よく)確かめる

6 私のかばんを棚に入れていただけますか？

Could you put my bag into the overhead compartment? overhead compartment＝(上にある)手荷物入れ

7 離着陸時はパソコンの使用をお控えください。

You're prohibited from using your laptop during take-off and landing.

8 座席を元にお戻しいただけますか？

Could you put your seat upright?

put ～ upright＝～を垂直にする

1 旅行

機内で

9 当機はまもなく離陸いたします。
We'll soon take off.

10 機内食は、いつかな？
When will the in-flight meals be served?

in-flight meal＝機内食

11 牛肉になさいますか、それとも魚になさいますか？
Would you like beef or fish?

💬「牛肉をお願いします」は Beef, please.

12 お飲み物はいかがですか？
Would you like anything to drink?

💬「コーヒーをください」は Coffee, please.

13 スパークリングワインはありますか？
Can I have sparkling wine?

14 温かい飲み物はありますか？
Do you have any hot drinks?

🔵 毛布 a blanket

15 機内は乾燥しているね。
It's dry in the plane.

16 のどが、からからだ。
I'm really thirsty.

thirsty＝のどが渇く

17 テレビが壊れているようです。
☞ **The TV set seems to be out of order.**

out of order＝故障して

18 まもなく映画が始まります。

The in-flight movie starts soon.

in-flight movie＝機内映画

19 座席を倒してもいいですか？

☞ **May I recline my seat?**

❗ 後ろの人に声をかけるときに使う。

20 トイレは今、使えますか？

Can I use the restroom now?

21 トイレは今、使用中ですね。

The restroom is occupied.

22 海外に行くと、時差ぼけと下痢に必ず悩まされます。

Whenever I go abroad, I suffer from jet lag and diarrhea.

jet lag＝時差ぼけ　diarrhéa［ダイアリーア］＝下痢

23 香港への到着予定は何時ですか？

What time are we expected to arrive at Hong Kong?

be expected to ～＝～することが予測される、～するはずだ

24 当機は定刻通り到着予定です。

The plane will get in on time.

25 現地時間は何時ですか？

☞ **What's the local time?**

26 これより着陸体勢に入ります。

We're beginning our landing approach.

旅行

機内で

1 旅行

入国審査

1 職業は何ですか？
What's your occupation?

occupation＝職業

2 旅行の目的は何ですか？
What's the purpose of your trip?

visit

3 観光です。
I'm here on vacation.

🔄 仕事 business

4 滞在予定はどのくらいですか？
How long do you intend to stay?

💡「およそ3週間です」は For about three weeks.

5 どこに滞在する予定ですか？
Where are you staying?

💡「ロンドンのABCホテルです」は At ABC Hotel in London.

6 両手の人さし指を機械に押し当ててください。
Please press both your index fingers on this machine.

index finger＝人さし指

7 税関へ行ってください。
Please go to customs.

customs＝税関

8 申告するものはありません。
☞ **I don't have anything to declare.**

9 申告書です。
Here's my declaration.

10 荷物引換券と搭乗券をどうぞ。
Here are your claim tags and your boarding card.

11 荷物はどこで受け取れますか？
Where do I pick up my baggage?

12 カートはどこですか？
Where are the baggage carts?

13 荷物が出てこなかったのですが。
☞ **My baggage didn't come out.**

14 制限を超えた荷物の料金はいくらですか？
What are the charges for excess baggage?

15 両替したいのですが。
I'd like to change some money.

16 両替所はどこですか？
Where's the money exchange counter?

money exchange counter＝両替所

17 5万円をドルに両替してください。
I'd like to change 50,000 yen into dollars, please.

1 旅行

入国審査

18 今日の換算レートはどのくらいですか？
What's today's exchange rate?

exchange rate＝換算レート

19 手数料はどのくらいかかりますか？
How much commission do you charge?

commission＝手数料

20 ホテルまではどのくらいかかりますか？
How long does it take to get to the hotel?

21 エアポートバスはどこから出ていますか？
Where do airport buses leave?

22 バスの運賃はいくらですか？
How much is the bus fare?

23 空港からABCホテルまでは、いくらかかりますか？
What's the fare from the airport to ABC Hotel?

24 DDCレンタカーはどこですか？
Where's the office for DDC Rent-A-Car?

25 快適なフライトだったね。
It was a really smooth flight.

↩ 長い long

26 少し、乗り物酔いしたみたい。
I felt a little airsick.

1 旅行

ホテルにチェックインする

1 やっとホテルに着いた。
We've finally reached the hotel.

2 ようこそ、ABCホテルへ。
Welcome to ABC Hotel.

3 ツインの部屋を予約してあります。
We have a reservation for a twin.

4 予約した川崎です。チェックインをお願いします。
My name is Kawasaki. I'd like to check in, please.

5 宿泊カードにご記入ください。
Plese fill out the visitor's card.

fill out=記入する

6 アメリカンエクスプレスのトラベラーズチェックは使えますか？
Do you take American Express traveler's checks?

7 お部屋は304号室になります。
Your room number is 304.

8 荷物をお願いします。
Take my baggage, please.

1 旅行

ホテルでくつろぐ

CD3 Track 58

1 私あてにメッセージは届いていますか？

Are there any messages for me?

2 ドアを閉めたらオートロックになります。

It automatically locks when you shut the door.

3 セーフティボックスを利用したいのですが。

I'd like to use the safe.

safe＝金庫、貴重品保管庫

4 何なりとフロントまでお申し付けください。

Please ask for anything you need at the front desk.

5 レストランはどこですか？

Where's the dining room?

❗ ホテル内のレストランなので restaurant より dining room がよい。

6 売店の営業時間は、午前8時から午後10時です。

The hotel shop is open from 8 a.m. to 10 p.m.

7 部屋でインターネットを使えますか？

☞ **Do I have an Internet connection in my room?**

8 ここの代金は、部屋につけておいていただけますか？

Could you charge this to my room?

9 伝票にサインをお願いします。

Please sign your name on the check.

10 ここでは、ちょっとしたカジノが楽しめるみたいだね。

They have a little casino here.

11 民族舞踊のショーも楽しみだ。

I'm looking forward to the folk dance show.

12 このホテルのエステは評判だよ。

The beauty-treatment clinic at this hotel has a good reputation.

reputation＝評判

13 眠くなるまで、バーでカクテルでもどう？

How about having cocktails at the lounge bar until we feel sleepy?

cócktàil [カクテイル]

14 ルームサービスは、まだやっていますか？

Is room service still available?

15 クリーニングをお願いします。

I'd like laundry service.

láundry [ローンドゥリ]

16 レンタカーの手配をお願いできますか？

Can I get a rental car at the hotel?

17 目覚ましは、ベッド脇の時計でセットできます。

You can use the alarm clock next to your bed.

1 旅行
ホテルでのトラブル

1 鍵を部屋に置いたまま、ロックしてしまいました。
☞ **I've locked my key in my room.**

2 鍵をどこかで失くしてしまいました。
I lost my key somewhere.

3 セーフティボックスが開きません。
I can't open the safe.

4 暗証番号を押してください。
Please enter your PIN number.

PIN number＝暗証番号

5 お湯が出ません。
I can't get any hot water.

6 お風呂があふれて、床が水浸しです。
The bathtub is running over and the floor is flooded.

7 トイレがつまってしまいました。
The toilet is clogged.

clogged＝(管などが)詰まった

8 インターネットに接続できません。
I can't connect to the Internet.

connect＝接続する

9 エアコンの調子が悪いのですが。

Something's wrong with the air-conditioner.

「クーラー」は和製英語。air conditioner で「冷房」と「暖房」の両方を表現できる。

10 すぐに直りますか？

Will it be repaired soon?

repair＝修理する

11 少し時間がかかります。

It'll take a while.

12 隣の部屋がうるさくて眠れません。

The room next door is too noisy for me to sleep.

next door＝隣の

13 部屋を替えてもらえますか？

I'd like to ask for a different room, please.

14 医者を呼んでください。

Please call a doctor.

「薬はありますか？」は Do you have medicine?

15 熱があります。

I have a fever.

16 氷と水を持ってきてください。

Please bring some ice and water.

17 平熱に下がりました。

My fever is down to normal.

normal＝標準　＊ここでは熱の標準で「平熱」。

― 1 旅行 ―

― ホテルでのトラブル ―

1 旅行

ホテルをチェックアウトする

CD3 Track 60

1 チェックアウトをお願いします。
I'd like to check out, please.

2 冷蔵庫の飲み物を飲みました。
I had some drinks from the mini-bar.

3 クレジットカードを見せていただけますか？
Could I have your credit card?

4 支払いはトラベラーズチェックでもいいですか？
Could I pay by traveler's check?

5 チェックアウト後の2時間ほど、スーツケースを預かっていただけますか？
Can I leave my suitcase here for two hours after check-out?

leave＝残す、置きっぱなしにする

6 最寄りの駅はどこですか？
Where's the nearest station?

the nearest station＝最寄りの駅

7 歩いて行けますか？
☞ **Is it close enough to walk there?**

8 歩いて20分くらいです。
It's about 20 minutes on foot.

on foot＝歩いて

1 旅行

街を楽しむ

1 この街の地図はありますか？
Do you have a local map?

2 一番の繁華街はどこですか？
Where is the most famous shopping area?

3 ロックフェラー・センターまでお願いします。
Please take me to Rockefeller Center.
take me to ～＝私を～へ連れて行く

4 お釣りは結構です。
☞ **Please keep the change.**

5 ロックフェラー・センターのクリスマスツリーを見逃さないでください。
Please don't miss the Rockefeller Center Christmas tree.
miss＝見逃す

6 セントラルパークまで、歩いて何分かかりますか？
How long does it take to get to Central Park on foot?
タクシーで by taxi

7 公園の中に自動販売機はありますか？
Are there any vending machines in the park?

8 今晩のブロードウェイ・ミュージカルのチケットは、どこで買えますか？
Could you tell me where I can buy a ticket to tonight's Broadway musical?

1 | 旅行
観光名所を訪れる

1 観光案内のパンフレットはありますか？
Do you have a sightseeing brochure?
brochúre [ブロウシャ]

2 この地域の見所を教えてください。
Tell me about the tourist attractions in this area.

3 観光案内所はどこですか。
Where's the tourist information center?
tourist information center＝観光案内所

4 観光案内所に問い合わせてください。
Please contact the tourist information office.

5 日本語の案内はありますか？
Do you have information in Japanese?

6 日本語が話せる観光ガイドさんはいますか？
Is there a sightseeing guide who speaks Japanese?

7 なんて美しい建物なんだ！
This building is so beautiful!

8 夢にまで見た風景だ。
It's like a dream.

9 一度でいいから見たかったんだ。

☞ **I wanted to see it just once.**

just once＝一度でいいから

10 京都といえば金閣寺だね。

When it comes to Kyoto, Kinkakuji Temple is worth visiting.

11 清水寺も忘れちゃいけないよ。

We can't miss Kiyomizu Temple.

can't miss 〜＝〜を見逃すわけにはいかない

12 あの像を背景に、私の写真を撮っていただけますか？

Could you take a picture of me with the statue in the background? with 〜 in the background＝〜を背景に

13 一緒に写真に入っていただけませんか？

Could you get in the picture with me?

14 このボタンを押すだけです。

All you have to do is push this button.

15 入場料はかかりますか？

Do I need to pay an entrance fee?

entrance fee＝入場料

16 市内観光のツアーはありますか？

Are there any tours of the city?

17 夜のツアーバスを手配していただけますか？

Can you arrange for a night tour bus?

1 旅行

お土産を買う

1 この辺にお土産屋さんはありますか？
☞ **Is there a souvenir shop around here?**

2 近くに観光客向けのショッピングセンターがあります。
There's a shopping center for tourists near here.

3 お土産を見たいのですが。
I'd like to see some souvenirs.

4 これは友人へのお土産です。
It's a souvenir for a friend of mine.

5 お土産屋さんにお連れします。
I can take you shopping for souvenirs.

6 どんなお土産がいいですか？
What kind of souvenirs would you like?

7 何かもう、決めてるの？
☞ **Do you have anything in mind?**

8 少し珍しいものが欲しいです。
I want something a little unusual.

9 この地方の特産品がおすすめです。

I recommend some products from this area.

10 このお土産はどうですか？

How about this gift?

11 これは、かさばるな。

These are really bulky.

bulky=大きい、かさばる

12 妻へのお土産には、何がいいでしょうか？

What kind of souvenirs for my wife would you recommend?

13 彼女のお気に入りのブランドを思い出しているところです。

I'm trying to remember her favorite brand.

14 お土産の予算はどのくらいですか？

How much do you want to spend on souvenirs?

15 まだお土産を買う時間はありますか？

Do we have enough time to buy souvenirs?

16 このおもちゃは、何歳用ですか？

What age is this toy for?

17 税金払い戻しの方法を教えてください。

Tell me how to get a tax refund.

réfund [リーファンド]

1 旅行

国連見学ツアーに参加する

CD3 Track 64

1 国連ビルへは何線で行けますか？

Which line goes to the United Nations Headquarters?

2 国連ビルは何時まで開いていますか？

How late is the United Nations Headquarters open? 🟰 What time dose the United Nations Headquarters close?

3 見学者センターは午前9時から午後5時半まで開いています。

The Visitors Center is open from 9 a.m. to 5:30 p.m.

4 見学の入場は午後4時45分までです。

The visitors' entrance closes at 4:45 p.m.

5 見学ツアーは、数か国語で行われています。

Tours are offered in several languages.

several＝いくつかの

6 15名以上のグループは、メールか電話で予約しなければなりません。

Groups of 15 or more should reserve their tour by either e-mail or by phone.

15 or more＝15以上

7 日本語のツアーは、申し出てください。

A tour in Japanese is available upon request.

8 日本語のツアーは30分ごとに始まります。

Tours in Japanese depart every half hour.

every ～＝～ごとに、～おきに

9 ツアーのチケットを、チケット売り場で買ってください。

Please purchase your tour tickets at the cashier's desk.

púrchase [パーチェス] ＝購入する

10 5歳未満の子どもはツアーに参加できません。

Children under five years of age are not permitted on the tour.

permit＝許す

11 英語のツアーを、大人2枚ください。

Two adults for the tour in English, please.

12 ツアーの所要時間はどのくらいですか？

☞ **How long does the tour last?**

last＝続く

13 講演会は、個人客でも聞くことができますか？

Can an individual attend lectures?

indivídual [インディヴィジュアル] ＝個人的な

14 国連ギフトショップはどこですか？

Where is the UN gift shop?

UN＝United Nations＝国連

15 国連ギフトショップのほかに、ユニセフショップがありますよ。

There's also a UNICEF gift shop, in addition to the UN gift shop.

in addition to 〜＝〜に加えて

16 国連の組織について教えてくださり、ありがとうございます。

Thank you very much for telling us about the UN organization.

17 見学ツアーにご満足いただけてうれしいです。

I'm glad that you liked the tour.

1 旅行
旅先でのアクシデント

1 トラブルに巻き込まれました。
I got involved in a complicated situation.

get involved in ～=～に巻き込まれる　complicated=複雑な

2 事故に遭いました。
I just had an accident.

3 体調を崩してしまいました。
I felt out of sorts.

feel out of sorts=体調を崩す

4 どうすればいいのか、わかりません。
☞ **I don't know what to do.**

5 事故の様子を説明してください。
Would you tell me about the accident?

6 仲間とはぐれてしまいました。
I got separated from my companions.

get separated from ～=～とはぐれる

7 財布をすられました。
I've been pickpocketed.

be pickpocketed=すられる

8 お金を使いすぎました。
I spent too much money.

9 その人をつかまえて！
Stop that man!

10 ひったくりに遭いました。
My bag got snatched.

snatch＝ひったくる

11 大使館に行ったほうがいいよ。
You should go to the embassy.

embassy＝大使館

12 ホテルの部屋にパスポートを置き忘れました。
I left my passport in my room at the hotel.

13 飛行機のトラブルのせいでフライトが遅れた。
The flight was delayed due to trouble with the airplane.

due to ～＝～のせいで、～が原因で

14 荷物が行方不明なんです。
My baggage is lost.

15 この路線、事故のせいで不通なんだって。
The line is suspended because of the accident.

suspend＝一時的に止める、不通にする

16 緊急です！
It's an emergency!

17 警察を呼んでください！
Call the police!

救急車 an ambulance

1 旅行

旅先でのアクシデント

2 公共の場所
初めての街で

1 道に迷っちゃった！
I got lost!

2 おまわりさんに道をたずねよう。
I'll ask the policeman how to get there.

3 駅へはどう行けばいいですか？
How can I get to the station?

4 タクシーで行ったほうがいいですよ。
You should grab a taxi.

grab a taxi＝タクシーをつかまえる

5 歩いて行ける距離ではないのですね。
It's not within walking distance, is it?

6 歩いて30分はかかります。
It takes about 30 minutes on foot.

🔄 車で by car／電車で by train

7 この辺りにコンビニエンスストアはありますか？
Is there a convenience store near here?

8 すぐそこですよ。
It's really close to here.

9 行きすぎてますよ。

You went too far.

> 「少し戻ってください」と言うなら Please go back a little.

10 最初の信号を右です。

Turn right at the first traffic light.

11 歩道橋を渡ってください。

Walk over the overpass.

overpass＝歩道橋

12 そうすると、人通りの多い道に出ます。

Then you'll come to a busy street.

13 道なりに進んでください。

Just follow the street.

14 何か目印になるものはありますか？

☞ Are there any landmarks?

landmark＝目印

15 郵便局の向かいです。

It's across from the post office.

> 「反対側にコンビニがあります」は A convenience store is on the opposite side.

16 一緒に行きましょう。

I'll walk with you.

17 土地のものではないんです。

I'm not from here either.

2 公共の場所

バスに乗る

1 そこに行くには、バスが一番便利よ。
Buses are the best way to get there.

2 バスが来たよ。
Here comes the bus.

3 このバスはどこ行きですか?
Where does this bus go?

4 このバスは渋谷駅に行きますか?
Will this bus take me to Shibuya Station?

5 どこでバスを降りたらいいですか?
☞ **Would you tell me where to get off the bus?**

6 空港行きのバス乗り場はどこですか?
Where's the stop for the bus to the airport?

7 バスターミナルは、交差点を過ぎた3番目のビルです。
The bus terminal is the third building past the intersection.

8 高速バスが安くて便利だよ。
The highway express bus is cheap and convenient.

2 公共の場所

タクシーを拾う

1 タクシーはどこで拾えますか？

Where can I get a taxi?

2 どちらまで？

Where to, sir?

> 相手が「女性」の場合は madam？

3 新宿駅の南口までお願いします。

I'd like to go to the south entrance of Shinjuku Station.

4 時間がかかりそうですか？

Is it going to be a long ride?

5 渋滞ですね。

The roads are jammed.

> 「渋滞に巻き込まれた」は We got caught in heavy traffic.

6 この辺はいつも込んでいるんですよ。

This area is always busy.

> busy＝にぎやかな、車(人)が多い

7 次の信号で停めていただけますか？

Could you pull over at the next light?

> pull over＝車を止める、路肩に寄せる

8 ここで降ろしてください。

Let me (get) off here, please.

2 公共の場所

駅の構内で

1 東京まで、往復で1枚ください。
A round-trip ticket for Tokyo, please.

2 禁煙車でお願いします。
A non-smoking car, please.

3 始発は何時ですか？
What time is the first train?

↳ 終電 the last train

4 何番線から出ますか？
☞ **Which track does the train leave from?**

track＝プラットホーム

5 新幹線は5時30分発です。
The Shinkansen leaves at 5:30.

❗「新幹線」を bullet train（弾丸列車）と表すこともあるが、通常は Shinkansen（train）

6 電車が来たよ。
There's a train coming.

7 黄色い線の後ろに下がってください。
Please stay behind the yellow line.

8 この電車は秋葉原に行きますか？
Does this train go to Akihabara?

9 この電車は、途中までしか行きません。

This train only goes midway.

10 電車は2、3分前に出ました。

The train left a couple of minutes ago.

a couple of 〜＝2、3の〜

11 この電車は急行ですか、各駅停車ですか？

☞ **Is this an express or a local train?**

local train＝各駅停車

12 快速電車はその駅には止まりません。

The rapid train doesn't stop at that station.

rapid train＝快速電車

13 各駅停車に乗らないと。

You have to take a local train.

14 次の駅で地下鉄に乗り換えてください。

Please change to the subway at the next station.

15 地下鉄のほうが早いですよ。

The subway is faster.

16 事故の影響で、この電車の発車は遅れる見込みです。

This train will be delayed due to the accident.

17 車内放送で案内があります。

You can get information from the train announcement.

train announcement＝車内放送

2 公共の場所

病院の受付で

1. 診察を受けたいのですが。
I want to see a doctor.

2. 初診です。
This is my first visit to this hospital.

3. 予約しています。
I have an appointment.

4. 予約はしていませんが、すぐに見ていただけませんか？
I don't have an appointment. But could I see the doctor right away?

5. 治療は予約制ですか？
Are consultations by appointment?

6. 外来受付は午前中のみです。
The clinic is open for outpatients only in the morning.
outpatient＝外来患者

7. お連れの方はいらっしゃいますか？
Is anyone with you today?

8. 保険証を見せてください。
May I see your medical insurance card?
medical insurance card＝保険証　＊insurance card と略すこともある。

9 健康保険に入っています。

I have medical insurance.

medical insurance＝健康保険　＊家族の誰かと一緒に来た場合、主語は we になる。

10 保険証がない場合は、自費診療となります。

Without your insurance card, you'll have to pay for the treatment yourself.

treatment＝治療

11 窓口にある箱に診察券を入れてください。

Put your hospital card in the box at the counter.

hospital card＝診察券

12 診察券を忘れました。

I forgot my registration card.

13 どのくらい待ちますか？

How long do I have to wait?

14 名前、生年月日、住所をご記入ください。

Please write your name, date of birth, and present address.

present address＝現住所

15 何科にかかりたいのですか？

Which department would you like to see?

16 皮膚科はありますか？

Does this hospital have a dermatology department?

dermatology＝皮膚科

17 以前のレントゲン写真や検査結果などありましたら、お預かりします。

If you have any X-rays or other medical data, please show them to us.

2 公共の場所

病院の受付で

18 では、内科を受診してください。
Okay, go to the Department of Internal Medicine, please.

◎外科 Surgery

19 インフルエンザの予防接種は1週間前に受けました。
I had a flu shot a week ago.

shot＝皮下注射、予防接種

20 病院で処方された薬を常飲しています。
I'm currently taking some medicine prescribed by my doctor.

21 どんな薬ですか？
What kind of medicine?

22 何かアレルギーはありますか？
☞ **Are you allergic to anything?**

allérgic［アラーヂック］

23 合わない薬はありますか？
Have you had any reactions to medicine?

24 今までに大きな病気はされたことはありますか？
Have you had any serious illnesses before?

serious illness＝重病、大きな病気

25 体がだるいです。
I feel exhausted.

＝I feel heavy.

26 輸血を受けたことはありますか？
Have you ever had a blood transfusion?

blood transfusion＝輸血

2 公共の場所

診察を受ける

1 どのような症状ですか？
What seems to be wrong?

2 ちょっと熱があって。
I have a slight fever.

slight＝少しの、わずかな　fever＝熱

3 咳をすると胸が痛むんです。
I have a chest pain when I cough.

cóugh [コフ] ＝咳をする

4 いつからですか？
When did it start?

5 手がずっとしびれています。
My hands have been numb for quite a while.

númb [ナム] ＝まひした、しびれた

6 動悸が激しくて。
I have strong palpitations.

pàlpitátion [パルピテイション] ＝動悸

7 咳が止まりません。
I can't stop coughing.

8 熱湯で、右足にやけどをしました。
I burned my right foot with hot water.

burn＝(体の部分に)やけどをさせる

9 めまいがします。
I feel dizzy.

dizzy＝めまいがする

10 鼻がつまっちゃって。
My nose is clogged.

clogged＝詰まった

11 息苦しいんです。
I have difficulty breathing.

have difficulty ～ing＝～するのが困難である　＊I feel choked. という表現もある。

12 胃が痛くて。
I have a stomachache.

💡「胃がむかむかします」は I feel sick to my stomach.

13 どのように痛みますか？
What kind of pain is it?

14 空腹時にとても痛みます。
When hungry, I feel a strong pain.

pain＝痛み

15 どこが悪いのでしょうか、先生。
☞ **What do I have, doctor?**

16 たいしたことないですよ。
I don't think it's anything serious.

💡「ご心配なく」は Don't worry.

17 おそらく、飲みすぎと食べすぎでしょう。
Maybe you ate and drank too much.

2 公共の場所

検査を受ける

1 検査を受ける必要がありますか？
Do I need to have a physical checkup?

2 どんな検査をするのでしょうか？
What kind of medical tests should I have?

3 尿検査をします。
We'll check your urine.

úrine[ユーリン]＝尿

4 X線検査と血液検査を行います。
We'll give you an X-ray and a blood test.

X-ray＝X線

5 心電図をとります。
We need to give you an electrocardiogram.

electrocardiogram＝心電図

6 精密検査を受けたほうがいいですね。
You'll need to give you further tests.

7 検査の前日は、夜8時以降、水以外のものは飲食しないでください。
Don't eat or drink anything, except water after 8 p.m. the night before the test.

8 検査結果はいつ出ますか？
When can I get the results?

＝ When will I get the results?

2 公共の場所
手術を受ける

1 手術の手順について説明します。
Let me explain the operation procedure.
operation＝手術　procedure＝手順

2 手術は初めてです。
I've never had surgery before.
surgery＝手術

3 抗がん剤は使いますか？
Will you be using cancer drugs?

4 これは手術同意書です。
This is an operation consent form.
consent form＝同意書

5 手術は痛いでしょうか？
Will the procedure be painful?
❗ procedure は operation procedure（手術の工程）を省略したもの。

6 手術の時間はどのくらいかかりますか？
How long will the operation take?

7 ペニシリンにアレルギーがあります。
I'm allergic to penicillin.

8 この手術は腫瘍を取り除くものです。
This surgery is to remove your tumor.
tumor＝腫瘍

9 全身麻酔ですか？

Will I be given a general anesthetic?

general anesthetic＝全身麻酔

10 局所麻酔の手術となります。

You'll be under local anesthetic.

local anesthetic＝局所麻酔

11 何か後遺症が残りますか？

Will there be any after-effects?

12 また歩けるようになるまで、どのくらいかかりますか？

How long will it take for me to walk again?

13 ご心配はいりません。

There's no need to worry.

14 麻酔は2時間ほどで切れます。

The anesthetic will wear off in about two hours.

15 このチューブでお腹にたまった血液を出します。

This tube will drain the excess blood from your abdomen.

drain＝排出する　ábdomen [アブダメン]＝腹部

16 合併症が起こらないように、しっかり監視しますからね。

We'll closely monitor you for any signs of complications.

monitor＝監視する　complication＝合併症

17 傷口は痛みますか？

☞ **Is the incision painful?**

incision＝傷口

2 公共の場所

入院する

1 こちらが入院案内です。
This is a pamphlet for your hospitalization.
hospitalization＝入院

2 持ち物はこの案内に書いてあります。
Items that you'll need are in this guide.

3 よくお読みください。
Please read it through thoroughly.
thóroughly［ソーロウリ］＝完全に、徹底的に

4 これに記入して、入院窓口に提出すればいいのですね？
Should I fill in this form and take it to the admission's desk?
fill in ～＝～に記入する

5 保証人の署名が必要ですか？
Do you need a guarantor's signature?
guarantor＝保証人

6 入院日は4月2日です。
You'll be admitted to the hospital on April 2.

7 入院期間はどのくらいですか？
☞ **How long will I be hospitalized?**

8 消灯は午後10時です。
Lights go out at 10 p.m.

9 緊急時は、このボタンを押せばよいのですか？

Should we press this button in an emergency?

in an emergency＝緊急時

10 今日から入浴してもいいですよ。

You can start taking baths from today.

11 来週の月曜日に退院できます。

You can leave the hospital next Monday.

12 1週間後に外来に来ればいいですか？

Should I come to the outpatient clinic a week from now?

13 定期的に診察を受けたほうがいいのですね？

Should I see a doctor regularly for checkups?

14 次の予約は、3月5日になっています。

Your next appointment is scheduled for March 5.

15 バランスのよい食事をとってくださいね。

Try to eat a balanced diet.

diet＝食事、食生活

16 3日後に抜糸します。

We'll remove the stitches in three days.

17 お酒は控えてください。

Please refrain from drinking.

refrain from ～ing＝～するのをやめる

2 公共の場所

お見舞い

1 今日は、どなたにご面会ですか？
Who are you visiting today?

2 面会時間内に、またお越しください。
Please come again during visiting hours.

3 渡辺さんは何号室でしょうか？
What room is Mr. Watanabe in, please?

4 田中さんは検査中です。
Mr. Tanaka is taking medical tests.

5 30分くらいで戻ります。
He'll be back in about half an hour.

6 高橋さんは現在、面会謝絶です。
Mr. Takahashi is not allowed visitors at this time.

7 お見舞いに来てくれてありがとう。
☞ **Thank you for coming to see me.**

8 元気そうで安心したよ。
You look fine. What a relief!

9 顔色がよくなったね。
Now you have a nice complexion!

complexion＝顔色、肌の色

10 入院生活はどう？
How's the hospital care?

11 病院の食事にはうんざりだよ。
I'm getting tired of hospital food.

tired of ～＝～にうんざりして

12 ずっと点滴しているんだよ。
I've been getting IVs constantly.

IV＝intravenous＝点滴

13 ゆっくり休んで完全に治してくださいね。
Take your time and recover fully.

14 今度来るときに持ってきて欲しいものはある？
What should I bring you the next time I come?

15 いつ退院できるの？
When will you be able to leave the hospital?

＝ When can you leave the hospital?

16 また会いに来るよ。
I'll be back to see you.

17 早くよくなるように祈っています。
I hope you get better soon.

2 公共の場所

歯医者さんで

CD4 Track 11

1 歯が痛いのですが。
I have a toothache.

2 虫歯ですか?
☞ **A cavity?**

cavity＝虫歯

3 歯茎から血が出ているんです。
My gums are bleeding.

gums＝歯茎

4 詰め物が取れちゃったんです。
My filling came out.

filling＝詰め物

5 娘さんは歯の矯正が必要ですね。
Your daughter needs to have braces.

braces＝(歯)矯正器

6 口を開けたままにしてください。
Please keep your mouth open.

7 歯を抜きます。
We have to pull out your tooth.

pull out＝抜く

8 口をすすいでください。
Please rinse your mouth.

rinse＝すすぐ

2 公共の場所

薬を買う

1 この辺に薬局はありますか？

Is there a drugstore around here?

2 胃薬をください。

I'd like something for my stomach.

3 処方箋がなくても購入できる痛み止めはありますか？

Can I get a painkiller without a prescription?

prescription＝処方箋

4 この薬を飲んだあとは、車の運転を控えてください。

Please don't drive after taking this medicine.

take medicine＝薬を飲む　＊薬の場合 drink ではなく take を使う。

5 副作用で、眠気を感じることがあります。

A less common side effect of the medicine is drowsiness.

drowsiness＝眠気

6 飲むのは食後ですか？

☞ **Do I take this medicine after meals?**

7 錠剤は1日に3回、食後に2錠ずつ飲んでください。

Take two tablets three times a day after every meal.

tablet＝錠剤

8 カプセルは食前に1錠飲んでください。

Take one of the capsules before eating.

2 公共の場所

銀行

1 口座を開きたいのですが。

I'd like to open an account here.

account＝口座

2 どのような口座がありますか？

What kind of accounts do you have?

💡 「普通預金」は saving account、「定期預金」は fixed account、「積立預金」は installment deposit

3 6か月定期にします。

I want a six-month fixed deposit.

4 利息はどのくらいつきますか？

How much interest does it earn?

interest＝利息

5 100万円、引き出したいのですが。

I'd like to withdraw 1,000,000 yen from my account.

withdraw＝引き出す、下ろす

6 預金を解約したいのですが。

I'd like to cancel the deposits.

cancel＝解約する

7 通帳とお届け印をお持ちですか？

Do you have the deposit certificate and your personal seal?

deposit certificate＝預金証書　personal seal＝印鑑

8 公共料金を口座振替にしたいのですが。

I'd like to pay my utility bills by automatic transfer.

utility bill＝公共料金　automatic transfer＝自動振替

9 郵便局に振込みをしたいのですが。

I'd like to make a transfer into my post office account.

transfer＝振り込む

10 送金手数料はいくらですか？

How much is the remittance charge?

remittance charge＝送金手数料

11 今の時間、ATMは使えますか？

Are the ATMs available now?

ATMは automated teller machine の略。

12 ATMを使えば、手数料が割安です。

There's a cheaper charge for using an ATM.

13 ATMで、1日にいくらまで引き出せますか？

How much is the daily withdrawal limit at an ATM?

14 振り込め詐欺には注意してください。

Beware of remittance fraud.

remittance fraud＝振り込め詐欺　＊remittance＝送金、fraud＝詐欺。

15 インターネットバンキングも利用できます。

You can bank online.

16 融資の相談にのっていただけますか？

I'd like to talk to someone about a loan.

17 住宅ローンの借り換えをおすすめします。

We suggest that you refinance your mortgage.

refinance＝借り換える　mortgage＝住宅ローン

公共の場所

銀行

2 公共の場所
役所・警察署

1 住民課はどこですか？
Where's the Resident Affairs Division?
Resident Affairs Division＝住民課

2 転入の手続きをしにきました。
I moved in and I need to register.
move in＝転入する ＊「転出する」は move out.

3 税金の申告をしたいのですが。
I'd like to file my taxes.
file＝申告する

4 婚姻届の用紙をいただけますか？
Could I have a marriage registration form?
離婚届 divorce registration form／死亡届 death report

5 代理人の方は委任状が必要です。
The agent needs power of attorney.
agent＝代理人　power of attorney＝委任状

6 印鑑証明書を2通ください。
May I have two copies of the seal notification?
seal notification＝印鑑証明書

7 外国人登録書が必要です。
You need to get an alien registration card.
alien registration card＝外国人登録書

8 パスポートはどこに申請するのですか？
Where can I apply for a passport?
apply for ～＝～を申請する

9 ビザの更新はどうすればいいですか？

What's the procedure for renewing a visa?

procedure＝手続き　renew＝更新する

10 日本大使館に連絡する必要があります。

I need to call the Japanese embassy.

embassy＝大使館

11 免許更新の手続きをお願いします。

I'd like to renew my driver's license.

12 視力検査を行ってください。

You need to take a vision test.

vision test＝視力検査

13 免許証の写真を撮影します。

We need to take a picture for your driver's license.

14 交通安全講習は10時に開かれます。

The traffic safety lecture will be at 10:00.

15 ストーカーをされているみたいなのですが。

Wherever I go, a guy follows me.

16 不審者を見かけたら、警察に電話をしてください。

Call the police if you see someone suspicious.

someone suspicious＝不審者

17 拘置されている息子を引き取りにきました。

I came to get my son who was detained.

be detained＝拘置される

2 公共の場所

郵便局

1 番号を呼ばれるまでお待ちください。
Please wait here until your number is called.

2 80円切手を10枚とハガキを5枚ください。
Can I have ten 80-yen stamps and five postcards, please?

3 これは定形外です。
This is a non-standard-sized item.

non-standard-sized item＝定形外

4 速達でお願いします。
I'd like to send this by express.

書留 registered mail

5 明日の午前中までに届きますか？
Will this be delivered by tomorrow morning?

deliver＝配達する

6 航空便ではいくらになりますか？
How much would it cost to send this by airmail?

7 不在通知が入っていたのですが、これから配達していただけますか？
I received a delivery notice. Could you deliver my package today?

delivery notice＝不在通知

8 記念切手はありますか？
Can I get commemorative stamps?

commemorative stamp＝記念切手

2 公共の場所
美術館・博物館・図書館

1 ここではお静かに願います。
Please be quiet here.

2 撮影は禁止されています。
Taking pictures is not permitted.

3 作品に手を触れないでください。
Don't touch the works.

work＝作品

4 順路に沿って、ご鑑賞ください。
Please look at the works of art along the way.

5 一列になって順番にお進みください。
Please move ahead in line.

in line＝一列になって

6 館内に飲食物は持ち込まないでください。
Don't take food or drink in the building.

7 本を探していただきたいのですが。
☞ **Would you help me look for a book?**

8 本は一度に5冊まで、2週間、借りることができます。
You can borrow a maximum of five books in two weeks.

3 冠婚葬祭、年中行事

結婚式に出席する

CD4 Track 17

1 田中君から結婚式の招待状が届いたよ。
I got a wedding invitation from Mr. Tanaka.

2 挙式は、6月にA教会で行われるそうだ。
The wedding will take place at A Church in June.
take place＝行われる

3 ご祝儀はいくら差し上げたらいいのかな？
How much gift money should we give?
gift money＝ご祝儀

4 同僚だから、3万円が相場かな。
I think my colleagues usually give 30,000 yen.
colleague＝同僚

5 スーツを新調しなくちゃ。
I should get a new suit.

6 お名前と住所をご記帳願います。
Would you write your name and address in the guest book?

7 新郎新婦の入場です。
The bride and groom are making their entrance.

8 友人代表としてスピーチをさせていただきます。
☞ **This speech is on behalf of the friends.**
on behalf of 〜＝〜を代表して

9 本日はお日柄もよく、ご結婚を心より祝福いたします。

Today is a lucky day, and I'd like to extend our best wishes on your marriage.

extend=述べる

10 心からお祝い申し上げます。

I congratulate you from the bottom of my heart.

11 本当にお似合いのお2人だと思います。

You look great together.

12 お2人の末永い幸せをお祈りいたします。

☞ **Long life and much happiness to you both.**

13 お2人の前途を祝して乾杯!

Here's to a happy future for you!

14 今日は来てくれて本当にありがとう。

Thank you very much for coming today.

15 とてもすばらしい式だったよ。

It was a wonderful wedding.

16 二次会もつき合ってくれる?

Are you also coming to the second party?

second party=二次会

17 もちろん、とことんつき合うよ。

Sure, I'll go with you to the finish.

to the finish=最後まで、とことん

3 冠婚葬祭、年中行事

成人する

1 成人式の日は1月の第2月曜日です。

Coming-of-Age Day is the second Monday of January.

Coming-of-Age Day＝成人の日

2 成人式は日本特有の儀式ですか？

Is the Coming-of-Age Ceremony something peculiar to Japan?

peculiar to 〜＝〜に特有の、独特の

3 成人おめでとう！

Happy Coming-of-Age Day!

4 今日から大人だね。

You're an adult from today.

5 お酒もたばこもOKだ。

I can drink and smoke.

6 アメリカでは選挙権は18歳からだよ。

In the United States, people have the right to vote from the age of 18.

right to vote＝選挙権

7 大人になった実感がわかないな。

It hasn't really hit me yet that I'm an adult.

hit＝思い浮かぶ

8 これからは自分の人生に責任を持たなくちゃ。

I'm responsible for my own life from now on.

be responsible for 〜＝〜に責任がある

3 冠婚葬祭、年中行事

先祖を祀る

CD4 Track 19

1 祖父が亡くなり、喪に服しています。
I'm in mourning for my grandfather.

2 母はお墓参りを欠かしません。
My mother never fails to visit his grave.
never fail to ～=必ず～する

3 ご先祖様を敬うのが日本の伝統です。
It's a Japanese tradition to respect ancestors.
respect=敬う

4 今日は父の三回忌です。
☞ **Today is the second anniversary of my father's death.**
anniversary=記念日

5 この本は父の形見なんです。
This book is a keepsake from my father.
keepsake=形見

6 彼は私の心の中に生きています。
He's alive in my heart.

7 多くの日本人はお盆に帰省します。
Many Japanese go back to their hometowns during the Bon Festival.

8 お盆には故人の霊が戻ってくるといわれています。
It is said that our ancestors' souls return during the Bon Festival.
ancestors=先祖

3 冠婚葬祭、年中行事

故人を悼む

1 昨日、父が亡くなりました。

My father passed away yesterday.

pass away＝亡くなる ＊die の婉曲的表現。

2 今日はお通夜でした。

A wake was held today.

wake＝通夜

3 お葬式は明日、お寺で行われます。

The funeral will be held at the temple tomorrow.

funeral＝葬式

4 故人の遺志により、葬儀は身内のみで行わせていただきます。

A private funeral will be held by request.

❶「故人の遺志により、供花の儀はご辞退申し上げます」は No flowers by request.

5 ご愁傷様でございます。

I'm very sorry.

＝ My sympathies.／My condolences.

6 心からお悔やみ申し上げます。

👉 Please accept my deepest sympathies.

❶「お悔やみをいただいて感謝しております」は I really appreciate your sympathy.

7 惜しい人を亡くしました。

This is a real loss.

＝ We've all suffered a great loss.

8 故人には大変お世話になりました。

👉 He was always very kind to me.

9 あんなにお元気そうだったのに。
He looked so healthy.

10 突然のことで、驚いています。
This is all too sudden.

sudden=突然の、思いがけない

11 逝くには若すぎますね。
He was too young to pass away.

12 やりたいことが、たくさんあっただろうに。
He had a lot of things left to do.

left=残された

13 立派な最期でした。
He died a dignified death.

dignified=堂々とした、威厳のある

14 お亡くなりになった原因は？
How did it happen?

15 彼は天寿をまっとうしたと思います。
He died of natural causes.

16 これから寂しくなりますね。
We're all going to miss him.

17 安らかなお顔ですね。
He has a peaceful face.

3 冠婚葬祭、年中行事

年中行事

1. 日本人にとって、お正月は最も大切な祝日です。

   New Year's Day is the most important holiday for Japanese.

   New Year's Day＝お正月、元旦

2. お正月には、様々な伝統行事が行われます。

   Various traditional events take place on New Year's Day.

3. 節分では、「鬼は外、福は内」と叫びながら豆をまきます。

   On Setsubun, people scatter beans as they shout "Fortune in and demons out!"

4. バレンタインには、男性は女性からチョコレートをもらえるかどうかが気になります。

   Men worry about not getting chocolates from women on Valentine's Day.

5. ひな祭りには、たくさんの伝統的な人形を飾ります。

   We display a lot of traditional dolls during Dolls' Festival.

6. 春には外でお花見を楽しみます。

   We enjoy cherry blossom viewing outdoors in the spring.

7. 5月には、子どもの健やかな成長を願って、鯉のぼりをたてます。

   We display carp streamers to pray for children's health and happiness in May.

8. 七夕には、願い事を短冊に書くと、かなうといわれています。

   Our wishes will come true if we write them on strips of paper on Tanabata.

9 8月は帰省ラッシュで、高速が渋滞します。

The highways are crowded with people heading back home in August. head back home＝故郷へ向かう、帰省する

10 夏祭りには盆踊りを踊ります。

Bon dances are held at summer festivals.

> 「夏祭りでは盆踊りが開かれます」の意味。

11 日本には四季折々の行事がたくさんあります。

There are a lot of events in each season in Japan. in each season＝季節ごとに

12 日本には満月を愛でる慣習があります。

There's a custom of admiring the full moon in Japan. custom＝慣習　admire＝愛でる

13 9月は台風のシーズンです。

September is the typhoon season.

14 秋にはよく運動会が開かれます。

Athletic meets often take place in autumn.

athletic meet＝運動会

15 7歳、5歳、3歳の子どもたちは、神社で七五三を祝います。

Children who are seven, five and three have a celebration at the shrines. celebration＝祝賀　shrine＝神社

16 年末には、新年を迎えるために大掃除をします。

At the end of the year, we clean the whole house to greet the new year. greet the new year＝新年を迎える

17 除夜の鐘を聞きながら新年を迎えます。

We ring in the new year and ring out the old year with temple bells.

3 冠婚葬祭、年中行事｜年中行事

- ●監修者紹介

佐々木 隆
[ささき たかし]

武蔵野学院大学教授。平成3年4月、武蔵野短期大学国際教養学科専任講師となる。平成19年度より、同大学院国際コミュニケーション研究科国際コミュニケーション専攻修士課程教授に。現在、大学院で言語コミュニケーション特殊講義や国際文化交流特殊講義、大学で英米文学史、国際文化交流、英語講読などを担当する傍ら、英学史や国際文化交流の観点から、シェイクスピア、ワイルドなどの日本への受容史を研究中。World Shakespeare Bibliography国際委員日本代表、日欧比較文化研究会会長。http://ssk.econfn.com/

- ●英文校正――――David A Thayne（デイビッド・セイン）　いしもとあやこ　エートゥーゼット
- ●イラスト――――しおたまこ
- ●デザイン――――嶋岡誠一郎（プレーンワークス）　満冨優子
- ●DTP――――明昌堂
- ●CD制作――――爽美録音株式会社
- ●ナレーション――ドミニク・アレン　ビアンカ・アレン　瀬戸奈保子　福島孝広
- ●制作協力――――編集室ビーライン
- ●編集協力――――スリーシーズン（花澤靖子）

ネイティブ英会話フレーズ集3240 スーパーCD4枚付き

- ●監修者――――佐々木 隆［ささき たかし］
- ●発行者――――若松 和紀
- ●発行所――――株式会社西東社
〒113-0034 東京都文京区湯島2-3-13
営業部：TEL（03）5800-3120　　FAX（03）5800-3128
編集部：TEL（03）5800-3121　　FAX（03）5800-3125
URL：http://www.seitosha.co.jp/

本書の内容の一部あるいは全部を無断でコピー、データファイル化することは、法律で認められた場合をのぞき、著作者及び出版社の権利を侵害することになります。
第三者による電子データ化、電子書籍化はいかなる場合も認められておりません。
落丁・乱丁本は、小社「営業部」宛にご送付ください。送料小社負担にて、お取替えいたします。
ISBN978-4-7916-1868-2